From a Ministry *for* Youth to a Ministry *of* Youth

Australian College of Theology Monograph Series

SERIES EDITOR GRAEME R. CHATFIELD

The ACT Monograph Series, generously supported by the Board of Directors of the Australian College of Theology, provides a forum for publishing quality research theses and studies by its graduates and affiliated college staff in the broad fields of Biblical Studies, Christian Thought and History, and Practical Theology with Wipf and Stock Publishers of Eugene, Oregon. The ACT selects the best of its doctoral and research masters theses as well as monographs that offer the academic community, scholars, church leaders and the wider community uniquely Australian and New Zealand perspectives on significant research topics and topics of current debate. The ACT also provides opportunity for contributors beyond its graduates and affiliated college staff to publish monographs which support the mission and values of the ACT.

Rev. Dr. Graeme Chatfield
Series Editor and Associate Dean

From a Ministry *for* Youth to a Ministry *of* Youth

Aspects of Protestant Youth Ministry in Sydney 1930–1959

RUTH LUKABYO

Foreword by
STUART PIGGIN

WIPF & STOCK · Eugene, Oregon

FROM A MINISTRY FOR YOUTH TO A MINISTRY OF YOUTH
Aspects of Protestant Youth Ministry in Sydney 1930–1959

Australian College of Theology Monograph Series

Copyright © 2020 Ruth Lukabyo. All rights reserved. Except for brief quotations in critical publications or reviews, no part of this book may be reproduced in any manner without prior written permission from the publisher. Write: Permissions, Wipf and Stock Publishers, 199 W. 8th Ave., Suite 3, Eugene, OR 97401.

Wipf & Stock
An Imprint of Wipf and Stock Publishers
199 W. 8th Ave., Suite 3
Eugene, OR 97401

www.wipfandstock.com

PAPERBACK ISBN: 978-1-7252-8242-1
HARDCOVER ISBN: 978-1-7252-8243-8
EBOOK ISBN: 978-1-7252-8244-5

Manufactured in the U.S.A.   09/17/20

Dedicated to Alan, Hayley, Lucy, and Calvin.

Other forces have aided this development in youth work— ... the need of a movement *of* youth instead of the old idea of a movement *for* youth, so that leaders of the Church of the future may be trained by leadership in their own group; the need for letting young people develop their own genius for winning contemporaries outside the Church.[1]

---

1. This was a distinction made by some young people of the British Anglican Youth Council in speaking of the new fellowship groups which they regarded as part of a youth movement.
Anon., *Youth's Job*, 5.

Contents

List of Illustrations | viii

Foreword | ix
—STUART PIGGIN

Acknowledgements | xi

List of Abbreviations | xiii

1   Introduction: The Study of the History of Youth Ministry | 1
2   Youth Ministry in Australia Before 1930 | 27
3   Protestant Youth Ministry at University and the Formation of the Evangelical Union | 63
4   Protestant Youth Ministry at Schools | 92
5   The Fellowships: Denominational Youth Ministry in the 1930s | 122
6   Challenges to the New Methodology: Heterodox Theology and World War II | 151
7   Witness and Mission: Postwar 1945–1959 | 181
8   Epilogue: The Billy Graham Crusade 1959 | 211
9   Conclusion | 220

Bibliography | 227

Illustrations

Figure 1: The New Convention Normal Manual for Sunday School Workers | 43

Figure 2: The Crusader Union Badge | 102

Foreword

PROFESSIONAL HISTORIANS ARE GIVEN to arguing that their discipline, if not the only way to understand the present, is the best way. This valuable study challenges historians, such as myself, to concede that some areas of historical inquiry are more relevant to the contemporary scene than others, and that the discipline itself is enriched if it is informed by the contribution of other disciplines, especially psychology and sociology. Just as youth ministry is vital to the future of the church, so its history deserves much more attention from church historians than it has to date. I felt chastened when I read this illuminating analysis by the realization that I, as a practicing church historian, am just as culpable for neglecting this area of church work as denominational leaders and ministers of churches are for their inadequate provision for it. Furthermore, it is not only Christian youth workers and church leaders who will find this study of immense practical application to their present vocation, but so too will all professionals concerned with understanding the role and place of adolescents and young people in modern society.

Those eager to identify the keys to successful youth ministry will appreciate the rigorous exploration here of the four pillars foundational to the demonstrably powerful work in Sydney, Australia: ministry by youth to youth; the spiritual intimacy of fellowship based on the witness of peers; the preference for coeducational over single-sex programs; and the appeal of conservative evangelical theology and culture. These themes are explored in the context of church fellowships, schools, and university Christian groups. A major beneficiary of the effectiveness of this work in the 1930s and 1940s was Billy Graham whose 1959 Southern Cross crusade reaped a larger harvest among youth than any other age cohort, the significance of which is here powerfully demonstrated.

The story of such non-denominational Christian youth ministries as the Inter-School Christian Fellowship, the Crusader Union, the Sydney University Evangelical Union, and the InterVarsity Fellowship makes exciting reading, especially perhaps for those who have participated in them in more recent times. There are heartwarming accounts of able pioneers and leaders, women as well as men, in the area of youth ministry. But the reader will also be grateful for the attention paid to cultural context, the depth of research in primary as well as secondary sources, and the comparison of conservative with liberal movements. While the focus on Sydney gives the study coherence and depth, international perspectives add to the value of this study for a wide readership. It augurs well for the future of this critical area of ministry that its past is at last receiving the scholarship which is at once so expert and a joy to read.

Associate Professor Stuart Piggin
Centre for the History of Christian Thought and Experience
Macquarie University

Acknowledgements

I AM THANKFUL FOR the many people who have helped me along the way in researching and writing this book. I have learnt that I could never do it on my own, that research is not an individual pursuit but best done in community.

The main person I have to thank is Stuart Piggin. He is a remarkable model of Christian service and academic generosity and in our many meetings he was always good-humored, kind, and positive. He taught me how to write history and has mentored so many others. Australian evangelical history and the church are indebted to him.

There were other people who read my work and gave me valuable feedback. I want to thank Alanna Nobbs for her encouragement. Thanks to Anya Williamson for the many hours she gave up to edit the book so it would read well. Thanks to Hugh Chilton for his ideas on how to strengthen the argument and write clearly. Thanks to Greta Morris for editing the final work. Finally, thanks to Geoff Treloar, Malcolm Prentis, and Paul Cooper for their willingness to share their time and expertise. I have been amazed by the generosity of those who write Christian history. They really are a community of scholars who help and support one another in the pursuit of understanding the past.

I have loved belonging to various groups of researchers, as being a solitary researcher can be lonely and demotivating. My research writing group at Macquarie University has been a "safe place" to learn how to communicate ideas clearly. My year working at the Moore College postgraduate study room provided friendships and prayer support. The International Association of Youth Ministry has been invaluable as a place to present ideas and receive gentle feedback amongst those who are passionate about youth ministry.

I would also like to thank the librarians, archivists, and administrators who have helped me. Thanks particularly to Erin Mollenhauer, the archivist at Moore College Library. Thanks also to those who work at the Ferguson Library, Fisher Library, and the State Library of NSW. Finally, thanks to the administrators at Crusader Union, Scripture Union NSW, and Youthworks.

Some of my favourite moments in the research process were interviewing those involved with youth ministry in the past. What a privilege it was to hear their stories, especially stories of God working in their lives when they were young. I think many of them enjoyed the experience as much as I did.

To my friends and family, thank you so much for your help. Thanks to Rowan and Jenny Kemp who generously allowed me to stay at their house in Katoomba for numerous writing retreats. Thanks also to Ruby Holland, Catherine Thompson, Caroline Andrews, and Careena Street who retreated with me. Thanks to my work colleagues, students, and graduates of Youthworks College who have shared words of encouragement along the way. Thanks to Graham Stanton who convinced me to attempt the project in the first place and has always been my advocate. Thanks to many other kind friends who helped keep me sane. Finally, to those closest to my heart: Alan, Hayley, Lucy, and Calvin—thank you for your love and support.

Abbreviations

EU	Evangelical Union
CE	Christian Endeavour
CEF	Church of England Fellowship
CEFDOS	Church of England Fellowship Diocese of Sydney
CICCU	Cambridge Inter-Collegiate Christian Union
CSSM	Children's Special Service Mission
CU	Crusader Union
GFS	Girls' Friendly Society
ISCF	Inter-School Christian Fellowship
IVCF	InterVarsity Christian Fellowship
IVF	InterVarsity Fellowship
PFA	Presbyterian Fellowship Australia
PFU	Presbyterian Fellowship Union
REA	Religious Education Association
SCM	Student Christian Movement
SRI	Special Religious Instruction
SU	Scripture Union
SVM	Student Volunteer Movement

VPSC   Varsity and Public Schools Camps
WSCF   World Student Christian Federation
YFC   Youth For Christ
YMCA   The Young Men's Christian Association

I

Introduction: The Study of the History of Youth Ministry

Why Study the History of Youth Ministry in the Early Twentieth Century?

THE 1950S IS A contested decade in Australian memory. The 1950s has been described positively as a decade of family values and community spirit,[1] and negatively as a decade of suffocating conformism.[2] In Protestant church life, church members describe a time when parents sought to nurture their children as Christian citizens, and when Sunday schools and youth groups were overflowing.[3] This research was first inspired by stories of the burgeoning Sunday schools and youth groups in Sydney during the 1950s and early 1960s. These stories raised significant questions, especially for those engaged in ministry to young people. Why was this period one of particular growth for ministry amongst youth and what methods were used at the time that we could learn from today? In the course of this research, it became apparent that answers to these questions could only be found by studying the methods of youth ministry developed in the 1930s and 1940s. This study will,

---

1. Murphy, *Imagining the Fifties*, 5.

2. The famous Australian book *My Brother Jack* by George Johnston portrays the suburbs in this way, as the protagonist breaks free of a life that is imprisoned by consumer values and an unhappy marriage. Johnston, *My Brother Jack*. For accounts of the 1950s, see Murphy, *Imagining the Fifties*; "Shaping the Cold War," 544–67; Brett, *Robert Menzies*; Senyard and Lees, *1950s*; Curthoys and Merritt, *Australia's First Cold War*; Ward, *Nation for a Continent*.

3. For example, interview with Rex Harris.

therefore, address the question: What were the methods used in Protestant ministry during 1930 to 1959 and how did they develop?

This question is a historical one, but it remains pertinent today. The period from 1930 to 1959 was one of seminal thinking and practice for modern youth ministry. The foundation laid in these earlier decades led to the flourishing and expansion of youth ministry in the 1950s and early 1960s and still shapes the principles and methods of youth ministry today. The effectiveness of Protestant youth ministry in the twentieth century may help to explain the relative health of conservative Protestant churches in Sydney in the twenty-first century. Despite the setbacks of the mid-1960s and 1970s when numbers within Sunday school and youth groups fell,[4] these churches have proved highly resilient.[5] There is still a vibrant subculture of young people involved in Protestant churches and ministries in Sydney. In these churches, the number of young people involved has a growth rate higher than that of adults. The total number of youth regularly attending Sydney Anglican churches has increased from 3,548 in 2005 to 4,601 in 2011.[6] Each year KYCK (Katoomba Christian Youth Convention) is held in the Blue Mountains west of Sydney, over three consecutive weekends.[7] KYCK is an interdenominational conference with Bible talks geared to youth, Christian music, and opportunities for those who do not identify as Christian to make a public decision to do so.[8] In 2017 around six thousand high school students attended the conference. One reason for this continuing vitality may be the methodology of youth ministry that was developed between 1930 and 1959.

At the heart of this project is a concern to understand the nature and effectiveness of Protestant youth ministry in Australia. However, because

---

4. For more on the 1960s and Christian faith in Australia, see Hilliard, "Religious Crisis," 209–27; Chilton, "Evangelicals"; Hilliard, "Australia: Towards Secularisation," 75–91; Carey, *Believing in Australia*.

5. In Australia, monthly church attendance has more than halved from 36 percent in 1972 to 15 percent in 2014. The percentage of those who are Christian has declined radically, but Christians continue to be an influential minority in the population. The biggest decline in church attendance has been within the Roman Catholic denomination and mainstream Protestant churches, but this has been offset by more evangelical churches such as the Pentecostals and the Sydney Anglican Diocese. Attendance at churches of the latter grew by 9 percent between 1996 and 2001. Bellamy and Castle, *Occasional Paper 3*. On the resilience of a more conservative evangelical faith, see Tamney, *Resilience of Christianity*; Smith, *American Evangelicalism*; Hilliard, "Religious Crisis."

6. Ballantine-Jones, *Inside Sydney*, 214.

7. The Katoomba conventions were inspired by the Keswick conventions in England, holiness conferences.

8. See Anon., "KYC."

so little research has been done in this field to date, it was not considered feasible to attempt to write a comprehensive history of Australian youth ministry. This study, focusing on one Australian city over a relatively short though critical period, is one contribution to which others may add. It may be that there have been factors in the development of Sydney Protestantism which made it exceptional.⁹ The extent to which changes in youth ministry in Sydney reflects wider trends in Australia is yet to be tested. This research provides a narrative of a period in the history of Protestant youth ministry in Sydney, despite the many different strands and institutions involved. To achieve a coherent narrative, there will necessarily be an emphasis on grouping similar ways of thinking, shared presuppositions, and similar methods used in youth ministry. Ultimately, two major streams will be identified.¹⁰ If at times this generalizing requirement precludes closer investigation of distinct contributions and different strands, it is hoped that other researchers may do further work on the various youth ministries and institutions. No less important than the other goals is the hope that this unified narrative will inform those involved in ministry with young people of the legacy they inherit and the story of which they are now part.

The Extent of This Study: Youth, Sydney, 1930–1959

For the purpose of this study, it is necessary to resolve the meaning of *youth*. Historians have found it difficult to agree on a definitive sense of the term, and some have argued that attempting precise definition is futile, as its

---

9. Historians have sought to understand the phenomenon of Sydney Anglicanism and in particular, the conservatism and vitality of this branch of the church. Stuart Piggin has argued that the key time when the conservative evangelical character of Sydney Anglicanism was set in concrete was 1938 under Archbishop Mowll and T. C. Hammond. Piggin, "Properties of Concrete," 185. Some historians have commented on the dissimilarity between Sydney and other Australian cities, for example, Richard Campbell: ". . . there is a striking difference between Sydney and Melbourne right across the religious board . . . Religious life in Melbourne has always been more urbane, more ecumenical, more catholic in its social vision, more Tory in its conservatism, whereas Sydney has been more assertive." Campbell, "Character of Australian Religion," 183. See also Cameron, *Phenomenal Sydney*; Ballantine-Jones, *Inside Sydney*; Kuan, *Foundations of Anglican Evangelicalism*.

10. The more conservative evangelical stream represented by the EU (Evangelical Union) and CEFDOS (Church of England Fellowship Diocese of Sydney) and more liberal evangelicals represented by the SCM (Student Christian Movement) and the PFA (Presbyterian Fellowship Australia).

meaning has changed over time.¹¹ Youth is not just a biological or psychological concept but a historically conditioned social construct.¹² Historians have come to treat youth as a legitimate category of historical study in much the same way as some have used class or gender.¹³ In this study, youth will be defined as the inbetween years of ages twelve to twenty-one, a transitional developmental stage between childhood and adulthood. This transitional stage has been classically described as *adolescence* by the sociologist, August Hollingshead, who defined it as "the period in the life of a person when the society in which he functions ceases to regard him (male or female) as a child and does not accord to him full adult status, roles and functions."¹⁴ In Australia in the early twentieth century, the youth in these in-between years were often still financially dependent upon their parents, and many were involved in education in an apprenticeship, secondary school or university. At the same time, they were beginning to make adult decisions about career, marriage, and life direction.

The geographic focus of this study is the state of NSW and in particular the city of Sydney. The churches studied are Protestant, and most of the primary sources consulted regarding local church ministry are from the Church of England and Presbyterian churches, as well as the movements within them: the PFA (Presbyterian Fellowship Australia) and CEF-DOS (Church of England Fellowship Diocese of Sydney). These were the two largest Protestant churches in NSW during the relevant period. More research could be done on the youth ministries within the Methodist, Baptist, Congregational, and Catholic Churches. The other youth organizations studied here are the Evangelical Union (EU), the Student Christian

---

11. For a helpful discussion on different ways of defining youth and a historiographical overview, see Hendrick, *Images of Youth*, 1–12. Also Kett, *Rites of Passage*, 11–37; Springhall, *Coming of Age*, 13–37.

12. Since the landmark work of Philippe Ariès, it has been generally accepted that the concept of "youth" itself was a modern invention, and before the Industrial Revolution there were simply dependent children and responsible adults. Philippe Ariès argued there was no real concept of an in-between time; a young person was either dependent (child) or independent (an adult). Ariès, *Centuries of Childhood*, 25–29. See also Springhall, *Coming of Age*, 8.

13. Other historians that focus on youth as a legitimate category of historical study include: Gillis, *Youth and History*; Fass, *Damned and the Beautiful*; Fowler, *First Teenagers*; Savage, *Teenage*; Garland et al., "Youth Culture," 265–71; Comacchio, *Dominion of Youth*; Todd, "Flappers and Factory Lads," 715–30; Humphries, *Hooligans and Rebels*; Springhall, *Youth, Empire, and Society*; Springhall, *Coming of Age*; Kett, *Rites of Passage*; Macleod, *Building Character*. There are also historians who have studied young women: Dyhouse, *Girls Growing Up*; Johnson, *Modern Girl*; Todd, *Young Women*.

14. August Hollingshead, an early sociologist, quoted in Mitterauer, *History of Youth*, 17.

Movement (SCM), the Crusader Union (CU), and the Inter-School Christian Fellowship (ISCF). One benefit of studying these interdenominational societies is that the researcher gains an overall picture of youth ministry that is not limited to two denominations. Future studies could include more investigation of the impact of the Christian Endeavor Society (CE) and its influence on other youth organizations.

The time period of this study is from 1930 to 1959. These years saw important and long-lasting shifts in Protestant youth ministry. The influential work of Mark Senter has proposed three phases in the history of youth ministry, and while his analysis is overly schematic, it is useful.[15] The first phase from 1740 to 1880 was shaped by the evangelical revivals. During this time, many young people were converted and motivated to serve Christ sacrificially and to participate in the "evangelisation of the world in this generation."[16] In the second phase of youth ministry from 1880 to 1930, there was a shift from a focus on *conversion*[17] to prioritizing *nurture*.[18] Youth ministry was an initiative of adults who sought to transform society through the nurture of young people as Christian citizens. Finally,

15. Senter, *When God Shows Up*.
16. Mott, *The Evangelization of the World*, 2.
17. There are important histories that have analyzed conversion as both a psychological and sociological phenomenon. A. D. Nock wrote a classic book on conversion which stressed crisis and discontinuity. Conversion was "re-orientation of the soul of the individual, his deliberate turning from indifference or from an earlier form of piety to another, a turning which implies that a great change is involved, that the old is wrong and the new is right." Nock, *Conversion*, 7. Sociologists and historians have built upon this definition, highlighting change not only in belief, but in affiliation of a group and changes in ethical behavior, that are expressed through the performance of ritual. See Geoff Oddie's summary in Oddie, *Religious Conversion Movements*, 1–14. Lewis Rambo has described conversion as a process over time, with distinct stages, not just a single event or crisis. He argues that it must be understood as contextual, involving relationships, expectations and situations, and that there are multiple causes for conversion. Rambo, *Understanding Religious Conversion*. See also Potter, "Making of Missionaries," 103–21; Bebbington, "Evangelical Conversion," 102–27; Hindmarsh, *Evangelical Conversion Narrative*.

18. Sarah Potter argues that this change was not just because of a change in theology but because of the development of youth organizations such as Sunday school and Christian Endeavor societies as well as the influence of an evangelical home. In the early nineteenth century, many young people were sent away from home to be apprentices in peer groups that encouraged deviancy. In an attempt to resolve guilt and adjust to adult life, they sought conversion and a new peer group. "The Church offered, too, an alternative set of social relations to the adolescent peer groups, and a number of missionaries describe how, at their conversion, they deserted their former companions for the people of God." In the institutions of the late nineteenth century, young people were protected and rather than dramatic conversions, gradual growth in religion became the experience of most young evangelicals. Potter, "Making of Missionaries," 109.

in 1930, Senter identifies a swing back to conversion and the promotion of the initiative of young people themselves.[19] This study draws on Senter's categories and begins its study at the beginning of the third phase in 1930. It is here argued that in this decade, there was a change of paradigm in Protestant youth ministry in Sydney, reflecting a change occurring throughout the Western world. The period researched ends with the Australian Billy Graham Crusade of 1959, which it will be argued was the high point of the success of the new model of youth ministry.

Generational Theory, Subcultures and Agency

Several schools of thought amongst historians and sociologists have proved particularly helpful for the methodology of this research. Generational theory argues that a generation is shaped by the experiences and events it lives through. Moreover, sociologists have also come to identify and study specific subcultures within a given generation. In addition, increasing consideration is being given to the agency of youth themselves in historical research.

The sociologist Karl Mannheim's theory of generations has influenced historians to consider age as a historical category. Manheim first developed his theory in 1923, arguing that *generation* was a category within the social and historical process comparable to class, and that the generation a person belongs to will shape their view of themselves and their way of looking at the world. This is because they are born into a particular time and place, and have experienced events at a particular age.[20] Each new generation inherits the culture of its parents, yet brings a new sensibility, which makes it an agent of cultural change.

This theory was extended by Talcott Parsons and then by the Birmingham Centre for Contemporary Studies to include the concept of subcultures. Talcott Parsons, in his famous essay in the 1940s,[21] emphasized the

---

19. Mark Cannister has written a short history of youth ministry in the US. He points out that youth ministry has been understood in a dichotomized way as being largely concerned with evangelism *or* discipleship, missional youth ministry *or* religious education. He claims that the history is one of excesses and correctives as the emphasis swings from one extreme to the other. Cannister, "Youth Ministry's Historical Context," 78.

20. Mannheim, *Essays*, 168. Mannheim understood human progress as a dialectic process of tension between new and old generations and their ways of thinking that impelled historical change. The younger generation will therefore always be an agent of change.

21. Parsons, "Age and Sex," 604–16.

importance of age rather than class as he analyzed adolescents in America. He argued that a generational consciousness was growing amongst youth in the US that could be called a *youth culture*. This culture was in tension with the adult culture and assisted young people to move through the transition of adolescence, from carefree childhood to responsible adulthood.[22] High school was the place that fostered these relationships and helped create a *youth culture*.[23] In Birmingham beginning in the 1970s, sociologists examined generational change through the prism of conflict. They claimed that the youth of the postwar generation were trapped between the working-class culture of their parents and the new values of capitalism and consumption.[24] The groundbreaking aspect of the Birmingham group was their analysis of youth as *subcultures* rather than as one undifferentiated generational group. These subcultures were analyzed according to their "style" and the culture that made them distinctive.[25] These sociologists have informed historical writing about youth, helping historians to analyze generational ways of thinking and behaving, as well as recognizing youth subcultures.[26]

This study will consider the effect on Christian youth of the generation they were born into. Young people in the period from 1930 to 1959 were a generation affected by the Depression and two World Wars, momentous events that shaped their view of the world.[27] Young people were also

22. Parsons, "Age and Sex," 606.

23. Many of the key sociologists who argued for the idea of *generations* formed their ideas in the 1960s and were themselves shaped by their own key experiences of being the young generation at a time of great social change. They defined themselves as the *boomer generation* and began to define others around them in generational terms.

24. Hodkinson, "Youth Cultures," 1–21. Other important sociologists who studied youth subculture: Brake, *Sociology of Youth Culture*; White, *Youth Subcultures*; Hebdige, *Subculture*; Hall and Jefferson, *Resistance through Rituals*; Hodkinson and Deicke, *Youth Cultures*; Willis, *Profane Culture*; Milson, *Changing Society*.

25. For example, groups such as the "Teddy Boys," the "Mods," and "Rockers." In their observations about subcultures, the Birmingham group tended to focus on subcultures of rebellion that expressed a subversion of the dominant culture of their parents through style and music. Current researchers have questioned the way their research focused on the deviant and rebellious minority of young people. The majority of young people did not take drugs, drop out, run away from home, become wildly promiscuous, and engage in street violence or petty crime; and they were pushed to the sidelines of academic concern. Cohen, *Rethinking the Youth Question*, 194.

26. One of the criticisms of this group of sociologists is that they are products of their own generation. They were part of the baby boomer generation who had a strong sense of the *generation gap* between them and their parents' generation. This experience may predispose them to analyze according to conflict between generations. This is a gap that many generations do not feel.

27. There are historians that have taken up generational theory and particularly how a time of trauma and crisis can create the character of a particular generation. The

growing up at a time of great change, with access to more consumer goods and disposable income than their parents.[28] They were consuming movies, jazz music, magazines, and American culture, while the parental generation fretted about the rise of juvenile delinquency.[29] The education of this generation was influenced by the new disciplines of psychology and sociology, which challenged some basic Christian presumptions about sexuality and religion. These generational characteristics made it harder for the parental generation to hand down the Christian faith to their children in a way that they could appropriate and apply. These factors heightened the importance of having younger Christians not too far removed from the new generation to communicate the Christian faith to the youth.

This study will consider young Protestants as a subculture within their generation.[30] Sociologists have argued that conservative evangelicalism has been particularly effective in creating a strong subcultural identity within groups and has "provided its adherents with both a distinct identity (belonging) and a strong purpose (meaning)—both of which are difficult to discover and maintain within the pluralism of a globalized world."[31] Christian Smith has argued that evangelicalism in contemporary America is flourishing because of a strong subcultural identity or "morally orienting collective identity."[32] This subcultural identity is formed:

> through the use of socially constructed symbolic markers that establish group boundaries. It is through language, rituals, artefacts, creeds, practices, narratives—in short, the stuff of human cultural production—that social groups construct their sense of self and difference from others.[33]

1914 generation of Robert Wohl, for example, focused on young men who had experienced the horrors of war and were forever scarred and "lost." Wohl, *Generation of 1914*.

28. Kociumbas argues that in Australia, youth were caught between these two different worldviews and values. "Between the wars, a start had been made in transforming working class culture from self-disciplined thrift to conspicuous consumption and the pursuit of pleasure." Kociumbas, *Australian Childhood*, 194.

29. See Matthews, *Dance Hall*.

30. For example, Ward, *Participation and Meditation*, 3; Root, *Relational Youth Ministry*, 32, 48; Smith, *American Evangelicalism*, 89–119.

31. Root, *Relational Youth Ministry*, 65. Andrew Root explains that subcultural identity involves defining the boundaries of who is in or out of the group and a self-understanding that shapes how each individual understands what *is* and what *ought* to be.

32. Smith, *American Evangelicalism*, 91. See also Evans, "Distinct Subcultural Identity," 467–77.

33. Smith, *American Evangelicalism*, 92.

This sub-cultural identity creates a kind of "sacred umbrella"[34] under which religious faith can thrive. Smith argues that the better a religious group is at constructing distinct identity boundaries, the more it will thrive and grow. This study will demonstrate the effectiveness of particular groups at creating a robust subcultural identity in which youth ministry can thrive. Protestant youth in Sydney differentiated themselves not only from their parents but also from other youth around them. What they wore, what they did on the weekends, their badges, uniforms, and the groups to which they belonged, all marked their identity.

Further strengthening the case for understanding Protestant youth as a subculture is the concept of *fellowship ties* which the sociologist David Olson investigates using this same terminology of *identity formation* and *subculture*. He argues that the idea of fellowship within modern evangelical groups is important for forming a religious identity. Fellowship within a group "facilitates interaction among persons who share a religious identity and shields many from significant exposure to religious pluralism,"[35] enabling members to sustain and pass on their beliefs to others. If correct, this would suggest that the strength of fellowship and relational networks was a key factor in the vitality and stability of these ministries among young people. Strong personal networks, defined as *fellowship*, were understood as a spiritual bond, like being part of the same family. You may not always like the people within your group, but you belonged to them. Olson concludes that "the ability of religious subcultures to transmit and maintain a real identity will vary with the depth and the number and strength of fellowship ties among participants and the number and strength of subcultural institutions."[36]

One consequence of theories of generation and subculture has been to legitimize youth as an agent of historical change amongst historians. As the Australian historian and social theorist Carole Cusack puts it, there has been a "shift away from focusing on the formal processes of young people's religious socialisation and a realisation that youth exercise considerable agency in their construction of personal and group identities."[37] In older research, youth were seen more as passive recipients of social processes. Primary

---

34. The sacred umbrella image is a response to the sociologist Peter Berger, and his image of a "sacred canopy." The canopy was a plausibility structure which made religious belief possible. He argued that in the modern world the sacred canopy of shared religious values and institutions was gone, and belief was becoming increasingly difficult. Berger, *Sacred Canopy*.

35. Olson, "Fellowship Ties," 35.

36. Olson, "Fellowship Ties," 37.

37. Cusack, "Some Recent Trends," 409.

sources for the study of youth were typically the reports of governmental and educational institutions and the writings of adults. Contemporary historians concerned with a *history of youth* have focused on the worldview and experiences of young people, and on primary sources that document these. In this study, there is a focus on identity formation and on the religious understanding and practice of young people themselves. Reports and autobiographies are key primary sources. In addition, this study seeks to hear the voices of young people themselves through the use of oral history. Unfortunately, at the time this research was conducted there were few people available to interview who retained sharp memories of the period under consideration. The research has relied on earlier taped interviews from the Moore College Donald Robinson Archives.

In the selection of sources, it is important not to overreact to weaknesses in earlier methodology. Young people were both the "products of change and agents of change."[38] For this reason, it remains valuable to study the primary sources written by adults, the institutional reports, newspapers, and journal articles on the assumption that the views of the adults around them influenced, if not determined, the self-understanding of young people.

The Emergence of Youth Culture

Whereas historians have accepted the idea of the agency of youth, the debate has continued over when *youth culture* emerged. That is, when did young people begin to create a culture of their own that was distinctive from their parents? Various time periods have been proposed. Ariès argued that *youth* developed as a concept during the Industrial Revolution. John Gillis has argued that it was invented by public schools in England in the late nineteenth century with the development of peer groups at boarding schools.[39] Other historians and sociologists have argued that the creation of a distinct youth culture happened after World War II,[40] suggesting

---

38. This is a phrase from Paula Fass who has written a history of youth in the US. She argues that youth culture was formed in the 1920s with the "burning youth" of the Jazz Age. Fass, *Damned and the Beautiful*, 5. The reason that youth culture developed earlier in the US than Canada or Australia was no doubt because high schools developed at an earlier time. Even so, it was the 1930s when American high schools radically expanded and Hollywood teenage stars like Mickey Rooney and Judy Garland symbolized teenage hopes and challenges. Mintz, *Huck's Raft*, 239.

39. Gillis, *Youth and History*, 105.

40. For example, Hodkinson and Deicke, *Youth Cultures*; Garland et al., "Youth Culture," and Australian writers: Irving et al., *Youth in Australia*; Stratton, "Bodgies and Widgies," 10–24.

that in the 1950s a teenage consumer market evolved when young people had disposable income for the first time and were able to fashion a cultural expression of their own.

More recently, there has been a trend within historical debate to argue that youth culture emerged in the 1930s and 1940s. Oded Heilbronner argues persuasively in his article on recent trends in historiography that: "The new periodization, the golden age of youth, with its negative and positive aspects, started not in the 1950s, as Jon Savage shows, but in the 1930s and the early 1940s, when many American youth idolized Frank Sinatra, young Germans served in tank-destroying units and many Jews fought for their lives in the East European ghettos."[41] Heilbronner goes on to state:

> This long period allowed deep changes in the patterns of youth cultures to take place: from cultures *for* youth to cultures *of* youth.[42]

This study postulates that the change at this time that led to significant agency amongst young people generally, was also evident among Protestant youth. It will also borrow Heilbronner's phrase "culture *for* youth to culture *of* youth"[43] as a useful tool to analyze the change in paradigm in youth ministry at this time.

One of the historians who documents the development of a youth generation through the changes in the interwar years is Cynthia Comacchio. She argues that in interwar Canada youth was first defined as a category between childhood and adulthood, distinct and "recognisable as never before."[44] The Great War was the end of the Victorian Age and heralded the beginning of modernity. The teenager emerged amidst these "new days" which included intensive developments in technology, medicine, psychology, education, cultural anthropology, family sociology, and a significant number of other "scientific advances" and "modern innovations."[45] Comacchio describes the teen emerging as a "Frankenstein's monster" to challenge the norms of the young nation. It was not the 1950s that created this monster, she notes. The "habits, behaviours and styles" of the teenager had already emerged. The 1950s were the time of mass media and production that enabled this already-developed teenage style to be communicated and accessed by all.[46]

41. Heilbronner, "Culture for Youth," 577.
42. Heilbronner, "Culture for Youth," 590.
43. Heilbronner, "Culture for Youth," 577.
44. Comacchio, *Dominion of Youth*, 1.
45. Comacchio, *Dominion of Youth*, viii.
46. Comacchio, *Dominion of Youth*, 3.

According to Comacchio, three massive events account for the emergence of the teenager: the Great War, the Depression, and World War II. The Great War was disruptive on an international scale. There was a general hope that after the "war to end all wars" there would be a new day led by the younger generation, and this idea was expressed by international writers and academics in a form of "romantic historicism."[47] The Depression was a second traumatic world event that meant that for many young people work opportunities and expectations for the future dried up. Finally, the Second World War disrupted the life patterns of youth, particularly those who did not sign up for military service. Comacchio applies generational theory to argue that these three world events shaped the identity of Canadian youth.[48] Consequently, the parental generation found it harder to transfer the values and beliefs down to the next generation, and there was more opportunity for conflict and alienation between them.

Many contemporary historians of youth are persuaded by Comacchio's argument that the roots of youth culture were in the 1930s and 1940s, although supporting Australian studies are scarce.[49] Compared to the volume of writing on the history of youth in other Western countries, there is very little written on youth in Australia and those who do continue to emphasize the 1950s.[50] Furthermore, Australian sociologists and historians have tended to focus on rebellious subcultural groups such as *larrikins*[51] and the *bodgies and widgies*[52] rather than on mainstream youth. There are reasons,

47. Comacchio, *Dominion of Youth*, 7.

48. Comacchio relies on the work of Norbert Elias who argued that the "usual rhythms of cultural transmission can be disrupted by intense social change of world events." Comacchio, *Dominion of Youth*, 11.

49. For example, historians who study youth in the US such as: Fass, *Damned and the Beautiful*; Mintz, *Huck's Raft*; Hawes, *Children Between the Wars*. Those who have studied youth in Britain: Fowler, *First Teenagers*; Todd, *Young Women*. Jon Savage also argues for a youth culture that develops before the 1950s. His book moves all over the Western world to examine the creation of a youth culture. It begins at the end of the nineteenth century and ends at what he calls "year zero" 1945. In this year the war ended, the magazine *Seventeen* was launched in the US, and Frank Sinatra was a national US hero. It heralds the formation of a distinct youth culture. Savage, *Teenage*, 455.

50. There are a few books written on the history of childhood in Australia that do include youth, the best being Kociumbas, *Australian Childhood*. See also Fabian and Loh, *Children in Australia*; Irving et al., *Youth in Australia*. Irving et al. focus on the relationship of youth to government and policy.

51. The larrikin is an Australian word for a young man who is uncultivated and rowdy, and acts with apparent disregard for social or political conventions. For example, Bellanta, *Larrikins*.

52. The bodgies and widgies were young men and women who embraced a particular style of dress and music influenced by American culture. They hung out at milk bars

however, for believing that the Canadian experience may also be reflected in Australian culture and that the key decades of change are in the 1930s and 1940s, not the 1950s. The present research suggests that Australians were similarly scarred by war and depression and faced the same life disruptions as Canadians. After the Great War, Australia was developing its national identity as a young nation and was loosening ties with "Mother England." Like Canada, the interwar years were ones in which the nation was "caught up in its own self-formation and transformation."[53] There were high expectations and fears for the young, who would be the "new generation" that would usher in modernity.[54] As will be shown in this study, church leaders shared these hopes and fears and believed that the young were the future of the church and needed to be encouraged to take up leadership. It was the particular atmosphere of the 1930s and 1940s that saw the emergence of a distinct generation, and new agency among youth in Sydney.

The Study of Youth Ministry: Historic Phases and the Influence of Theology

There has been significant research in the history of ministry to youth in the United States and Britain, but not in Australia. Historians who work in the field have identified broad changes in youth ministry methodology and goals over time. This study will argue that youth ministry in NSW fits into worldwide patterns of change and, following Senter's analysis noted above, that there were three distinct phases within this historical narrative. The first phase from the 1740s to 1880 was characterized by revival. The second phase from 1880 to 1930 was characterized by nurture. The third phase from 1930 to the present was characterized by witness. Senter's analysis goes beyond identifying phases and emphases to noting key methodologies in each phase, as follows:

---

and dance halls in the city and the press portrayed them as "juvenile delinquents." The bodgies were young men who wore zoot suits, leather jeans, and leather jackets and swept back their hair in a quaff. The widgies were young women who wore sleeveless blouses and straight skirts with a split up the back to make dancing easy. Braithwaite and Barker, "Bodgies and Widgies"; Stratton, "Bodgies and Widgies."

53. Fass, *Damned and the Beautiful*, 2.

54. Fass, *Damned and the Beautiful*, 1. Judith Bessant argues that a key way that Australians thought about youth was as the hope of the future. Australia was like a child to mother England, a child who needed to grow up and become independent. Bessant, "Patchwork," 82.

1. 1824–1875: Associations
2. 1881–1925: Youth societies
3. 1933–1989: Relational outreach

The heart of this study is concerned with the change from the second phase to the third, and the accompanying changes in methodology in youth work. Worldwide there was a shift in the 1930s and 1940s from a ministry *for* youth to a ministry *of* youth and this same change is evident in Sydney.

Senter argues that each cycle of youth ministry began with great vitality, but after about thirty years the ministry stagnated and needed to be reinvented. The first cycle, 1824 to 1875, he calls the period of associations; these included the temperance societies, the American Sunday School Union, and the YMCA. The second cycle, 1881 to 1925, he calls the period of youth societies, initiated by the Christian Endeavor Movement and then the denominational societies. Finally, the third cycle from 1933 to 1989 was the period of relational outreach, characterized by parachurch ministries such as Youth for Christ, Young Life, and the Miracle Book Club. Senter argues that each cycle had the same components: "a visionary, a simple system, media coverage, a spokesperson, and of course, the batteries, a sense of God's special working in a new generation."[55] Importantly, each was a response to social disruption and cultural change.

The analysis of Senter has strengths and weaknesses. An obvious strength is the clarity of his three cycles of youth ministry and its broad explanatory power. Another strength is his insight into the innovative nature and influence of parachurch youth organizations on church youth ministry. A weakness, however, is his heavy reliance on Max Weber's concept of institutionalization and the "routinization of charisma."[56] Weber's theory of institutional development argues that movements begin with a charismatic leader and grow quickly, but then become increasingly organized and institutional and eventually go into decline. Relying on Weber means that Senter emphasizes the development of the institution, rather than the historical context or the theology of youth ministry. Senter's cycles are also a little too schematic to make sense of the many different strands of youth ministry, but for this study, they are a good base to build upon.

The historian Joseph Kett, in contrast to Senter, describes only two phases in the history of youth ministry. He argues that in the period from 1880 to 1920 there was a change from ministry characterized by *conversion*

---

55. Senter, *When God Shows Up*, 82.
56. Senter, *When God Shows Up*, 42.

and *revival* to a focus on Christian *nurture* and *moralism*.[57] He argues that in the period after 1880, there was a change from the ministry *of* youth, to ministry *for* youth. Before 1880, youth had been at the forefront of leading the early institutions like the YMCA (Young Men's Christian Association). After 1880, youth became passive recipients of the ministry rather than leaders.[58] Kett supplements Senter in bringing to life the vitality of the first phase of youth ministry before 1890 and the enthusiasm and sense of mission fired by revival. In the revivals of the nineteenth century it was documented that the majority of those converted were young people, and often revivals began among youth.[59] Kett calls the conversions in revival the "supercharger" that harnessed the passion and energy of youth and often led to a life of religious activism.[60] The Sunday schools, YMCA, and the SVM, whose watchword was "the evangelization of the world in this generation," demonstrated this kind of activism.

After 1880, Kett argues that there was a change in leadership and goals within youth organizations largely through the influence of Horace Bushnell[61] and G. Stanley Hall.[62] Bushnell's theology was developed in reaction to the contemporary focus on conversion and revivalism. He believed that it was the responsibility of the family and church to nurture a child so they should "grow up a Christian and never know himself as being otherwise."[63] Hall further shaped ministry to youth, by introducing the psychological concept of adolescence. He described adolescence as a time of temptation, of "storm and stress," when a young person tries to form their identity and

57. Kett, *Rites of Passage*, 6.
58. Kett, *Rites of Passage*, 6.
59. Kett, *Rites of Passage*, 64–65.
60. Kett, *Rites of Passage*, 70.
61. Bushnell, *Christian Nurture*, 10. Horace Bushnell was an American Congregational minister who wrote the book *Christian Nurture* in 1847 and in his day was a controversial figure. He is often called the "Father of Christian Education," but it was not until almost fifty years later that his writing really influenced ministry to young people and education. See Kathan, "Horace Bushnell," 44; also Krahn, "Nurture Vs. Revival," 70.
62. G. Stanley Hall was an influential psychologist who is said to be the inventor of the concept of adolescence. In his book, *Adolescence*, which was published in 1904, he argued that adolescence was a tumultuous time of transition for a young person. In adolescence, character is formed, and animal spirits need to be curbed and redirected. Adolescence was a kind of "rebirth" into sexed life. Hall proposed creating a stage of life that would delay entry into the adult world and give young people more time in the protected environment of school. He also argued that adolescence was a time of heightened spirituality when the majority of Christians were converted. See Hall, *Adolescence*; Arnett, "G. Stanley Hall's Adolescence," 186–97.
63. Bushnell, *Christian Nurture*, 10.

grow into an adult. During adolescence, a young person should be given space without responsibility, in a "self-contained world in which prolonged immaturity could sustain itself." He argued that those who work with youth ought to defend them from "contamination by the alien culture."[64] Indirectly, Hall significantly influenced youth ministry as many adults came to believe they should protect adolescents during this vulnerable time of formation so they would not become "juvenile delinquents." The key leaders of youth ministry were adults concerned about the nurture of Christian citizens rather than about conversion.[65]

Kett's description and analysis of the change in youth ministry after 1890 is persuasive, but not without weaknesses. He does not identify a third period beginning in the 1930s, a period that this study will argue is crucial. He is also at times overly critical of youth organizations after 1890[66] and does not deal with the new ministries in the US such as fellowship groups, Youth for Christ, and Young Life ministries.[67] In these organizations in the US in the 1930s, there was a return to the leadership of youth and evangelism that revitalized a ministry *of* youth. Kett's analysis is also quite dichotomistic, contrasting conversion with nurture and activism with passivity. This way of conceptualizing tends to be unqualified and oversimplified, as youth organizations can be concerned for *both* conversion and nurture. However, allowing for these qualifications, his categories are useful in seeking to paint a big picture of change over time.

Andrew Root, an American theologian of youth ministry, has built upon the work of Kett and Senter. His focus is youth ministry since the late nineteenth century, and he documents a change from institutional to relational youth ministry. He argues that before the 1940s, adults were motivated by fear "that their children would be swept away by the currents of modernization."[68] According to his analysis, in the 1940s parachurch organizations responded to changes in culture such as the development of high schools and the rise of the youth peer group. These organizations managed to retain conservative theology while communicating a vision of the Christian life that was modern and engaged, "a biblical faith that was

---

64. Kett, *Rites of Passage*, 110.

65. Kett points to the example of Christian Endeavor as an illustration of this mission. Christian Endeavor focused on the children of Christians rather than those outside the church and the goal of the ministry was "training," which kept young people busy without giving them real responsibility. *Rites of Passage*, 194.

66. He even uses the pejorative term "hollow youth" to describe the way that the concept of adolescence disempowered youth. Kett, *Rites of Passage*, 243.

67. For more on the third phase see Pahl, *Youth Ministry*.

68. Root, *Relational Youth Ministry*, 30.

fully engaged in American life."[69] The goal of youth ministry changed from protecting youth from temptation and training them for future service, to "evangelistic engagement through nationalistic and relational strategies."[70] The reasons Root presents for this change are shaped by the historical context rather than an inevitable institutional change over time. He claims that a change to a more relational style of youth ministry was due to modernization, the rise of psychology, the rise of the high school, peer groups, and youth culture in the 1940s.[71]

The narrative of the history of youth ministry in Britain is not as coherent as that of the US but is arguably more fruitful for understanding the history of youth in Australia.[72] British historians John Gillis, John Springhall, and Harry Hendrick have examined youth movements in the nineteenth and early twentieth century through the prism of class.[73] They present young people as oppressed by adults who are motivated by anxiety about religion and the social order because of their fear for the empire and for racial survival.[74] Gillis calls these adults "child-savers," who believed working-class youth were being corrupted by city life and were tempted into juvenile delinquency. In response, the adults ran ministries such as boys' clubs, Boys Brigade, and later Scouts. Gillis argues that "through games, rituals, juvenile pursuits of all kinds, the Victorian-era youth leaders had set out to free the young from the bonds of an urban-industrial civilization grown rigid and corrupt in their eyes by virtue of its own material progress."[75] Increasingly, this youth work focused on physical and psychological health rather than conversion and Christian maturity.[76]

Supplementing this more sociological analysis, evangelical historians such as David Bebbington consider theological motivations for youth

69. Root, *Relational Youth Ministry*, 50.

70. Root, *Relational Youth Ministry*, 48.

71. Root, *Relational Youth Ministry*, 30–52.

72. It will be demonstrated in this paper that English models used by the student evangelist Howard Guinness were particularly influential.

73. These historians believe that youth movements were, for the most part, instruments of social conformity. Adults sought to "train, supervise and control" the young and "consolidate their powerlessness." Hendrick, *Images of Youth*, 250, 259; Springhall, *Coming of Age*, 16. They point to the liberation from this adult oppression in the 1950s and 1960s with the rise of a youth culture when young people themselves would no longer allow themselves to be the object of conformity. The three British historians fail to take religious motivations for youth ministry seriously, instead seeing youth work through the Marxist lens of oppression of one class by another.

74. Springhall et al., *Sure and Steadfast*, 44; Springhall, *Coming of Age*, 16.

75. Gillis, *Youth and History*, 141–42.

76. Gillis, *Youth and History*, 141–42.

ministry. Bebbington has described traditional evangelicalism through the prism of a quadrilateral of priorities: *conversionism, activism, biblicism,* and *crucicentrism*.[77] These priorities shaped early evangelical youth ministry, especially the parachurch organizations of the nineteenth century, the Children's Special Service Mission (CSSM, 1867), and Scripture Union (SU, 1897), which adopted a revival-based model that dominated until 1890. They saw the need for outreach, camps, and discipleship for young people, particularly those who had graduated from Sunday school, as well as for children who were unchurched. In the early twentieth century, however, some evangelicals wrestled in their attitude to the authority of the Bible in the light of modern thought and biblical criticism and called themselves *Liberal Evangelicals*.[78] Bebbington argues that *conservative evangelical*[79] leaders believed the way to respond to the challenge of liberal theology in the church was to focus on youth, to "win the next generation to the truth."[80] New organizations such as Young Life in 1913, and later the Bash camps,[81] Crusaders, Pathfinders, and the IVF were all theologically conservative and were established to evangelize young people and help them reach other young people.[82] Bebbington argues that these interdenominational youth organizations developed many

77. Bebbington, *Evangelicalism*, 3.

78. Bebbington, *Evangelicalism*, 181–228. Theological liberalism was a movement which was particularly influential in the late nineteenth century and early twentieth century. Liberal evangelicalism was a response to new academic thinking about the Bible as well as the flourishing of new academic disciplines such as sociology, psychology, and evolutionary biology. It was an attempt to make the evangelical faith "up to date" by rethinking Christian doctrines and engaging with modern thought. It was also in reaction to an individualistic conversionist faith, to a faith that was concerned to transform society. See Randall, *Evangelical Experiences*; Mark Edwards, "Can Christianity Save Civilisation?," 51–67; Rogers, *Liberal Evangelicalism*. For the influence of liberal evangelicalism in Australia see Barnes, *Half-Way House*; Emilsen, *Whiff of Heresy*; Lawton, "Better Time to Be."

79. Conservative evangelicalism was a movement that defended orthodox faith. Conservative evangelicalism in Britain and Australia can be distinguished from the American-style Fundamentalism though it has many similarities. It longed for revival, had a strong Bible focus, and defended the authority of the Bible and traditional doctrines, particularly the atonement of Jesus. It can be argued that the movement was not as sectarian in Australia, perhaps because many who would claim that description were part of the established Church of England and committed to the institution. See Treloar, "Some Reflections," and Treloar, *Disruption of Evangelicalism*, 5–17, for some interesting reflections on distinguishing between liberal and conservative evangelicalism and the danger of polarizing these evangelicals rather than seeing them on a spectrum.

80. Bebbington, *Evangelicalism*, 226.

81. Eddison, "*Bash*." E. J. H. Nash ("Bash") ran camps for elite public schoolboys in England from 1932 to 1965.

82. Bebbington, *Evangelicalism*, 258.

INTRODUCTION: THE STUDY OF THE HISTORY OF YOUTH MINISTRY

influential evangelical leaders and led to a resurgence of conservative evangelicalism in the Church of England.[83]

Pete Ward has studied the history of youth ministry in Britain, building upon the work of Bebbington. He documents a change in method in youth ministry from *telling* to *discovering* in the nineteenth century. He explains that the Sunday school movement, YMCA, and Boys Brigade had all tried to shape the character of young people through teaching them Christian doctrine and values. In the late nineteenth century, there was a general realization that more was needed to provide fellowship with other Christians for young people who were old enough to leave Sunday school. In response, ministries were established based on small groups for fellowship, such as Christian Endeavor, Crusader groups, the Varsity and Public Schools Camps (VPSC), and the Student Christian Movement (SCM). The structure of these groups was no longer didactic but had moved from telling to "discovering, training and sharing"[84] and they proved outstanding at training and developing leaders and reaching middle-class youth. They formed a "pattern for the development of youth work"[85] and had an enormous impact on middle-class youth. Ward's critique is that success in youth ministry in England has been largely within the middle and upper classes, unlike youth work in the US, which has been more successful in reaching working-class youth.[86]

Those writing the history of youth ministry in Britain have described it as having two distinct models. The first model was increasingly secular, was based on nurturing good character and citizenship, and was aimed at the working class. The second model was led by the parachurch organizations and emphasized the importance of conversion. Those involved in this latter model of ministry tended to have conservative theology, whereas those involved in the former tended to be more liberal. The dominant model before 1880 was the conversionist, but between 1880 and 1930 the dominant model became that of nurture and citizenship. Although they were not culturally dominant, the parachurch organizations continued to uphold a conversionist model, and after the 1920s new youth organizations were formed that reenergized this approach.

The research into the history of youth ministry in the US and Britain helps us to establish a narrative of change over time. This study will adopt

83. Bebbington, *Evangelicalism*, 258.
84. Ward, *Growing Up Evangelical*, 27. Ward here is quoting from Cliff, *Rise and Development*, 169.
85. Ward, *Growing Up Evangelical*, 33.
86. Ward, *Growing Up Evangelical*, 11.

the time periods of Senter as the most persuasive and will seek to apply this same model to Protestant youth ministry in Sydney. This review of literature also alerts us to some key explanatory concepts and potential hypotheses for the reasons for such change. Concepts such as conversion and nurture are significant for understanding the methodology of youth ministries. The writers have also alerted us to the significance of the para-church organizations and their impact on church youth ministries. We will see this, for example, in the influence of the Young Men's Christian Association (YMCA) on the Presbyterian Fellowship Union (PFU) and other church fellowship groups and the Evangelical Union (EU) and its influence on church ministries.

Causes of Change

This book will argue that there was a change of paradigm in Protestant youth ministry in the 1930s and 1940s in Sydney. It will conclude that four key causes of this change can be identified. These agents of change were social forces, changes in the theological outlook of the church, new organizations and institutions, and key individuals.

The social forces at work in the interwar years meant that young people in Australia were beginning to develop their own youth culture and were given greater agency. The young generation was affected by the wars and the Depression and influenced by a parental generation that was both fearful of the future and hopeful about the young who were to build a new nation. The young were seen as the future of the nation and also of the church. This meant that young people were encouraged to lead the fledgling youth organizations, to take initiative, teach, and do ministry amongst their peers.

Another significant social force that shaped the youth culture was the development of secondary education in NSW. Until the 1930s and 1940s in Australia, all children except the elite left school and joined the workforce when they turned fourteen years. During the 1930s and 1940s, there was a rapid expansion in secondary education.[87] The historian Paula Fass has emphasized the importance of high schools for creating a youth culture and peer groups in the US in the 1920s. For the first time, young people spent most of their day with peers rather than with parents or other adults. These

---

87. There were approximately sixteen thousand young people involved in NSW state post-primary education in 1920 and eighty thousand in 1948. NSW Department of Education, "Enrolments."

There were many more young people receiving secondary schooling in church and independent schools.

peer groups were important in socialization and "they controlled and directed habits, attitudes, and values but could not be completely directed or controlled by older and adult institutions."[88] High schooling in Sydney was at least a decade behind the US, but by the 1930s, high schools in Sydney enabled peer groups and youth culture to develop. As we shall see, peer groups were to have an important influence on youth ministry.

There was also a change in the theological landscape in the Protestant churches. The 1930s saw the beginning of a worldwide resurgence in conservative evangelical belief.[89] Early in the century, the liberal evangelical writers and leaders within the church had shaped ministry to youth. They had focused on nurturing Christian character and citizenship. In the 1930s, conservative evangelicalism became more influential. The interwar period has been characterized as a time of infighting and sectarianism. Joel Carpenter's history of evangelicals in the US, however, points out that in this period American Fundamentalists[90] were very active in building new institutions such as Bible colleges, journals, and radio stations. Their strength in the 1950s was because of the investment of time and resources in the

---

88. Fass, *Damned and the Beautiful*, 57.

89. The story of evangelicalism in Australia has to be seen as a "trans-global movement with local expressions." See Chilton, "Evangelicals," 16; Piggin, "American and British Contributions," 290–309; Dickey, "Evangelical Anglicans Compared," 215–40.

90. Fundamentalism was a conservative evangelical movement that reacted against theological liberalism in America. It defended orthodox Christian belief, a six-day creation, and the imminent return of Christ. For a classic reading of Fundamentalism see Marsden, *Fundamentalism and American Culture*. Fundamentalism as a movement was characterized by a concern to identify the essential doctrines of Orthodox faith ("the Fundamentals"), but also by a tendency to withdraw from traditional denominations in order to form new institutions. Historians have found it difficult to define the parameters of Fundamentalism, as there was a spectrum of beliefs and approach within evangelicalism. John Stackhouse has helpfully used a sociological model of "Church vs. Sect" rather than defining Fundamentalism and liberalism in purely theological categories. The Sect deliberately separates from culture and has no status within it. The church remains within culture and enjoys a status within it. He describes Fundamentalism as "militant opposition to modernity—especially modern ideas (liberal theology, biblical criticism, and evolution chief among them)—and separation from all who are not wholly pure in their convictions and associations." Stackhouse, *Canadian Evangelicalism*, 12. Treloar uses Stackhouse's model and argues that in Australia, like Canada, the degree and influence of Fundamentalism was not nearly as great as in the United States; it was not as militant, nor as sectarian. It could be argued that the continued importance of the Church of England within evangelicalism in Sydney moderated the retreat towards Fundamentalism, as it was held in high regard as a quasi-established institution within Australian culture. Evangelicals continued on the whole to engage in public debate, particularly on issues of public morality. Treloar, "Some Reflections," 9; Parker, "Fundamentalism." See the discussion in Bebbington and Ceri Jones, *Evangelicalism and Fundamentalism*, 1–14.

1930s and 1940s.[91] Brian Stanley has argued that in these years there was a global resurgence of conservative evangelicalism when evangelicals became intellectually credible as they invested in academic work, writing, and teaching.[92] This strengthened the movement and helped to slow the drift of young people into liberal evangelical churches. The Australian historian, Geoff Treloar, has argued that there was a change in evangelistic priorities from working men to youth.[93] In the Anglican Diocese of Sydney (a diocese is a district under the pastoral leadership of a Bishop) in the 1930s, conservative evangelicals took control of the key institutions, establishing a conservative evangelical diocese that would influence the other Protestant churches.[94] The resurgence of conservative evangelicalism strengthened the branch of youth ministry that emphasized the importance of conversion, which came to dominate the *nurture* branch by the 1950s.

As well as theology, there were institutional causes of change. New organizations emerged in the 1930s that were to influence ministry in the following decades with their particular model of ministry. In 1930 the Evangelical Union (EU) and the Crusader Union were formed in Sydney. In 1934 the Inter-School Christian Fellowship (ISCF) began. In 1930 the Presbyterian Fellowship Australia (PFA) was formed and in 1934 the Church of England Fellowship (CEF) was established. These new organizations at university, schools, and churches began to overshadow the older societies that had previously been popular such as the Student Christian Movement (SCM), Christian Endeavor (CE), the YMCA, Boys Brigade, and Girls' Friendly Society (GFS).

Finally, there were individuals who were agents of change. A key person to be noted in this respect is Howard Guinness.[95] His model of ministry to young people emphasized leadership by the young, peer ministry, and evangelism. He was the founder of the EU and the Crusader Union, and his model subsequently shaped the ISCF and influenced fellowship groups. The model of ministry that was first applied in the university was

---

91. Carpenter, *Revive Us Again*, 3–12.

92. Stanley, *Global Diffusion*, 13, 96.

93. Treloar, *Disruption of Evangelicalism*, 238; Judd and Cable, *Sydney Anglicans*, 246.

94. Judd, "Defenders of Their Faith"; Judd and Cable, *Sydney Anglicans*, 225–50.

95. Howard Guinness was a British evangelist and pastor. As a student he had been involved in the founding of the London Inter-Faculty Christian Union in 1923. When the InterVarsity Fellowship was established in 1928, he became the Vice Chairman. He was sent as an itinerant evangelist to the British colonies and established student and schools work in Canada, New Zealand, and Australia. Braga, "Guinness"; Guinness, *Journey among Students*.

later brought into the churches. Paul White[96] was an important leader and mentor both within the EU and the schools ministry. Other agents were the Anglican Archdeacon T. C. Hammond[97] and Archbishop Howard Mowll[98] who shaped the theological outlook of the Anglican Diocese of Sydney. Key influences in the fellowship movement were exercised by John Jamieson[99] in the Presbyterian Church, Alan Walker[100] in the Methodist church, and Graham Delbridge[101] in the Anglican church. There was also a myriad of

96. Paul White was an Australian missionary doctor, evangelist, and author. When Guinness came to Sydney in 1930, White became a key leader in the newly formed EU and Crusader Union. He became the General Secretary of the Australian InterVarsity Fellowship in 1943 and remained involved in the Crusader Union and Scripture Union for the rest of his life. He was a dynamic Christian speaker and wrote the famous Jungle Doctor books for young people. Loane, "White"; White, *Alias Jungle Doctor*.

97. T. C. Hammond was an Irish Anglican evangelist with a background in philosophy and logic who worked with the Irish Church Missions. He was involved in matters of controversy and law in Ireland in a tumultuous time. He was invited to be the Principal at Moore Theological College in Sydney by Archbishop Mowll in 1935 to give some academic weight to the conservative evangelicals. In 1936 he published his influential book *In Understanding Be Men* for the IVF. He was a popular speaker at the EU, at conventions and house parties. Nelson, "Howard"; *T. C. Hammond*.

98. Howard Mowll was a student leader, missionary, and church leader. He was President of the Cambridge Inter-Collegiate Christian Union (CICUU) in 1910, the year that they broke away from the SCM. He became a missionary bishop in China in 1922. Then in 1933 he was invited to become the Anglican Archbishop of Sydney, where he served until his death twenty-five years later. He was a big man who was charismatic and energetic, who led the expansion of conservative evangelical ministry in Sydney. He was a keen advocate of youth ministry. Loane, "Mowll"; *Archbishop Mowll*.

99. The Reverend J. C. Jamieson was born in New Zealand and was a leader in Presbyterian youth ministry in his native country and in Australia. He was involved in the Bible Class Movement in New Zealand, the YMCA, and the student movement. In 1911 he left New Zealand to become the travelling secretary of the Methodist Welfare of Youth Department NSW and to support the Presbyterian Fellowship Union. In 1924, he became the travelling secretary for youth work in Melbourne. In 1927, he became the Director of Youth Work in Melbourne until he retired in 1948. He was a noted leader and speaker and he wrote the manual for the Fellowship Association as well as many Bible Class books. "Register"; Jamieson, "Modern Fellowship Association."

100. Alan Walker was a Methodist minister and evangelist. He ran a significant ministry in Waverley from 1944 to 1954 with an outreach to youth and a community center. He led and preached at the Mission to the Nation from 1953 to 1956 and ran the Wesley Mission in Sydney from 1958 to 1978. He also founded the Lifeline telephone crisis service. Wright, *Conscience of the Nation*.

101. Graham Delbridge was a charismatic mentor of young people as well as an Anglican church leader. He was a protégé of Archbishop Mowll who appointed him to be Sydney Diocesan chaplain for youth in 1943, a role he remained in until 1952. In this role, he formed a youth department that acquired campsites and ran camps, rallies, and leadership training. Under his ministry, the department energetically sought to evangelize youth. Later he became the Bishop of Wollongong, and then the Bishop

student leaders who took up positions of leadership and became agents of change as their generation shaped the culture of the ministry. Finally, the influence of Billy Graham[102] must be assessed. He was the evangelist par excellence, whose model of revivalism was embraced in Sydney in the 1950s and beyond partly because of the model of ministry amongst youth that had already been in operation since the 1930s.

Structure

In chapter two, the paradigm of youth ministry in Australia before 1930 will be described. This chapter will compare the paradigm of those involved with youth ministry in Sydney before 1930 with the approach taken after 1930. It will argue that the paradigm of youth ministry from 1890 to 1930 was one based on ministry *for* youth. It emphasized nurturing the faith of young Christians to form Christian citizens and used a religious education model and the *Foursquare* approach. *Nurture* will be understood as a methodology based on the slow cultivation of faith through care as well as though biblical and moral teaching. *Religious education* will be defined as a pedagogical model of teacher to student, imparting Christian truths. *Foursquare* was a psychological educational system that posits four aspects of the person: spiritual, social, intellectual, and physical, and that all four need to be developed in the young person.

In the 1930s and 1940s, the paradigm changed from a ministry *for* youth to a ministry *of* youth. Youth, rather than adults, led the ministries themselves. The paradigm focused on the conversion of young people rather than on nurture. It encouraged young people to be involved in *peer ministry*, defined as serving each other within their peer group and seeking to *witness*[103] or evangelize other young people. This model emphasized *fellowship*,

---

of Gippsland. Dickey, "Delbridge, Graham Richard (1917–1980)"; Loane, *Mark These Men*; Harris et al., *Delbridge Years*.

102. Billy Graham was a conservative American Baptist pastor and speaker who became a global celebrity. As a young man, he was involved in the "Youth for Christ" movement as an evangelist. He became well known and supported as an evangelistic speaker both in the US and overseas and in his career spoke at 400 crusades in 185 countries. In 1959 he spoke at the Billy Graham Crusade in Sydney that led to the conversion of many young people. He was a key leader amongst the new evangelicals and he led a "revival of revivalism" in the 1950s. Carpenter, *Revive Us Again*, 211–32; Graham, *Just As I Am*.

103. Witness was a key word within youth ministries and the catchphrase of the EU: "I will be witnesses unto you," Acts 1:8. It was understood by young Christians as being faithful to Jesus in the way they lived their life, doing good deeds and taking up opportunities to actively proselytize their friends.

which should be understood as deep relationship with God and with each other. It was *coeducational*, that is, it brought men and women together in fellowship. It was a relational rather than an institutional model.

In chapters three to five, this new *ministry of youth* paradigm will be examined through the development of key youth ministries of the time including university ministries, school groups, and church fellowship groups. The paradigm was expressed in a *methodology*, that is, a particular way of doing ministry and practice within the organizations. In all the institutions a similar methodology was used that included leadership by young people, peer ministry, and the participation of both men and women. Despite the consistent methodology, there were two distinctive goals which expressed two different theological branches. All were seeking the Christianization of Australia, but in the theologically conservative parachurch organizations and the conservative fellowships this meant revival through the conversion of many young people. In the more liberal evangelical churches, the aim was to inspire young people to be part of a universal Christian youth movement that would bring about a new social order. The conservative vision was to become more dominant during this time period.

In chapter six, the study examines two challenges to the paradigm in the late 1930s: World War II and the Sinless Perfection movement. During the war, the youth ministries lost many of their key leaders (particularly men) and in many ways, the ministry was put on hold and numbers did not grow. The war did lead many to consider the reconstruction of society, and many within the church to consider how they might contribute to building a Christian civilization. The churches invested money and resources in the youth ministries. Along with war, Sinless Perfectionism challenged the model of ministry. This movement developed within the conservative youth organizations and threatened to divide organizations and damage the effectiveness of the ministries. The characteristics that had made the youth ministry strong were distorted in this movement: idealistic youthful leadership, conservative pietism that emphasized holiness, and a strong emphasis on fellowship. The model of youth-led ministry proved vulnerable, and there was a perceived need for older leaders to step in and take the leadership away from the young people in order to get the youth organizations back on the right track.

In chapter seven, the success of the model is demonstrated after the war until 1959. A clear paradigm had been established and now ministries were able to grow. Numbers increased and there was a new confidence and energy. Camping ministries became more important as they were viewed as the most effective way to evangelize young people and train leaders. There was an optimistic belief in the imminence of revival. There were many "youth to youth" missions at the university and churches, as Christians recognized the necessity of young people leading their own groups and engaging in peer ministry. The conservative vision of revival overshadowed the liberal vision of a new social order, and witness became the undisputed goal of ministry. The Billy Graham Crusade of 1959, the subject of chapter eight, showed that the model was effective. The decades of youth ministry cultivated the ground that the crusade sowed, and in the crusade itself, thousands of young people made a decision to become Christians, causing the youth ministries to grow exponentially. Throughout this book, the four causes noted above will be clearly in evidence: social forces, changes in the theological outlook of the church, new organizations and institutions, and key individuals.

2

Youth Ministry in Australia Before 1930

IN ORDER TO APPRECIATE the changes in youth ministry methodology during the 1930s, it is necessary to understand what was happening before 1930. In the previous chapter it was observed that there were changes over time in the way that youth ministry was conducted in the US and Britain, and that these changes have been conceptualized in three broad phases: 1740 to 1880, voluntary associations focused on conversion and personal reformation; 1880 to 1930, youth societies focused on nurture; and from the 1930s on, relational outreach focused on witness. This chapter will turn to Australia and will argue that this same pattern is evident. It will become clear that ways of thinking about youth ministry which originated in the US and Britain came to influence methodology in Australia also. This chapter will describe generally the first two phases of youth ministry in Australia and then turn to the immediate background of the 1930s. After the Great War, in the midst of the Depression, and with many children and young people leaving the church, the question was: What should be the vision for youth ministry in such a changed world? There was a sense of crisis in mission to youth, and a reappraisal of the methodology by which it should be conducted.

In Australia from the start of European colonization in 1788 until 1880, youth ministry was influenced by the evangelical concepts of revival and moral reformation. For these purposes, young people were viewed in much the same way as adults. The vision of those engaged in ministry was that young people would hear the gospel message and be converted. Their lives would be reformed, and this, in turn, would lead to the reformation of society. These assumptions can be seen in the methodology of ministries as diverse as the Sunday schools, the Scripture Union, Band of Hope, and the YMCA. After 1880, the assumptions and methodology changed through the influence of liberal religious educational thinking. Youth were now to receive a type of ministry distinct from ministry to adults that nurtured them to become future church members and Christian citizens. These new goals can be seen expressed in the Sunday schools, Christian Endeavor, Boys Brigade, and the GFS.

1788–1880: Revival and Reformation

Sunday Schools

The first phase of youth ministry was dominated by the impact of the evangelical revival across the English-speaking world. The mission of the Protestant Church in the age of revival was the evangelization of the world through teaching the message of the Bible and caring for the needy. Believers sought an awakening of people both at home and abroad to "true" (personal) religion. It was believed that this would lead to a reformation of the individual's life and ultimately to the reformation of society.[1] Revival thus led to an activism both in evangelistic endeavor and in charitable activity. The primary means in both cases was the formation of Christian associations and societies. Evangelical revival in England and the Second Great Awakening in the US had an enormous influence on young people in particular. There is evidence that the majority of those converted in the revivals were under the age of twenty five.[2] Many of those who had been converted in turn

---

1. In his influential book, William Wilberforce argued that in revival the fundamental doctrines of Christianity had the power to transform the morals of individuals and, in turn, to transform nations.
"If indeed, through the blessing of Providence, a principle of true religion should in any considerable degree gain ground, there is no estimating the effects on public morals and the consequent influence on our political welfare." Wilberforce, *Practical View*, 277.

2. David Bebbington studied conversion accounts, many from a more Calvinist background between 1750 and 1850, finding that 82 percent of conversions were at the age of twenty-five or below, and that adolescence was the peak time for conversion. Bebbington, "Evangelical Conversion," 110. Michael Watts studied Dissenters from around the same time and his results were that 74 percent of conversions were under the age of twenty-five for Dissenters. Watts, *Dissenters*, 121.

focused their energy and time on ministry among the young, particularly in the Sunday schools[3] and later in other youth societies.[4]

The colonization of Australia in 1788 came at a time when the influence of the evangelical revival was still strong, and many believed the role of Christian leaders was to provide for the evangelization and reform of those who arrived in the penal colony. Evangelical leaders such as William Wilberforce worked to ensure that there would be an evangelical ministry in the Sydney colony and looked for a suitable chaplain to send with the First Fleet. In 1786, the Reverend John Newton wrote to Wilberforce:

> To you, as the instrument, we owe the pleasing prospect of an opening for the propagation of the Gospel in the Southern Hemisphere. Who can tell what important consequences may depend on Mr Johnson's going to New Holland . . . This small beginning may be like the dawn which advances to a brighter day, and lead on to the happy time when many nations, which now sit in darkness and in the region of the shadow of death, shall rejoice in the light of the Sun of Righteousness.[5]

It seems that colonization in New South Wales was seen by evangelical leaders as an opportunity. Criminals would be plucked out of their home context with its bad influences and be taken to the colony where they would hear the gospel and reform their lives. In Australia, a godly nation could be created through the power of the gospel that would be the beginning of God's kingdom in the southern hemisphere.[6]

This evangelical mission to bring about conversion and reform through the teaching of the message of the Bible found expression in the formation of Sunday schools. The first Australian Sunday school was established in Parramatta in 1813 by Thomas Hassall who was only nineteen years old.[7] Two years later, he became the secretary and superintendent of the newly formed

---

3. For example, the historian Anne Boylan argues that many of the organizers of Sunday schools were those who had recently experienced conversion in the Great Awakening. Boylan, *Sunday School*, 10.

4. For more on societies formed after the Evangelical Revival, see Wolffe, *Expansion of Evangelicalism*, 176–82.

5. Wilberforce and Wilberforce, *Correspondence*, 15.

6. Piggin argues that the evangelicals saw the colony as a means to bringing revival and reformation to the world. Through it, there would be reformation of the convicts as well as outreach to the indigenous peoples, and the beginning of a mission to the South Seas. Piggin, *Spirit, Word and World*, 3.

7. Thomas Hassall was the son of a London Missionary Society missionary Rowland Hassall who was sent to preach to the natives of the South Seas but came to settle in the Sydney colony assisting the chaplains in their ministry. Gunson, "Hassall, Thomas."

Sunday School Institute. Hassall formed his Sunday school after he met a young Irish boy, Jemmy Mullins, who knew nothing of the Bible. He invited Jemmy into his living room to teach him to read, and soon other children joined them. After a few years, Jemmy died, but because of the Sunday school, Hassall praised God that he would be in a "better world at his death."[8] The first Sunday school was established to bring salvation to young souls, but also to bring reform through education and reading the Bible.

Over time, more Sunday schools were established in Sydney with the goal of bringing about moral reformation, especially for the children of convicts. The Sunday schools were intended to rescue poor and benighted children from bad influences, including parents and friends.[9] The editor of the *Sydney Gazette* recorded in 1821 that the Sunday school at the Carters' Barracks of 150 boys:

> . . . is intended for the moral culture and reclamation of poor convict boys, who have (by early depravity) been exiled from friends and kindred in Europe to the distant shores of New South Wales, where the benign intention of our mild laws are, at length, evidently becoming blessed in their fullest completion.[10]

It was hoped that these children would be awakened and reformed through being taught the Bible: "by that instruction which will not only, it is hoped, restore them to society, but also fit them for hereafter."[11] It was even hoped that Sunday school children might reform their convict parents.[12]

The Sunday schools relied on the teaching of the Bible to bring about conversion and reformation in children. The Bible was central to evangelical faith as the authoritative basis of faith and values.[13] In the Sunday schools

---

8. Earnshaw, *Fanned into Flame*, 16.

9. The preeminent historian of the Sunday school movement, Lacquer, argues that the early Sunday schools in England were similarly motivated. "For some, the new institution was an instrument for the moral rescue of poor children from their corrupt parents, thereby at one stroke insuring the happiness of the little ones and the regeneration of society." Lacquer, *Religion and Respectability*, 4.

10. *Sydney Gazette and NSW Advertiser*, September 1, 1821, 3. The newspaper recorded that there were now Church of England and Methodist Sunday Schools in Windsor, Liverpool, and Parramatta, and three Wesleyan Sunday schools in Sydney.

11. *Sydney Gazette and NSW Advertiser*, September 1, 1821, 3.

12. *Sydney Gazette and NSW Advertiser*, September 1, 1821, 3.

13. Lacquer argues that evangelicals had a passionate belief in the Bible to regenerate lost souls and therefore literacy was a high priority. "[T]he word of God contained all that was necessary for the salvation of the soul. And, since evangelicalism was a highly individualistic form of religion, a religion of the spirit, it was thought essential that everyone have direct access to the truth of scripture." Lacquer, *Religion and Respectability*, 9.

teachers read the stories of the Bible and taught children to memorize passages of Scripture and to learn the basic catechetical material (that is, some basic doctrinal teaching in the form of question and answer).[14] The Sunday school children were examined once a year to encourage learning and were given incentives such as medals, books, and tracts. Although the methodology was formal and didactic, the ultimate goal was that the child would experience an authentic evangelical conversion. Many believed that this typically occurred in the middle to late teenage years.[15] For a lot of children, the ultimate incentive for involvement was the Sunday school anniversary service which was followed by a feast of plum cake, wine, and sugar water, donated by a wealthy patron.[16]

By 1880, it seemed that the Sunday schools were achieving their ambitious goals—this year was the centenary of the first Robert Raikes'[17] Sunday school, and in Australia, the Protestant churches were involved in celebrations. There were multiple conferences and services leading up to the centenary, and in June a large celebration took place in the Garden Palace with eleven thousand Sunday school children and their teachers.[18] In a public address at the conference, it was claimed that the growth of Sunday schools in Australia was now greater than in Britain[19] and that Sunday schools were teaching about half of all those under fifteen.[20]

Despite these large numbers, there was still anxiety that the Sunday schools were not effectively evangelizing older students. Sunday school supporters were concerned many adolescents graduated from Sunday school but were never converted. Some argued that rather than treating adolescents as

14. For example, in the 1830 examination at St. Philip's York St., some of the boys had memorized all of the book of Matthew. "To the Editor of the Sydney Gazette," *Sydney Gazette and NSW Advertiser*, June 5, 1830, 3.

15. Lacquer, *Religion and Respectability*, 92.

16. After the examination in 1830, the children were fed on plum cake and fourteen or sixteen bottles of wine and a surfeit of sugar and water (this was before the influence of the temperance societies). "To the Editor," June 5, 1830, 3.

17. Robert Raikes was a British philanthropist who is credited with the founding of the Sunday school movement beginning in England and spreading to the rest of the world. Anon., "Robert Raikes"; Cliff, *Rise and Development*; Lacquer, *Religion and Respectability*; Orchard and Briggs, *Sunday School Movement*.

18. "Sunday School Centenary," *Sydney Morning Herald*, July 6, 1880, 6.

19. "Sunday School Centenary," *Sydney Morning Herald*, July 6, 1880, 6. It was claimed that in Britain there were three million pupils involved in Sunday schools out of a population of eighty million, which is roughly equivalent to one in ten. In Australia, there were one hundred thousand children in Sunday schools, so one in eight people were in Sunday school.

20. Kelley, "Nurseries for Christians," 256.

children, there needed to be new ministries that focused on them as a distinctive group. At a Church of England Sunday school conference in 1880, Mr. Alex Gordon[21] spoke on *How to Retain the Hold of the Church upon our Elder Scholars* and recommended that "Bible Classes" should be established.

> For them, there must be some organization outside the Sunday School, such an organization as a Bible Class, conducted by someone who would make it felt to be a distinction by the youths who gather around him.[22]

These classes would involve serious study of the Bible and discussion. A Sunday school teacher or the minister would conduct them on a Sunday afternoon for an hour, in a room separate from the Sunday school. Despite Gordon's challenge, the Bible Class did not catch on in Australia as it did in New Zealand and America.[23]

Youth Associations

In the mid nineteenth century, societies were being formed in Sydney concerned for the revival and reform of young people and they supplemented the work of the Sunday schools. The YMCA[24] was an association in Sydney that did cater for older children and young men and sought to both evangelize and reform them. It was particularly concerned for young workers and the temptations they might face in the corruption of the industrialized city, and for *larrikins* (the Australian vernacular term for juvenile delinquent).[25]

---

21. Alex Gordon was a QC, Chancellor of Sydney Diocese of the Church of England, and became a member of the council of the Church of England Sunday School Institute. "Church of England Sunday School Institute," *Sydney Morning Herald*, August 6, 1884, 11.

22. "Sunday School Centenary," *Sydney Morning Herald*, July 6, 1880, 6.

23. The Bible Class movement was particularly championed by the Presbyterian Church in those countries. The question of why the Bible Class movement did not take off in Australia may be answered by the fact that the Presbyterian Church in NSW championed its new youth organization, the Presbyterian Fellowship Union, as a substitute to the Bible Class movement.

24. The YMCA was the foremost evangelical youth organization of the nineteenth century according to Joseph Kett. Kett, *Rites of Passage*, 199. It began in 1844 in London and its goal was to reach young men, particularly those who were leaving home to work in industrial cities. The American revival preacher Moody was a key leader in the movement in America and Britain in the 1870s and 80s. The first YMCA in Sydney was established in 1853; see Shedd, *World's Alliance*; Hopkins, *History of the Y. M. C. A.*; Massey, *Y. M. C. A. in Australia*.

25. The historian Anthony Platt has called the youth movements of the nineteenth century the "child saver" movement and believes they were a response to adult concern

It was aggressively evangelistic and organized Saturday night meetings for young men, distributed tracts at the wharves to the sailors, and waited at the dock to greet young male emigrants to give them Christian support and counsel. At the very first YMCA lecture in 1853, the Reverend George King explained that the goal of the YMCA was:

> . . . to win the mind away from vulgar and degrading scenes of amusement which court attention at every corner of the streets. And in the case of the newly arrived immigrant, who may have left the bosom of a happy family, to come and spend his days amongst us, while they in some measure remind him of home in by-gone days . . . The object, then, towards which our labours will be directed is man—man as a social being, and man as an immortal being; and the practical working of this Association will consist in bringing within the reach of the youth around us the various moral appliances, healthful mental exercise, and religious instruction.[26]

The YMCA methodological priority was to evangelize, but also to provide young men with healthy entertainment, educational and religious lectures, and a virtuous peer group, to keep them away from temptation.

Another association seeking revival and reform in the nineteenth century in NSW was the Band of Hope Union.[27] The Union was formed in 1856 when local temperance groups were brought together in the one association. The groups met in churches and were often linked to Sunday schools, though they were not officially church organizations. Like the YMCA, they were concerned for larrikins, especially younger boys who might be wandering the streets and vulnerable to evil influences.[28] The purpose of the Band of Hope Union was to "interest and train the child for temperance and good citizenship."[29] By focusing their efforts on younger children, organizers aimed at a double reformation, to save the child from the clutches of

---

and fear of juvenile delinquency. See Platt, *Child Savers*.

26. "The YMCA," *Sydney Morning Herald*, October 8, 1853, 4.

27. Trimmer, "Children," 151. It is difficult to find hard numbers of how many children and young people were involved in the Band of Hope. In 1890 there were over four thousand in Australia. "Band of Hope," *Sydney Morning Herald*, November 7, 1890, 7. Later, in the 1920s there seems to be a new peak of 24,575 members. "Australian Band of Hope," *Sydney Morning Herald*, September 25, 1925, 12. It became a revival movement through engaging young people in the church.

28. Bessant, "Patchwork," 82.

29. Stanton, "An Old Movement, Band of Hope Revival," *Sydney Morning Herald*, November 14, 1933, 11.

alcohol through early instruction, and—by elevating the child to the status of paragon—to issue a message to the wider community.[30]

Scripture Union (SU) and the Childrens' Special Service Mission (CSSM) were also associations that sought to evangelize children and young people.[31] In NSW the Scripture Union was founded in 1880 by Eliza Hassall (the daughter of Thomas) in Parramatta. Young people were encouraged to join branches and were then sent a membership card with Bible readings for a year. In 1884 an Australian CSSM was formed as an association and members were encouraged:

> To always remember that the end of all Scripture is "to make wise unto salvation through faith in Jesus Christ," and the distinct aim of the Scripture Union is "to bring to present decision to Christ, and to feed and to strengthen those who have eternal life in him."[32]

In Australia, the two associations became branches of the one organization, the Scripture Union and Childrens' Special Service Mission. Their method was to preach the Christian message in the open air at beaches and to call on children to make a decision for Christ. Those who responded were then encouraged to grow in faith by reading the Bible regularly. The founder of the CSSM in Britain, Joseph Spiers, believed that the CSSM was the missing link between Sunday school and a young person finding a personal faith. The beach missions could be "reaping times" after the "sowing" of the Sunday schools.[33] By 1886 there were 170 Scripture Union branches in NSW and ten thousand members.[34] In 1888 the first beach mission was held at Manly on a Saturday afternoon.[35] The peak of the Scripture Union was 22,500 in NSW in 1892, numbers not exceeded until after the Billy Graham Crusades of 1959.[36]

---

30. Sleight, "Sake of Effect," 4.

31. For more on the history of the Scripture Union and CSSM see Pollock, *Good Seed*.

32. Shrimpton, "Letter to Members," October 30, 1884, "Scripture Union and CSSM Australia, Council Minutes Vol. 1, 1884–1906."

33. Pollock, *Good Seed*, 27.

34. Prince, *Tuned In to Change*, 19.

35. Prince, *Tuned In to Change*, 24.

36. Prince, *Tuned In to Change*, 29.

The Student Movement

The student movement[37] does not quite fit into Senter's scheme, but its importance merits separate treatment. By date, it belongs to the later era of societies, but in character, it has more in common with the earlier evangelical associations with their concern for conversion and roots in revival.[38] The movement began in the US in response to the Moody-inspired revivals of the nineteenth century.[39] In 1886, John Mott,[40] a convert of Moody's, spoke at a conference at Mount Hermon, Massachusetts. After some stirring talks, students were encouraged to sign a declaration that they would become missionaries. One hundred students signed their names, and the Student Volunteer Movement (SVM) was born.[41] Mott then founded the World's Student Christian Federation (WSCF) in 1895 as he travelled around the world visiting Christian organizations in universities and colleges and YMCAs to unite them in an international movement. The ultimate goal of the movement was "the evangelisation of the world in this generation,"[42] and many students were inspired by Mott's incredible optimism about the spread of God's kingdom, inspired by his postmillennial theology.[43] Mott

---

37. University student ministry is not always included within discussion on youth ministry. We are defining youth ministry as Root defines it, as an "age-specific ministry to young people," and *youth* as the time between childhood and adulthood, a transition period of semi-dependency upon parents. University ministry fits within these parameters. Root, *Relational Youth Ministry*, 26.

38. There were strong links between the youth movement and the YMCA too, particularly through the influence of Mott.

39. Dwight L. Moody (1837–1899) was an American Evangelist and leader in the YMCA whose evangelistic campaigns in the UK and America in the late nineteenth century, it is said, led to the conversion of millions. See Evensen, *God's Man*; Bebbington, *Dominance of Evangelicalism*.

40. John Mott (1865–1955) was the leader of the YMCA movement, the Student Volunteer Movement, and the World Student Christian Federation. See Hopkins, *John R. Mott*; Treloar, *Disruption of Evangelicalism*.

41. Trimmer, "Children"; Hopkins, *John R. Mott*, 60. Harder claims that by 1920, twenty thousand students had been recruited for missionary work. Harder, "Student Volunteer Movement," 142.

42. Harder, "Student Volunteer Movement," 26.

43. Mott was shaped by the postmillennial theology. Postmillennialism is a philosophy of history that states that there will be a *golden age* for the church for a symbolic one thousand years before Jesus Christ returns. Mott believed that God's kingdom on earth was being progressively realized through advances in mission, education, and science. His goal was to "enthrone Jesus Christ as King among all nations and races of men," that is, to preach the gospel in order to Christianize non-Western countries and that when that was accomplished, Jesus would return. Mott, *Evangelization of the World*, 8; *Student Missionary Uprising*, 19; Koester, "Future in Our Past," 137–44.

and other leaders of the student movement became influential in the ecumenical movement. Their vision was not a union of churches, but rather a union of Christian youth in cooperation and intercommunion that would transform the world.[44] The WSCF sought to evangelize and enlist students to be part of this great mission. The three goals were:

> (a) To lead students to become disciples of Jesus Christ as only Saviour and God (b) To deepen the spiritual lives of believers (c) To enlist students into the work of extending the Kingdom of God throughout the whole world.[45]

University students were encouraged to organize services and study groups, to witness to their friends and to consider the possibility of future missionary service.

Christian ministry amongst university students was based on a particular understanding of how to transform society. Mott's strategy was to target young men who would be the future leaders in the church, government, and professions. While they were at university, they were open to being molded and having their life direction set upon Christian service. Mott said that these were "the vision-forming years, the habit-forming years, the years of determining life attitudes and tendencies, the years of discovering, of invention, of creation."[46] Mott was influenced by missiologists such as Alexander Duff,[47] who in the mid nineteenth century, attempted to educate and Christianize upper caste Indians, believing that the knowledge of Christianity would eventually filter down the social ladder. This came to be known as the *downward filtration* theory of evangelism.[48] Mott's goal was to Christianize non-Western nations and to ensure that Western nations maintained their Christian heritage. A key phrase in the student movement was: "Students—strategic points in the world's conquest."[49] Mott saw the student movement as a strategic military camp in training, and himself as the commander-in-chief responsible for military strategy.[50]

---

44. The organizations YMCA, SVM, and WSCF were all driving forces within the ecumenical movement. Treloar, *Disruption of Evangelicalism*, 219–22.

45. Hopkins, *John R. Mott*, 130.

46. Howe, *Century of Influence*, 38.

47. Alexander Duff (1800–1878) was a missionary of the Church of Scotland to India in the nineteenth century.

48. Kalapati, "Early Educational Mission," 140–55; Heredia, "Education and Mission," 2332–340.

49. Rouse, *World's Student Christian Federation*, 23.

50. Harder, "Student Volunteer Movement," 144.

The student movement was highly effective in its early years in raising up young leaders who were committed to self-sacrificial service. This commitment was fostered by the holiness theology espoused by Mott and Moody.[51] Central in holiness theology was the idea of *consecrating* one's life as a response to the Christian gospel; a radical giving up of one's own will to obey the will of God. This experience of self-consecration, an act of faith similar to conversion and sometimes described as a second blessing of the Spirit, was characterized by Randall as a "crisis and subsequent process in Christian experience."[52] It was understood as a daily process, of "making Jesus Lord" in your life, or as one of the holiness slogans put it, Jesus "wants to be Lord of all, or he will not be Lord at all."[53] The experience of consecration led many within the SVM to great religious passion and activism, particularly in missionary service. Kett suggests that following the experience of understanding the sacrifice of Christ to save them, self-consecration in dedicating one's life to sacrificial service was like a "super-charger." This subsequent commitment "acted not only as a resolution of religious and vocational anxieties but also as a supercharger, propelling then into religious careers characterized by lofty aims and extraordinary sacrifice."[54]

The Australian student movement began at Sydney University in 1896 when Mott arrived on his world tour. As a result of his visit, the

---

51. For a clear explanation of the nature of Keswick movement see Randall, *Evangelical Experiences*, 1–10; Harford, *Keswick Convention*. In Sydney, the Keswick movement continued to be a significant influence on Protestant Christian youth well into the 1950s. The Katoomba Christian Convention which was a Keswick-style convention, a kind of spiritual clinic, taught this view of holiness, as did many of the CMS missionaries, particularly those who had experienced revival in East Africa. Lawton, "Better Time to Be," 23. The visit of Keswick speaker George Grubb to Australia in 1890/1891 had also led to the conversion of many and influenced many future leaders of evangelical youth ministry in their focus on evangelism. Piggin, "Bicentennial History," 30; Deane, "New Evangelical Movements."

52. Randall, *Evangelical Experiences*, 27.

53. Randall, *Evangelical Experiences*, 29–30.

54. Kett, *Rites of Passage*, 70. The finest example of students exercising this kind of radical service was C. T. Studd who was one of the so-called "Cambridge Seven." Studd was a wealthy student who was converted after hearing Moody preach at a mission in Cambridge in 1885. He then had a second experience of consecration after reading a holiness book. This experience of consecration led him to give up his place in the English cricket team and to give away every cent of a sizable fortune in order to become a missionary. The Cambridge Seven toured the US in 1886 and inspired the leaders of the SVM. He worked in China, India, and Africa persevering through poverty, ill-health, and loneliness to die in Africa at the age of 70. In his book *The Chocolate Soldier*, Studd called on students to sacrifice all in Christian service as soldiers of Jesus Christ. "For me to live is Christ, to die is gain. I'll be a militant. A man of God. A gambler for Christ. A hero." Studd, *Chocolate Soldier*, 1; Grubb, *C. T. Studd*.

Australian Student Christian Union (ASCU, later named the Student Christian Movement or SCM) and the SVM were formed that year. Both these organizations were originally very popular with students and effective in encouraging evangelism and missionary service.[55] The students organized study groups, services, and "house-parties" (time away in a holiday house or campsite). The national movement was able to employ travelling secretaries (often young graduates) who would travel around the country encouraging the student leaders and organizing national events, but the real work was done by students themselves.

1880–1930: The Societies and Nurture

The youth ministry in Sydney before 1880 was thus based on a model of revival and reformation, largely inherited from youth ministries begun in England in the evangelical revivals. At the time of the Sunday school anniversary in 1880, it seemed that with such large numbers attending Sunday schools in Australia, success in evangelism and the formation of a Christian nation was in sight. It soon became obvious, however, that there were challenges to be faced and that new methods would be necessary for the modern age. The introduction of compulsory free education in 1880 meant that Sunday schools had to reassess their raison d'etre. Another challenge was the continued leakage of older scholars from the Sunday schools. In addition, there were intellectual currents that were to shape a new methodology of ministry to youth. These included liberal evangelical theology, the emerging discipline of psychology, and new educational methods exhibited in the religious education movement. Revival historian Robert Evans claims that this led to a change in the expectations of evangelicals about conversion and ministry to young people:

> There was a widespread turning away by many Christians from the stereotype that conversion should normally be sudden and powerful to the idea that Christian education could produce slow conversions, in the young especially, and that this was more desirable.[56]

In youth ministries in Sydney, there was a consequent move away from conversionist evangelism to the nurturing of Christian character.

---

55. Stanley Addison was the main administrator of the SCM in 1906 and he estimated that at that time about one sixth of Australian university students attended Bible classes. This figure does not include the other students who attended conferences, meetings, and camps. Howe, *Century of Influence*, 81.

56. Evans, "Collecting for Revival," 66.

A significant challenge was the Public Instruction Act of 1880[57] which meant the Sunday schools had to reexamine their purpose. Through this act, the state provided free compulsory education for all children aged six to fourteen years. State funding of denominational schools ended, and many churches had to give control of their parochial schools to the state government. They did so in exchange for the assurance that they would have access to the state schools through Special Religious Instruction (SRI),[58] and that Sunday schools on the Sabbath would supplement the SRI. Sunday school was no longer a vehicle of education and reformation of the poor, but a foundational religious education for all children, to supplement what they were learning in school. Clergy saw it as primarily their responsibility to give religious education to the young in both contexts, and much time was devoted to teaching large SRI classes,[59] as well as encouraging Sunday schools.[60]

Another challenge to ministry was the fact that older children continued to leave the Sunday schools. There was a real concern for the "elder scholar" that was becoming more urgent. In *The Methodist* in 1899, the Reverend J. Woodhouse claimed that the greatest failure of the Sunday schools was their inability to retain the elder scholars; there was a *chasm* or *leakage* between Sunday school and full church membership.

> The idea that the Sunday School is *for* children, clings to its very organization and stands in the way of improvement in this direction. Wherever success has been won in gaining or retaining scholars of advanced years (say beyond sixteen or seventeen) a change of name has been adopted.[61]

Woodhouse argued that there should be a different department, a senior department of the Sunday school, that would be in a different location and time and would encourage the young people in personal service of the church.[62] Although he was not the only person advocating a senior depart-

---

57. Earnshaw, *Fanned into Flame*, 35.

58. In the legislation, an hour of class a day was to be given over to Special Religious Instruction by a denominational minister. This hour was called *scripture*.

59. Not just primary schools but the growing number of secondary schools too.

60. Despite the changing purpose of Sunday schools after 1880, the popularity of the institution remained high, particularly amongst younger children. The peak of numbers was probably in 1906, with the Methodist Church leading the way. According to Earnshaw's numbers, over 60 percent of children in NSW were members of Sunday schools in 1906. Earnshaw, *Fanned into Flame*, 62.

61. "Sunday Schools: Their Strengths and Weaknesses; With Suggestions to Improve Methods," *The Methodist*, February 11, 1899, 6.

62. An important factor in the problem was that many young people were leaving

ment, very few Sunday schools had success in this area and the problem of leakage persisted. In the Church of England, when a young person turned fourteen, they were confirmed and were expected to become a fully-fledged member of the congregation. Instead, many young people often left the church after confirmation. For example, at St Paul's Anglican Church in Chatswood in the 1920s, confirmation was seen as the "the done thing," and "often treated as a graduation service out of Church life."[63] In all churches, there was a desire to combat this attitude. As early as 1902, three hundred Sunday school teachers gathered at St Paul's Anglican in Redfern to hear a lecture on "How to retain our young people."[64]

Another force of change was the new discipline of psychology. Psychology was influential in the universities, in education and in the church. There was a growing concern that educators should cater to the psychological needs of the young person, not merely teach the content of the Bible. There was also an emphasis on adolescence as a psychological stage that must be addressed. In this study, it has been noted that Kett and other historians have highlighted the influence of G. Stanley Hall and in particular his analysis of adolescence as a difficult time of transition between childhood and adulthood. There were other writers, such as William Forbush's *The Boy Problem* (1901),[65] who wrote about the "problem" of the adolescent boy. The boy problem emerged in adolescence because the adolescent boy was influenced by "sex instincts" and the "herd mentality" at a time of life that would shape character and life forever. The problem was exacerbated by an increasingly urban life, which provided temptations for the boy such as alcohol, cigarettes, sex, and gangs. If he gave into temptation, this problem could develop into "juvenile delinquency."[66] The response required was for adults to provide for boys' psychological nurture, and youth societies were formed to do this. According to Hendrick, youth societies were created for:

---

school and working at the age of 14. The challenge was how to retain the working young person.

63. Hicks, *City on a Hill*, 123.
64. Earnshaw, *Fanned into Flame*, 66.
65. William Byron Forbush (1868–1927) was an American Congregational minister who became the expert on church work with adolescent boys and published many popular books on boys that became essential reading for Australian Sunday school teachers and other youth societies. For more on Forbush and the adolescent boy see Macleod, "Act Your Age," 3–20.
66. Forbush argued that the gang mentality of youth can lead to juvenile delinquency. The answer was to understand the psychology of the adolescent boy and engage with him accordingly. For example, adolescent boys are prone to hero worship, so older mentors and the example of Christ are very important. Forbush, *Boy Problem*, 20, 23.

... keeping boys "off the streets": actively teaching the value of discipline, spreading the public school *esprit de corps*, and generally advocating the intangible virtues of "character."[67]

Youth societies sought to develop a strong Christian peer group with shared values and a strong devotion to one another, much as one would find in the English public schools. This was described as *esprit de corps* and strengthened by providing healthy entertainments and group-building exercises such as team sports, camping, hikes, and military-style drills. It also corresponded with the muscular Christianity movement which sought to nurture character and values such as Christian manliness. This focus on nurturing character had an impact on the nineteenth century youth organizations in Australia. Those in leadership believed that adolescence was the most critical stage of life and they began to teach leaders that their role involved understanding and responding to the psychological needs of youth rather than simply teaching the content of the Bible, as will be shown in this study.

As well as psychology, liberal theology shaped ministry to youth. The years 1880 to 1930 were arguably the high point of liberal evangelicalism in Australia.[68] Liberal theology had challenged the old literal way of reading the Bible and the Bible had become for some, a "somewhat uncertain source of information."[69] This led many to believe that there should be a greater emphasis on social ramifications of the faith rather than an individualistic emphasis on salvation.[70] Many of the educational leaders were shaped by liberal theology and aspired to be open to modern schools of thought such as psychology and the theory of evolution. The historian David Setran has argued that:

> Such a theological stance made for an easy transition from religious to character education, from explicitly doctrinal notions to ethical precepts derived from human experience.[71]

---

67. Hendrick, *Images of Youth*, 159. The muscular Christianity movement began at the end of the nineteenth century inspired by the novels of Charles Kingsley and Thomas Hughes. They were concerned that the Oxford movement was making the Church of England effeminate. They sought to encourage "manliness" in Christians through public school values such as "esprit de corps," games, and sport. Watson et al., "Development of Muscular Christianity," 2.

68. In the 1920s in Australia Piggin argues that the liberal evangelicalism "star was in the ascendant." Piggin, *Spirit, Word and World*, 79.

69. Hansen, "Churches and Society," 51.

70. Hansen, "Churches and Society," 53.

71. Setran, "Morality," 111.

There was a theological transition from doctrine to ethics. Conversion and revival became less of a goal, and instead, leaders sought to foster a holistic education shaped by current academic thought.

Psychology and liberal theology were to influence ministry in Australia particularly through the Religious Education Association (REA) established in 1903 in the US and led by educationalists such as George Albert Coe,[72] William Rainey Harper,[73] and George Hamilton Archibald.[74] This organization brought together Sunday school leaders, executives of YMCAs, and leaders of other organizations to forge new ways of thinking and a new methodology of ministry. The REA stated that:

> The religious and moral instruction of the young is at present inadequate, and imperfectly correlated with other instruction in history, literature and the sciences, and that the Sunday School, as the primary institution for the religious and moral education of the young, should be conformed to a higher ideal, and made different for its work by the gradation of pupils, and by the adaptation of its material and method of instruction to the several stages of mental, moral, and spiritual growth of the individual.[75]

The REA sought to influence those who did ministry with youth to engage with modern thought and the best of biblical criticism. They advocated

---

72. George Albert Coe (1862–1951) was a professor of philosophy at Northwestern University from 1891 to 1909 and then at Union Theological Seminary from 1909 to 1922. Coe began life as an orthodox evangelical, but doubts about orthodox notions such as atonement, sin, and conversion led him to embrace liberal Protestantism. He stressed the significance of religious experience and ethical living within communities and nations and wrote about character formation and the significance of developing religious and moral character in young people. Setran, "Morality," 107–44.

73. William Rainey Harper (1856–1906) was appointed the first president of the University of Chicago in 1891. He was influenced by the work of liberal biblical scholars such as Welhausen and sought to harmonize higher criticism with the truth of the Bible. Lee, "Higher Criticism," 508–33.

74. George Hamilton Archibald (1858–1938) had been trained at the Springfield College of YMCA and later taught at the Westhill Training College in England which became a "training Institute for Sunday School Workers" and was founded with the patronage of George Cadbury, the chocolate king. He also worked as an extension lecturer for the English Sunday School Union. Archibald sought to embrace new ideas of biblical scholarship and teach in a way that recognized Scripture as biblical narrative and poetry rather than mere prose. Cliff claims that Archibald changed the face of Sunday school in all denominations across the world. In 1903 he ran a child study unit at the Sunday School Union Centenary convention in the US—this was the first articulation of the "New Methods." Cliff, *Rise and Development*, 206; Orchard and Briggs, *Sunday School Movement*, 235.

75. A purpose statement of the REA in 1903, quoted by Kathan. See Kathan, "Horace Bushnell," 52.

that Sunday schools abandon the old ideal of universal Sunday school lessons, and instead write materials that were aimed at specific age groups, that is, different lessons for the different stages of psychological development (graded lessons): beginner, primary, junior, intermediate, and senior. These were called the New Methods. They also sought to train Sunday school teachers in child developmental theory (as illustrated in fig. 1) so that they might be able to teach according to the new methods.

	PREVIEW OF THE SECOND			DIVISION—THE PUPIL.		
General	The BEGINNER is considered as follows:	The PRIMARY PUPIL is considered as follows:	The JUNIOR PUPIL is considered as follows:	The INTERMEDIATE PUPIL is considered as follows:	The SENIOR PUPIL is considered as follows:	The ADULT PUPIL is considered as follows:
	I. PHYSICALLY.			I. PHYSICALLY.		
Energy	1. Restless	1. Active	1. Energetic	1. Energy Lessened	1. Energy Greatly Increased	1. Endurance
Physical Dependence	2. Dependent	2. Less Dependent	2. Growing Independence	2. Self Sufficient	2. Self Reliant	2. Aggressive
	II. MENTALLY.			II. MENTALLY.		
Attention	1. Attention Brief	1. Attention Growing in Power	1. Voluntary Attention	1. Voluntary Attention Strengthened	1. Attention to the point of Application	1. Attention to the point of Concentration
Curiosity	2. Curiosity	2. Curiosity Strong	2. Inquisitive	2. Investigative	2. Independent thinking	2. Original Research
Memory	3. Memory but Slightly Developed	3. Memory Rapidly Developing	3. Verbal Memory at Height	3. Memory Based on Association of Ideas	3. Logical Memory	3. Philosophical and Practical Memory
Imagination	4. Imagination "Run Riot"	4. Imagination Imitative	4. Imagination Toned Down	4. Imaginative Literature a Delight	4. Imagination Productive of Ideals	4. Imagination Creative
	III. SOCIALLY.			III. SOCIALLY.		
Play	1. Plays Alone	1. Plays with Companions	1. Plays with the Gang	1. Plays with Team	1. Plays as Exhibition of Skill and Strength	1. Plays for Recreation
Egoism	2. Self Centered	2. Sensitive	2. Social Nature Developing	2. Self Conscious	2. Self Sacrificing	2. Service
	IV. SPIRITUALLY.			IV. SPIRITUALLY.		
Religion	1. Impressionable	1. Conversion a Possibility	1. Great Evangelistic Opportunity	1. Religious Crisis	1. Choice of Service	1. Life of Service

Note—This Chart in enlarged form, wall size, for class use, may be had from the Sunday School Board.

Figure 1: The New Convention Normal Manual for Sunday School Workers 1911[76]

The REA was shaped by the writing of Horace Bushnell and his concept of Christian nurture. He was called the "spiritual father" of the religious education movement.[77] In his book *Christian Nurture*, he argued that the church and Christian parents should cultivate Christian faith and affections in their children at a very young age.[78] Importantly, he asserted that if there has been adequate nurture, the child would not need to go through an experience of conversion.

76. Kett uses this manual to illustrate the fourfold psychological view of young people used by the Sunday Schools and YMCAs. "On page after page, the authors sliced the pupil into chronological segments and then tucked him into physical, mental, social and spiritual compartments of development." Kett, *Rites of Passage*, 209.

77. Kathan, "Horace Bushnell," 55.

78. Bushnell, *Christian Nurture*, 21.

> In other words, the aim, effort, and expectation should be, not, as is commonly assumed, that the child is to grow up in sin, to be converted after he comes to a mature age; but that he is to open on the world as one that is spiritually renewed, not remembering the time when he went through a technical experience, but seeming rather to have loved what is good from his earliest years.[79]

Bushnell also argued that ministry to youth in the past had failed because of its focus on the doctrinal rather than ethical.

> He believed the church had failed by making Christian education a purveyor of doctrine and facts rather than a transmitter of a Christian lifestyle characterized by deliberate and conscious obedience to God.[80]

Instead of teaching doctrine, Christian nurture must focus on the development of character and the deliberate modelling of Christian adults. According to Archibald, the way to nurture character would be to focus on the child rather than the subject (the content of the curriculum). Archibald argued: "Study the child and he will show you what to do."[81] These became basic presuppositions of the REA.

The REA and their New Methods influenced many writers and Sunday school teachers in Australia. After 1910, they began to talk of Sunday school as the "nursery of the Church" and that scholars were "young plants" to be nurtured. The child was to "be nurtured, instructed, and graduated for consistent membership and effective service."[82] There was a rewriting of Sunday school materials with different material for different age groups.[83] Instead of rows of chairs in classes, the layout of many Sunday schools changed to small circles of gathered desks and smaller rooms for each of the departments. New methods of teaching were based on small groups

---

79. Bushnell, *Christian Nurture*, 10.

80. Reed and Prevost, *History of Christian Education*, 334.

81. Archibald was inspired by the words and teaching of Frederich Froebel. Cliff, *Rise and Development*, 230.

82. Woodhouse, "Sunday Schools: Their Strength and Their Weakness," *The Methodist*, February 11, 1899.

83. In 1913 an Australian curriculum was developed in line with graded lessons and Sunday Schools were encouraged to develop senior departments and extracurricular activities. There were also youth departments established in the Presbyterian and Methodist Churches. There were some who resisted the new methods and continued a "Bible-centered" course of study with stress upon instruction, catechism, and memory work. Kelley, "Nurseries for Christians," 174, 175, 180. For more on the impact of the graded Australian curriculum see Keen, "Feeding the Lambs."

and discussion as children got older. In 1912, Archibald came to Sydney on a world tour with his wife and daughter. They gave lectures on these new methods with topics such as "Adolescence" and "Nurture *by* Activity." They also gave public demonstrations or exhibitions of Sunday schools in action so that teachers could watch and imitate their methods.[84]

The New Methods introduced in Sunday schools still retained a place for conversion, even though nurture now was the primary task. The liberal educator had a different view of conversion from the conventional paradigm of guilt, repentance, and then joy in the realization of forgiveness. Instead, they taught that conversion was the time when young people made a decision *for Christ*, an exercise of the will to live as a Christian and to imitate Christ. They believed that it was important to call young people to this decision around the age of fifteen to sixteen years.

> And whereas in the younger departments a decision for Christ may be left to the promptings of the scholar's inner consciousness—rather than forced on from without at an untimely moment—we feel that in the early Senior Department years decision must be pressed as imperative and urgent. We dare not allow any of our young people to dally now, lest the ardour of youth be allowed to cool with the great choice indefinitely postponed.[85]

Conversion had its place within Christian nurture but was merely part of the process.

The YMCA after the 1880s was also influenced by this emphasis on Christian nurture and liberal education theory. The YMCA had been established in NSW with a priority on evangelism, but it was also a "mutual improvement society." The YMCA developed a psychological theory of adolescent health and character development based on the *Fourfold* (or Foursquare program); that each young person should develop the physical, mental, social, and spiritual aspect of their personality.[86] The belief was that this program would lead to balance or symmetry in a person.[87] For

---

84. "The Archibald Lectures," *Newcastle Morning Herald and Miner's Advocate*, September 6, 1912, 6.

85. Hayes, *Child in the Midst*, 19.

86. The fourfold program had been particularly championed by Luther Gulik at the international YMCA training school at Springfield in the US from 1898 to 1903. Gulik was the inventor of the YMCA triangle that represented spirit, mind, and body. Kett, *Rites of Passage*, 203.

87. The one verse in Luke 2:52 was used extensively to explain the object of symmetry: "Jesus increased in wisdom and stature and in favor with God and man." A US YMCA manual even explained that this meant that "Jesus Christ had the most symmetrical life of all the men that have ever lived." Macleod, "Live Vaccine," 21.

example, at a public speech the Australian Prime Minister Alfred Deakin in 1910 praised the YMCA and its fourfold educational program:

> As one of the most essentially modern, and yet perhaps in Spirit one of the most ardent of those voluntary associations, the YMCA stands today, recognising how aptly the institution meets the four-fold rich lands of its principles: the physical, the mental, the social, and spiritual or moral uplifting of its members.[88]

In practice, this meant that the program of the YMCA included educational lectures, a lot of sport and gymnastics, but increasingly, less attention was paid to Bible study and spiritual nurture.[89] The historian Massey also argues that in the nurturing of young people in the YMCA, "there has been rather too much done for than by youth."[90] That is, young people became passive as older men led and shaped the movement.

The Christian Endeavor Movement established in 1881 was another Christian youth organization much influenced by Bushnell and his teaching on nurture. The founder, Dr. Francis Clark, was explicit in accepting the arguments of Bushnell about nurturing a child's faith so that they would never know themselves not a Christian. He claimed to be combining both the revival model as well as the nurturing model within his ministry. As well as seeking to nurture young Christians, its commitment to evangelism should not be overlooked.

> While I believe heartily in revivals, and in many revivalists, and in special periods of religious awakening, I also believe that there is a place for the Timothy conversion as well as for Pauline, and that the Mother Eunice and Grandmother Lois may be as much used by God in bringing their children to Christ, as the fieriest and most eloquent evangelist.[91]

In his own ministry with youth, Clark used a model which organized events to incorporate outsiders and nurture Christian youth. However, he believed that the future of the church lay not in revival, but in nurture. He

---

88. "Mr Deakin's Speech," *Clarence and Richmond Examiner*, May 7, 1910, 5.

89. John Massey claims that "[a] reference to records will indicate that the programme of all early Australian Associations was mainly in religious activities. Later there developed an emphasis on the fourfold idea with a diminution of expressly religious work, which, however, has been increasingly 'integrated' into 'all round programmes.'" This reflects changes in British youth societies in the twentieth century that focused on the psychological and social to the neglect of the spiritual. Massey, *Y. M. C. A. In Australia*, 59; Gillis, *Youth and History*, 141–42.

90. Massey, *Y. M. C. A. In Australia*.

91. Clark, *Children and the Church*, 22; Senter, *When God Shows Up*, 142.

believed that revivalists like Moody and Finney focused too much on the outsider and that true kingdom growth will be "growth from within rather than conquest from without."[92] The real challenge for the church was not to convert those from non-Christian families but to provide a place in the church after Sunday school so that Christian youth were not lured away by other entertainments.[93] The "youth problem" was not the number of unconverted youth in society, but rather that young people were disengaging and leaving the church.

The Christian Endeavor movement was established in 1888 to work alongside the church to nurture Christian citizenship and to train youth through pledges and committees.[94] Its societies were for young people aged thirteen to thirty.[95] To become an active member, one needed to make a pledge similar to that of the temperance societies to uphold allegiance to private devotion and weekly church attendance.

> Trusting in the Lord Jesus Christ for strength, I promise Him that I will try to do whatever He would like to have me do; that I will make it the rule of my life to pray and to read the Bible every day, and to support my own church in every way, especially by attending all her regular Sunday and mid-week services unless prevented by some reason which I can conscientiously give to my Saviour; and that, just as far as I know how throughout my whole life I will try to lead a Christian life.[96]

The other key aspect of the methodology of the movement was the training of young people. It was expected that every member would attend both the weekly hour-long Christian Endeavor services and the monthly consecration service. They were also to participate in a committee of

---

92. Clark, *Children and the Church*, 28.

93. Senter, *When God Shows Up*, 155.

94. Little argues that Christian Endeavor: "had to do with the usual functions of a congregation: worship, study, stewardship, fellowship, and service, interpreted for youth." Little, "Youth Ministry."

95. After the Sunday schools, Christian Endeavor was easily the biggest youth movement in Australia in the late nineteenth century and early twentieth century. In Australia, the peak number of members was in the mid-1930s at almost 100,000 members. These numbers fell away at an alarming rate during the war and never recovered; in 1947 there were only 45,000 members. "Christian Endeavour Tenth Endeavour Convention," *Northern Star*, Lismore, NSW, August 1, 1938, 10; Sorrell, "National Christian Endeavour Convention Summarised Report," *The Methodist*, November 8, 1947, 1. Godman states that in 1905, one in forty Australians was a member, a striking statistic. These came largely from the Methodist Church, but also Congregational, Presbyterian, and Baptist. Godman, "Mission Accomplished," 10.

96. Clark, *Christian Endeavor Manual*, 59.

service such as the prayer committee or look-out committee and to take part in the services by leading, praying or giving talks. Christian Endeavor was to be a "training school for the Church."[97] At large annual conventions, the talks tended to be a "blend of inspirational-devotional and social concern."[98] During the interwar period, the historian P. W. Godman claims that the Australian movement followed the international movement in turning away from the old focus on holiness to emphasizing social responsibility and transforming the world.[99]

Although the intention of Christian Endeavor was to empower the leadership of young people and train them to be useful in the future in both their churches and communities, in practice this vision was not realized. Godman argues that in Australia the movement was increasingly led, and events were organized, by adults rather than youth.[100] The American historian, Joseph Kett claims that Christian Endeavor was part of the late nineteenth century move away from societies organized by youth themselves to those organized by adults for youth.[101] Youth were made passive within the church rather than taking an active role.[102]

The year after the establishment of Christian Endeavor, the Presbyterian Fellowship Union (PFU) was established in NSW in 1882. It was the first denominational youth ministry in Australia, and its significance has been too little acknowledged.[103] Like the Sunday schools, YMCA, and Christian

---

97. Clark, *Children and the Church*, 57.

98. Godman, "Mission Accomplished," 38.

99. Godman, "Mission Accomplished," 44, 46. Mark Senter argues that the international movement changed its focus on personal salvation and holiness to changing society. Senter, *When God Shows Up*, 62.

100. Godman, "Mission Accomplished," 97.

101. Kett, *Rites of Passage*, 190. As early as 1917, Erb argued that the movement was at this time increasingly adult led. Erb, *Young People's Movement*, 107.

102. Kett claims that Christian Endeavor kept young people busy by pledges and training, but they were not given a real influence in the affairs of the church. The pledge was "devoid of any theological content and nearly devoid of moral content. It was not a pledge to do anything in particular. The act of pledging and the ardor it summoned up were more important than what was being pledged. In other words, the focus had shifted from content to process and from involvement to substitutes for involvement." Kett, *Rites of Passage*, 195.

103. The first fellowship group began at St. Stephens, Phillip Street Sydney, in 1874, with an hour-long meeting of devotion for young men. It was called the *Young Mens' Christian Fellowship*. A few other fellowship associations were established and in 1882 they were brought together as the *Young Mens' Sabbath Morning Fellowship Union*. Not intending to exclude women, it became known as the Presbyterian Fellowship Union of NSW. In 1931 the state unions were amalgamated into the Presbyterian Fellowship of Australia (PFA). See Prentis, "Fellowship," 1–14.

Endeavor, it sought to nurture the faith of young people and retain them in the church. It was also influenced by current psychological and educational thought. There were ways, however, that this organization stood apart as a forerunner of later models of youth ministry. The name of the organization *fellowship*[104] rather than society or association pointed ahead to a more relational methodology. The methodology of the PFU was very similar to that of Christian Endeavor and YMCA, but the fellowships were more successful than the Christian Endeavor in empowering the leadership of young people.[105] The PFU meeting was typically held on Sunday morning at ten am, the same time as Christian Endeavor. At this meeting, a study circle was conducted with methods similar to that of the Bible Class or Sunday school senior department. The study circle would involve the members taking turns at giving a paper and then leading a discussion on a Bible passage, Christian biography or social issue suggested by the curriculum. Apart from the Sunday meeting, social events such as tennis, hikes, and picnics were organized. The PFU embraced the fourfold program of the YMCA and sought to provide for all the psychological needs of the young person: worship, study, service, and recreation.

The methodology of the PFU seems to reflect a tension between the goal of evangelizing and allowing youth to lead the movement, and the goal of retaining, nurturing, and training. The first travelling secretary of the PFU, the Reverend John Jamieson[106] claimed that:

104. It was the PFU that first used the word "fellowship" as the description of a youth group in Australia. The term can first be traced to the YMCA in Scotland in the mid-nineteenth century. The YMCA ran weekly meetings "for devotion and friendly discussions" and at some stage these groups were called fellowship meetings. Indeed, for a time the association was called the "YMCA and Fellowship Unions." See "Correspondent from the YMCA Conference," *Scottish Guardian*, September 30, 1859. The Moody revivals in 1874–75, 1883, and 1892 energized the fellowships as there were many young people converted and they were encouraged to join a group. The purpose of these first fellowship groups was to nurture the faith of new Christians after their conversion, and to protect young men from the temptations of ungodly living in the city, a similar function to John Wesley's classes. See also, White, *Challenge of the Years*, 244. There is evidence that D. L. Moody encouraged these kinds of classes or fellowship groups. Moody met with two thousand church leaders in Glasgow in 1874 to discuss how to follow up after the fruit of the revival. He stated that Scotland needed a Wesley, to organize young people into classes to be nurtured. See Sprange and Reed, *Children in Revival*, 315.

105. The early leaders of the PFU were directly influenced by the YMCA and Fellowship Associations in Glasgow. Neil Livingston, for example, was converted in 1859–60 in a revival in Glasgow and then was active in fellowship work. When he immigrated to Australia in the late nineteenth century, he sought to establish the same kind of ministry in his new country. Jamieson, "Modern Fellowship Association," 5, 13.

106. Jamieson came to Australia from New Zealand to become the travelling

> The aim of the modern Fellowship Association is the all-round development of its members, physical, mental, spiritual and social. It seeks by the study of the Bible and by the discussion of the deeper problems of life to awaken their powers, enlist their energies in the service of others, and thus develop the vast possibilities that lie hidden within every young man and young woman.... Bible study, however, is the one thing essential. The other features are optional but highly desirable.[107]

Jamieson wanted to emphasize the priority of the spiritual, but he was influenced by the Foursquare psychological approach. He elsewhere listed the objects of the organization, but they seem to have had a different focus:

1. retain girls and boys outgrowing the Sunday school
2. attract the outsider to the church
3. be an evangelistic strategy, through Bible study come to make a definite decision
4. be a training school for future workers.[108]

The objects seem to be dedicated to the needs of the church, that is, to retain and attract new young members and to train them to be workers in the church. Jamieson's goals display a tension here between the two models of youth ministry, the nineteenth century religious education model of nurture and a more relational model based on the young person taking up leadership and service.

The PFU was successful in empowering young leaders and, although the Fellowship Association was run by older men, the local groups were led by the young people themselves in the offices of President, Vice President, and Secretary etc. and they were encouraged to take responsibility for their own activities and governance. Jamieson argued that the young person in the past had been treated like a child, "chilled and repressed by 'lessons' when she ought to have been warmed by comradeship and developed by

---

secretary of the PFU. He had been involved with Bible classes and youth evangelism. He claimed that his three influences were George Troup of the Bible Class movement in New Zealand, D. A. Budge of the YMCA Montreal, and John Mott of the student movement. From Troup he learnt the "co-operative method," that is, sharing the leadership among the young people, while the adult "stimulates and supplements the work of the members." From Budge he learnt the Foursquare method. From Mott he caught a vision of being part of a worldwide evangelical youth movement. Jamieson, "Modern Fellowship Association," 5, 13.

107. Jamieson, "Modern Fellowship Association," 9.
108. Jamieson, "Modern Fellowship Association."

being trusted with responsibility."[109] Jamieson encouraged the leadership of the young people themselves that the ministry might be *by* youth rather than *for* youth.

> ... work *for* youth must be abandoned in favour of work *by* youth. Work by the member is better for the member and the future church than better work done by the Leader.[110]

In 1913 Jamieson sought to establish in the PFU the kind of youth leadership that only began in other denominations in the 1930s.

Other Victorian-era youth societies that were influenced by the concept of Christian nurture were the uniformed associations. They had a particular concern for adolescent boys and the *boy problem*. The answer to this boy problem was to provide healthy entertainment and activities that would shape character and "keep boys off the streets." For example, the Boys Brigade was brought to Australia in 1890 and focused on adolescent boys from fourteen to seventeen years.[111] They organized activities each week such as sports, games, drills, camps, woodwork, and Bible study. The Boys Brigade had uniforms, earned badges, and practiced marches to encourage military-like discipline. They sought to develop an *esprit de corps*; an English private school virtue developed in sports that encouraged comradeship, pride, and standards of character.[112] In the nurture of character, boys' societies sought most of all to build *manliness*. The Boys Brigade aim was:

> The advancement of Christ's kingdom among Boys and the promotion of habits of Reverence, Discipline, Self-Respect, and all that tends towards a true Christian manliness.[113]

The importance of manliness had already been highlighted by the muscular Christianity movement, which talked about the importance of producing manly leaders to keep the empire strong.[114] Manliness was felt to be under threat because the church was effeminate and urban life was sedentary.[115] The founder of the Brigade, William Smith, was greatly influenced

109. Jamieson, "Modern Fellowship Association," 48.
110. Jamieson, "Modern Fellowship Association," 11.
111. Springhall et al., *Sure and Steadfast*, 68.
112. Hendrick, *Images of Youth*, 81, 159.
113. Quoted in Springhall et al., *Sure and Steadfast*, 39.
114. Historians such as John Springhall and Carol Dyhouse have argued that part of the motivation of this movement was a concern for the empire and its strength, particularly after the recruiting of young men for the Boer War had found so many unfit for service. Springhall, *Coming of Age*, 59; Dyhouse, *Girls Growing Up*, 110.
115. Anne O'Brien argues that this masculinized Christianity was influential on the

by the muscular Christianity movement. One of his fellow teachers spoke of Smith as a model of Christian manliness:

> He knew the difficulties of mind and body that beset the life of a boy entering upon the adolescent period. He knew the tremendous pull that was being exercised on the boy's imagination and desires and of the vital need of having that led into a healthy environment. He placed himself alongside the boy and consciously passed onto him the help and guidance he most needed. . . . His was a manly, robust religion which found expression in the common ground of everyday life.[116]

Smith and the Boys Brigade, therefore, sought to redirect the animal spirits of boys that they too might develop into robust, manly leaders of the future.

There were other Protestant boys' societies in Australia. The Boys Brigade was very popular in Baptist churches, but the Anglican equivalent was the Church of England Boys Society (CEBS).[117] In the Methodist Church, a different kind of society began; the Methodist Order of Knights (MOK or just OK).[118] It sought to nurture virtues of chivalric masculinity, to retain boys within the Methodist Church, and provide for their psychological needs: physical, mental, spiritual, and social (the Foursquare).[119] Masculinity was nurtured by a veneration of King Arthur and the Knights of the Round Table and earning badges based on the Foursquare. The MOK members wore regalia, and they used rituals and secret passwords (similar to Masonic clubs) in order to shape a culture of belonging and masculinity.[120]

In NSW, along with the boys' societies there were also societies established to nurture Christian character in girls. The Girls' Friendly Society (GFS) was established in 1881[121] with the object:

> To unite for the glory of God in one fellowship of prayer and service, the girls and women of the Empire, to uphold purity in thought word and deed, and to encourage dutifulness to parents, faithfulness to employers, temperance and thrift.[122]

---

church in Australia. O'Brien, "Church Full of Men," 449.

116. Springhall et al., *Sure and Steadfast*, 45.

117. O'Brien, "Church Full of Men," 437–57.

118. The Order of Knights began in 1914 and grew quickly with a peak in the 1930s. O'Brien, "Church Full of Men," 449.

119. Anon., *Methodist Order of Knights*, 7.

120. Hunt, *This Side of Heaven*, 334.

121. "News of the Day," *Sydney Morning Herald*, June 15, 1881, 5.

122. *Year Book of the Diocese of Sydney, 1923, NSW, Australia*, 214.

Its focus was working-class girls, and its aim was to nurture feminine virtues so that they might aspire to be godly wives and mothers. The virtues were sexual purity, modesty, respect, and hard work. They were taught by the earning of badges, but also by connecting girls into a virtuous peer group with older women as mentors.[123] Another society for girls was Girls Comrade, a girls' equivalent of the MOK. Its object was, "To provide for the physical, intellectual, social, and spiritual welfare of the members and to present them a worthy conception of womanhood."[124] Like the GFS it used the Foursquare and sought to cultivate feminine virtues.[125]

In Sydney, apart from the formal societies, there were more informal boys' and girls' clubs that sought to provide Christian nurture. For example, at St Paul's Wahroonga a boys' club began in 1916 with its goal being to attend to the "spiritual, mental and physical well-being of the members."[126] It was a club for boys aged from eleven to eighteen years, and at its inception, forty boys signed up. The group time consisted of half an hour of Swedish exercise, after which a speaker would give a short talk to the boys. A girls' club and girls' guild were established at around the same time, with the purpose of raising money for the church as well as training young girls, no doubt in their conventional feminine role as fundraisers and voluntary workers.[127]

The boys' and girls' societies in the churches in Sydney between 1880 and 1930 were guided by a particular view of Christian education and nurture that was shared by Sunday schools, the YMCA, and Christian Endeavor. The Foursquare view of the young person shaped their teaching and activities. Increasingly, groups began to stress the psychological and physical rather than the spiritual. Many of the societies were single-sex and sought to nurture the virtues of masculinity and femininity as well as Christian virtues. Behind the establishment of these organizations lay a real anxiety about adolescents and the psychological challenges they faced, as well as a fear of juvenile delinquency.

123. Carol Dyhouse argues that the GFS and Snowdrops "aimed to purify and exalt femininity, to persuade girls that the essence of womanhood lay in innocence, modesty, gentle devotion to duty and domestic tasks. Both feared that adolescent girls of the working class were too soon removed from the influence of family and school: they needed the restraining hand of adult authority, ideally the contact with 'cultured' benevolent ladies of the middle or upper class who could serve as models, as surrogate mothers, providing images of refined, feminine behavior." Dyhouse, *Girls Growing Up*, 110. See also Hancock, *Modern Methods*.

124. Porter, *Methodist Order*, 2.

125. Porter, *Methodist Order*.

126. Nobbs, *You Are God's Building*, 95.

127. Nobbs, *You Are God's Building*.

The Challenge of the 1930s

The years leading into the 1930s saw a confluence of social forces which helped produce a reevaluation of the place of young people in Australian society. This presented new challenges for Protestant churches, leading them to modify the methodology used to reach youth. The historical context of the aftermath of war and the impact of the Great Depression shaped a generation of young people. The disruption of war led to a questioning of the cultural authority of Christianity, particularly in the face of diverse new currents of thought. Fears were held over the potential rejection of social norms by young people, but at the same time, youth movements were seen as holding promise for a better world. The sharp rise in the proportion of youth involved in secondary education and consuming cinema, music, and magazines further facilitated the development of a distinct youth culture. The old approach of youth ministry, using the Foursquare to nurture young Christians, no longer seemed persuasive. Young people were viewed differently in society, and in the churches, there was a need for youth ministry that allowed young people to take agency and lead ministries themselves.

The far-reaching effects of the Great War on Australia included a reshaping of how Australian society viewed youth. In the aftershock of war, the Victorian-era belief in the inevitable progress of civilization was harder to believe.[128] Family life was damaged by the loss of fathers who did not return from the war, or who came home physically but were emotionally incapacitated.[129] There was a general sense of guilt at having sent Australian young men to be slaughtered on the Western Front so far from home,[130] and a belief that civilization had been threatened by the atrocities of the war and remained in crisis. It was up to the young people of the new generation to rebuild the world.[131] Historian Renate Howe relates that many university students of the

---

128. Treloar, *Disruption of Evangelicalism*, 229.

129. The statistics on the devastating casualties of the Great War on Australia are sufficient explanation for the nation's postwar psychic malaise. There were about 60,000 men killed, 156,000 injured, gassed or imprisoned in a population of under five million. Many of these were young men and even boys younger than eighteen who had lied about their age. This compares to the Second World War where the casualties, in keeping with the percentage of population, was only a quarter as heavy. Higgins, "Australians at War."

130. For more on the impact of the Great War on that generation and Christian faith, see Wohl, *Generation of 1914*; Linder, *Long Tragedy*.

131. Howe, *Century of Influence*, 232. This was the case in America as well, where youth were seen as crucial to the fate of civilization and the "cult of youth" was encouraged by the work of Wyndham Lewis. Lewis, *Doom of Youth*. See also Bergler, "Winning America," 45.

1930s felt themselves to be a doomed generation, "growing up in the shadow of the War and the Depression." In her history of the SCM, she evokes their sense of duty as Christian citizens who had a great responsibility: "They felt they had a duty to make positive contributions to society, especially in trying to bring about peace if at all possible."[132] Geoff Treloar has argued that in the churches there was a shift of primary concern away from working-class men and onto youth. He attributes this to the losses of war and the recognition that church and society needed to be reborn through the efforts of the next generation. Moreover, the absence of those who did not return from the war to take up leadership in the churches made the raising up of a new generation vital for the survival of the church, to replace the "lost generation." Treloar cites a statement often made by Protestants at this time, "the future of our churches depends on the young."[133]

After the war, Australia faced the further challenge of the Great Depression. Following the rapid industrial growth in the first decades of the twentieth century, there had been a general expectation of a continued increase in incomes and wealth. The shock came in the 1930s with high unemployment and shrinking of the economy which led to poverty and hardship for many. Young people faced leaving school with no jobs available for them and many adults believed that Australia had failed the young.[134] David Potts, in his assessment of the Depression in Australia, argued that it was a time in flux between the traditional and modern worlds:

> In the 1930s their values drifted between declining nineteenth century work ethics (including stoicism), and ascending consumer ethics (which emphasized comfort and pleasure). Those who managed did so partly because they chose between the two to their best advantage on their available incomes, even if intuitively. Nevertheless, they still favoured non-material values and experiences when reflecting on what mattered most to them.[135]

It was young people who were caught between these two sets of values, attracted by the world of popular culture and consumption, yet still committed to family values and service of God and country.

---

132. Howe, *Century of Influence*, 232.

133. Treloar, *Disruption of Evangelicalism*, 238.

134. The experience of young people in the Depression was mixed. There were accounts of many employers deliberately employing youths because they were cheaper than adults, and then firing them as they got a little older. On the other hand, many young people had a sense of pride in getting some work and contributing to the very tight family finances. Fabian and Loh, *Children in Australia*, 156.

135. Potts, *Great Depression*, 338.

The war and the Depression brought into question the version of the Christian faith that had emphasized an optimistic, progressive view of society and humankind. At the same time, there were new ideologies that challenged the cultural authority of Christian faith. Socialism, in particular, challenged the accepted understanding of the place of work and class in a society, and how to live the *good life*. These new currents of thought were of course particularly attractive to the young and idealistic and they posed a challenge in the transmission of Christian faith from one generation to another. New academic disciplines such as psychology, sociology, and evolutionary biology were at times difficult to harmonize with Christian faith. Modern thought and an increasing secularist outlook were undermining the cultural authority held by Christians in the Victorian era.[136]

There was a changing view of youth portrayed in the media in the late 1920s and 1930s which reflected a certain anxiety but paradoxically also an idealization of the young.[137] Many books were written and public talks were given about the *revolt of youth*.[138] This anxiety about the *revolt* or *problem of youth* came from a belief that young people were rejecting their families and religion and were disillusioned with the state of the world. For example, Charlotte Nevin (the world secretary of the YMCA) in 1933 explained that the revolt of youth was against family, religion, and institutions of the past:

> It is a result of the war, and we cannot shut our eyes to it, nor do we wish to condemn the younger generation which seems to find it impossible to accept anything that has been thought good in the past, merely because it was in the past, and they feel that they must discover it themselves.[139]

Alongside the anxiety about the youth problem, there was an idealization of youth in the media. Writers spoke of the enthusiasm, idealism, and sacrifice of young people, especially evidenced in the war. There was a belief that youth around the world were "on the move" and a general optimism about the new world they would create.

---

136. Treloar, "Some Reflections," 13.

137. This was true in other countries such as the US. The historian Paula Fass explains the *youth problem* in the 1920s was part myth and part reality. Older people believed that, after the war, young people were rejecting the beliefs and behaviors of the previous generations. Young people were both denounced by the media or idealized, either the *damned* or the *beautiful*. Fass, *Damned and the Beautiful*, 13, 15.

138. For example, Lindsey and Evans, *Revolt of Modern Youth*; Coe, *What Ails Our Youth?*

139. "The Revolt of Youth," *Sydney Morning Herald*, June 27, 1933, 3.

> We are told that the younger generation is up against what I consider the narrow outlook, and the futile aims of the older generation, and is determined to use its energy and power to bring about what it considers are improvements in the present day situations.[140]

The media noted that there were *youth movements* all over the globe; youth banding together to change the world. They pointed to the German youth movement, the Bündische Jugend,[141] as an inspiration to youth elsewhere. The media also called the International Scouting Association, Student Christian Movement (SCM), and the YMCA "youth movements" that would lead to social change. This sense of a movement was encouraged by international conferences held after the war, such as the YMCA conference at Helsingfors in 1926. Young people from all over the world, including Australia, came together to discuss the issues of the modern world and how to solve them.[142] These conferences and movements encouraged young people to see themselves as agents of change and to take leadership and initiative.

Church leaders were also very concerned about the youth problem, but generally idealistic about a Christian youth movement that might shape the church and society.

> Much has been written recently on the subject of youth and the Church. Conferences have considered these problems and published their findings, and press and pulpit have devoted much time to attacking or defending the young people of today. At the same time, many explanations have been offered of the revolt of youth against organized Christianity that has been so marked a feature of the war.[143]

---

140. Harker, "The Revolt of Youth," *The Methodist*, April 27, 1929, 6.

141. This movement was a combination of the old Wandervogel, a German nature movement, and the German Scouting movement. Laqueur, *Young Germany*.

142. Denham, "Worlds Youth, a Challenge," *Sydney Morning Herald*, September 25, 1926, 9.
In 1926, there was also a conference at High Leigh in England of the leaders of the Boys Brigade, Scouts, YMCA, WYCA, and GFS. Vodden and Martin state that at this conference, "they asked for a clear statement of the present world situation and how youth is blazing a trail in almost every nation of the world. . . . The outstanding feature of world movements today is the leading part which youth is taking in the life of every land. The world renaissance of a youth movement. Youth is blazing the trail. . . . The revolt of modern youth is different; it is the first of its kind; and it possesses means for making its will effective." Vodden and Martin, *Youth in World Service*, 11.

143. Hayes, *Child in the Midst*, 122. For example, Harris, *Problems of Youth*.

The churches believed that the heart of society's youth problem was that many young people were turning their back on the church and the Christian faith. A report was written for the NSW Methodist Church in 1936, entitled the *Challenge of Youth*.[144] In it, the nature of the youth problem was described as first, the numerical decline in Sunday school and other youth organizations, and second, the challenge of sex and popular culture which provided "undue sex stimulus."[145] The causes of the youth problem were described as the cataclysm of war, irreligious families, the increase of cars, Sunday drives, and the rise of secular ideologies, particularly fascism and communism.[146]

As noted earlier, there is good reason to accept that genuine youth culture emerged for the first time in the 1930s and 1940s. The way that the media talked about the revolt of youth and the challenge of youth presumed that *youth* had become a distinctive group and generation, different from their parents. Arguably the main reason for this development in NSW was the expansion of secondary education. Before the 1930s, secondary education had been seen as the preserve of the elite who would go to university, while all other children joined the workforce at the age of fourteen. This began to change in the interwar years, and between 1920 and 1932 enrolments at post-primary government schools rose from 6 percent of children and youth enrolled in schools, to 18 percent.[147] In 1920 there were approximately sixteen thousand children involved in post-primary education in NSW; in 1930, fifty-five thousand; and by 1940, seventy-nine thousand.[148] The NSW State Department of Education recognized the need for capable professionals for the modern world. The department was:

> ... acutely aware of the need to provide an efficient form of secondary education in order to build a technically proficient elite capable of taking the lead in developing Australia as a staunch bastion of the British Empire in the South Pacific.[149]

In response, the 1930s saw the creation of new high schools, technical secondary schools and post-primary sections in many primary schools.[150]

---

144. New South Wales Conference, *Challenge of Youth*.
145. New South Wales Conference, *Challenge of Youth*, 24.
146. New South Wales Conference, *Challenge of Youth*, 19–22.
147. Cleverley and Lawry, *Australian Education*, 134.
148. NSW Education and Communities, "Post-Primary Enrolments."
149. Cleverley and Lawry, *Australian Education*, 134.
150. There was an increase in numbers of separate secondary schools in NSW. In 1920 there were twenty-eight; in 1930, forty-eight; and by 1940, sixty. NSW Education and Communities, "Number of Government Schools."

Secondary education facilitated the creation of a youth culture by enabling the formation of peer groups. Young people were socialized in peer groups at the school where they were able to share common values and style without the interference of their parents.[151] Psychologists in the 1940s were able to analyze the phenomenon of adolescent peer groups that had developed in the interwar years. For example, Caroline Tyron noted that:

> ... children as they grow up, evolve their own standards or social values by which they guide their conduct and evaluate their behaviour. This is not to say that the children's value patterns do not reflect in some fashion those of the adult society which frames the particular child group ... But if we were to examine the pattern of values of any group of children we would see that they were in many respects distinctly different from the grown-ups around them. ... As far as we know, they emerge to a large extent, out of the needs of the group and initiation by members of the next older developmental level.[152]

They were influenced by their parents' generation but were able to establish their own values, especially with the help of those who were just a little older, as Tyron notes. Those who led the changes in the methodology of youth ministry in the 1930s and 1940s recognized the significance of peer groups and leadership of those young people who were just a little older than group members. Peer groups were seen as key to the establishment of values and of a Christian youth culture that would aid the transition of young people into adulthood. The challenge in this ministry was to allow the youth culture to "reflect in some fashion" the culture of their parents, yet be "distinctly different from the grown-ups around them."[153] Protestants embraced this challenge by allowing the youth ministry to move away from old models of Christian education and teaching to that of peer encouragement and dialogue.

Further contributing to the emergence of a distinct youth culture was the fact that young people had time for entertainment, and for some, the money to consume cinema, magazines, and other forms of popular culture.

---

151. Paula Fass has described the similar effect of secondary education in the formation of peer groups in the US: "high schools as well as colleges were thus crucial to the new patterns of youth socialization. They substituted youth centers for work centers, intensified age homogeneity, exposed youths to broader influences than home and local community, and provided the facilities and occasions for the homogenization of behavior and beliefs through peer-imposed conformity." Fass, *Damned and the Beautiful*, 220.

152. Tyron, "Adolescent Peer Culture," 236.

153. Tyron, "Adolescent Peer Culture," 236.

Australian historian Julia Matthews has demonstrated that young women especially were forming a distinctive form of youth culture influenced by American popular culture.[154] This culture was imported through the cinema and music of the dance halls, while "everywhere national elites watched with dismay as they saw their young people eagerly dancing to the mongrel tunes of the American pied piper."[155] The media denounced the morality of young people who seemed to prefer the cinema and dance halls to the church hall. The youth culture that emerged in the 1930s and 1940s meant that young people had different fashion, music, and attitudes to relationships with the opposite sex from those of their parents. The youth culture at times led to moral panic among the older generations.

There was a growing belief in the Protestant churches that old methods of ministry to youth were not working in the new modern society. For example, Katherine Niles of the REA studied eighteen societies for young people in 1929 and concluded that:

> In a society which has undergone many changes and developments, they have become misfits, even drags on the progress of religious work with youth. Their forms and techniques, which remain much the same as they were in the beginning, (i.e. the last decade of the nineteenth century) are no longer suited to modern society.[156]

Other writers stated that what was needed was not for adults to create a new ministry *for* youth, but for the church to resource and encourage the initiatives and leadership *of* youth themselves.

> In the past, there has been too much done "for" the young people. We have spoon-fed them too long, instead of making a big demand on them for adventurous and self-sacrificing service.[157]

They encouraged a new focus on "comradeship" and discussion as well as youth leadership and service, rather than educational classes. In keeping with the profound changes shaping the current generation of youth, new ministry methods were needed that reinvigorated the agency of young people.

---

154. Matthews, *Dance Hall*. Employment for unmarried young women was opening up in the 1920s and 1930s. As well as office work, there were also new professions, such as dental nursing, journalism, and physical education, that were deemed suitable for women. This meant, for the first time, they had some pocket money for entertainment and consumables. Fabian and Loh, *Children in Australia*, 152, 53.

155. Matthews, *Dance Hall*, 11, 68, 204.

156. Niles, "Survey and Critique," 534.

157. Clover, *Senior Department Handbook*.

The 1930s generation of young people was therefore shaped in deep ways by the historical events that their country had endured. In Australian society, in general, there were fears as well as hopes for the next generation. Conservative leaders were concerned by the psychological damage and the potential moral laxity of youth, in a world that challenged many conservative values. Protestant leaders were sensitive to the effects of the war. For example, in 1935, Bishop W. G. Hilliard[158] spoke of youth who were:

> Born in the fevered years of warfare, brought up in the debilitating atmosphere of its tragic aftermath, growing into manhood and womanhood during the greatest economic Depression in history, and amid a welter of conflicting thought: economic, social and theological, we need to be patient with them and to realize our heavy responsibility towards them.[159]

There was a sense of guilt as well as the responsibility to these children of the war and the Depression. Conservative leaders were not only fearful, they were also hopeful about the future; they believed that investing in the youth might empower them to be the leaders that society needed. Youth were the future of a Christian society, as well as the future of the church.

Conclusion

This chapter has argued that there was a changing approach to ministry to youth over time in Sydney. The first phase, 1788–1880, was characterized by revival and a desire for moral reformation. This is illustrated by the different youth associations: the Sunday schools, YMCA, Scripture Union, and Band of Hope Union. In the second phase, from 1880 to 1930, the Sunday schools, YMCA, youth societies, and brigades were influenced by the theology and methodology of Bushnell and the REA. Christian nurture and the formation of Christian character became the primary aim of these organizations. They were also influenced by a psychological understanding of the young person and of adolescence, and they adopted the Foursquare methodology to organize their teaching and activities. They sought to nurture masculinity and femininity in young people and were motivated partly by a concern for the strength of the empire.

---

158. William Hilliard was an exemplar of muscular Christianity and headmaster at Trinity Grammar School and later a bishop of the Sydney diocese. West, *Innings of Grace*.

159. Hilliard, "Synod Sermon," in *Year Book of the Diocese of Sydney, 1935*, NSW, Australia, 258.

Youth ministry in the 1930s faced new and complex challenges as a result of the powerful social forces of the time. Young people grew up in the shadow of the Great War and the Depression. Adults both demonized and idealized youth, but either way, believed that young people were the hope of the future. Therefore, young people were given more agency and leadership. Secondary education was expanded and this led to the forming of peer settings that shaped youth. In the 1930s and 1940s, a youth culture emerged that was distinctive from the culture and values of their parents. This generation of youth was shaped by its historical context as part of a new world, and new methods of ministry became necessary. This was a context that encouraged the development of leadership amongst the Christian youth and would require a movement away from a ministry *to* youth to the ministry *of* youth. In succeeding chapters, we will see this exemplified in the ministry of university students, the ministry amongst school students, and the youth ministry in local churches.

3

Protestant Youth Ministry at University and the Formation of the Evangelical Union

THE 1930S WERE CRITICAL years in the history of Protestant youth ministry in Sydney. Major social forces were changing the way youth viewed themselves and how they were viewed by others. At the same time, the liberal evangelical outlook of Protestant churches was giving way to a more conservative evangelical spirit. Emboldened by the influence of key individuals, Christians and churches responded to these changes by forming new institutions and developing new methods in ministry to the young. The number of new ventures in youth ministry that began in this decade is remarkable. Interdenominational institutions were formed that encouraged youth ministry[1] at university and in schools: the Sydney University Evangelical Union (EU) in 1930, the Australian Inter Varsity Fellowship (IVCF) in 1930, the Crusader Union (CU) in 1930, and the Inter-School Christian Fellowship (ISCF) in 1935. In Protestant parishes, fellowship groups for youth were also started during the 1930s.

In this chapter, the character and impact of the Evangelical Union (EU) at Sydney University will be examined. Accounts of the formation of the Evangelical Union have previously been written,[2] but this account will

---

1. University student ministry is not always included in historical discussions of youth ministry. We are defining youth ministry as "age-specific ministry to young people" and *youth* as the time between childhood and adulthood, a transition period of semi-dependency upon parents. University ministry fits within these parameters. Root, *Relational Youth Ministry*, 26.

2. Lake, *Proclaiming Jesus Christ*; Prince, *Out of the Tower*; Guinness, *Journey among Students*. For another account by the author see Lukabyo, "Protestant Youth

specifically attempt to identify the traits of this model of youth ministry that was to prove so influential.[3] It will be argued that the key characteristics were the empowering of youth leaders, theological conservatism, the encouragement of peer ministry, and the acceptance of coeducation. This university model of youth mobilization was, in turn, to influence other youth ministries to move from a ministry *for* youth to a ministry *of* youth as elements of the university student ministry were brought into ministry in schools and parishes; most notably a commitment to student leadership and empowerment.[4] Howard Guinness, the founder of the EU, also established the schools ministry of the Crusader Union. There was a significant overlap in these movements, with the same key leaders involved in both organizations. University students involved themselves in schools ministry and established the IVCF and the ISCF in Australia. Students also had an impact on churches through visitation and through the formation and encouragement of youth fellowships in parishes.

It was noted in chapter two that revival and moral reform had been the catalyst for student ministry before the 1930s. In the late nineteenth century, John Mott had established the Student Christian Movement, a strategic ministry that sought to raise up young leaders for the church and society. It was deeply influenced by holiness theology and the idea of consecration, committing one's life to the service of God. It fostered a passion for activism that helped motivate and empower the students. This activism was directed towards the theological goal of building God's kingdom throughout the world. The ultimate expression of this commitment was to give up worldly ambitions and become a missionary in a desire to serve the Lord and establish his kingdom on earth. One of the distinctives of this pioneering student ministry was the empowering of young leaders. In the 1930s this trait was retrieved from the earlier student ministry and reenergized, though with a changed emphasis and a foundation of conservative evangelical theology.

Ministry," 3–22.

3. The history of student ministry in other countries has been examined with particular interest in theological and sociological reasons for growth or decline. For example, Bruce, "Student Christian Movement"; Goodhew, "Inter-Collegiate Christian Union," 62–88. Recent research has compared liberal and conservative evangelical approaches and has argued for resilience within conservative evangelicalism. The formation of religious identity has been another important theme. Schmidt, "Crossing the Great Divide"; Lange, *Rising Tide*.

4. It has to be conceded that the percentage of Australians (born before 1927) who completed some form of higher education was lower than 10 percent. Australian Bureau of Statistics, "Generation to Generation," 2006. The argument of the chapter is that the university students were influential leaders, particularly in the schools ministry and in fellowship groups, despite their small numbers proportionally.

University Ministry and Liberal Evangelicalism in the 1920s and 1930s

The Student Volunteer Movement's goal of Christianizing the world by raising up large numbers of Christian leaders to be missionaries was not realized. In 1921, twenty-five years after Mott's Australian visit, the SVM was discontinued in Australia due to lack of volunteers (though the Australian Student Christian Movement at Sydney University remained strong).[5] The old assumption of the importance of Christianizing Eastern nations by bringing them the Christian faith and civilization were being undermined by secularism and the loss of Christian cultural hegemony. The collapse of the SVM was a challenge to the clear purpose of the student movement.

At the same time, the liberal evangelicalism which was influential in Sydney in the 1920s and 1930s was exerting a significant influence on university student ministry. Liberal evangelicalism was a theological adaptation to modernism, an intellectual movement that embodied a general optimism and idealism about the fruition of rational and intellectual thought, particularly scientific reasoning. Among the factors that led to this movement were the emergence of the new disciplines of sociology and psychology, as well as the victory of evolutionary science. The theological adaptation of modernism led to new thinking about the Bible in major theological colleges in Germany, England, and the United States. Liberal evangelicalism reflected the desire of some evangelical clergy and Bible colleges to rethink the Christian faith. For example, the Anglican Evangelical Group Movement saw its watchword as "the truth shall set you free."[6] "While clinging to the fundamental spiritual truths of evangelicalism," they "recognized the old doctrines had to be set forth in modern language."[7] Liberal evangelicals believed that evangelical faith had to be modernized.[8]

Liberal evangelicals, on the whole, still valued their evangelical heritage. The gospel message of the death of Jesus was to be preached, but a "moral view" of the atonement began to flourish in place of the old theology

---

5. Howe, *Century of Influence*, 155–57.

6. Wilson, "Development of Evangelicalism," 2.

7. Quoted in Randall, *Evangelical Experiences*, 46.

8. Over time, some evangelicals on the more "liberal" end of the spectrum began to eschew the name "liberal evangelical" for "liberal" as they could no longer uphold the authority of the Bible. There was a "broadening" of the evangelical movement amongst those who were liberal, until they were no longer within the camp. It is difficult to define when this transition happened in Sydney, but it was later than the time period being discussed. For a discussion of the narrowing and broadening of the evangelical movement see Treloar, *Disruption of Evangelicalism*, 67–90.

of substitutionary atonement.⁹ Conversion remained important but was recast as a commitment of the human will to establishing the kingdom of God, inspired by the love of Jesus and his example as the greatest and most sacrificial of all human beings. This imitation of Jesus included a great concern for society and issues of social justice. When combined with a postmillennial worldview, many liberal evangelicals began to see the goal of their ministry as the progressive realization of the kingdom of God through combatting evils in society and the establishment of the fatherhood of God and the brotherhood of all mankind.

Liberal evangelicals embraced biblical criticism as *the* way to understand the Bible, a methodology that emphasized the historical context of the Bible. They believed the Bible was a witness to human responses to a revelation from God, rather than God's authoritative word to human beings that was free from error. They argued that the Bible contained great truths from God, but the "husk" had to be cut away to find the "kernel of truth" within.[10] Some theologians were moving away from a literalist reading of the Bible and were seeking to interpret the message of the gospel for a modern scientific worldview that rejected such presumptions as the possibility of miracles, including the virgin birth and the bodily resurrection of Christ.

At what was then Sydney's only university, liberal evangelicalism influenced the student ministry largely through the teaching of Dr. Samuel Angus, the Professor of Theology at St. Andrew's College at Sydney University.[11] Angus helped train Protestant ministers at the Joint Theological Faculty of the Presbyterian, Congregationalist, and Methodist Churches. In 1923, Angus taught at an SCM conference at the King's School that the Bible was not to be treated as if it were "God himself." The Bible needed to be interpreted through the methods of biblical criticism in order to find the truth. Truth was also available through modern academic and scientific thought. Angus taught students that:

> Despite the suffocation of the Church, Christ habitually provoked men to think for themselves. It should not claim infallibility in a world which is constantly discovering new elements in the unsearchable riches of Christ. Life is the great iconoclast; it is ever outgrowing every static form of religion.[12]

9. Randall, *Evangelical Experiences*, 52.

10. This metaphor was used by Sydney liberal evangelicals such as the Reverend Arthur Garnsey. See Garnsey, *Arthur Garnsey*, 72.

11. Professor Angus (1881–1943) was involved in leading Bible studies and giving talks in the SCM. He faced charges of heresy in the 1930s. Dougan, "Angus, Samuel"; Emilsen, *Whiff of Heresy*.

12. Howe, *Century of Influence*, 167.

He brought a very "modern" approach to thinking about the Christian faith; that one must be open, make new discoveries and develop in new ways rather than being stuck in the past. In 1934 Angus wrote *Truth and Tradition* which challenged orthodox Christian belief including:

> ... the virgin birth, the physical resurrection of Jesus and the empty tomb; the death of Jesus as a "propitiation" and "all-sufficient sacrifice" for the sins of the world; the deity of Christ; the Trinity, not of the New Testament, but of fourth century speculation; the authority of the Scripture, and whatever the Westminster divines excogitated and systematized during the years of codification of their statements of Christianity.[13]

There were other liberal evangelical leaders who exerted influence within their churches and amongst young people at this time. The Reverend Arthur Garnsey[14] was the warden of St. Paul's College at Sydney University and in the 1920s and 1930s regularly spoke on matters such as love, freedom, and fellowship, and on social issues such as war and evolution.[15] Garnsey also sought to defend the Christian faith against the attacks of atheism and materialism, and as a result, the students of the SCM came to him for advice on matters such as responding apologetically to the Freethought Society[16] and dealing with the Evangelical Union.

Garnsey and Angus directly influenced the SCM at Sydney University. Both were involved in leading Bible studies and speaking at conferences. Angus's book *Discipleship* was used by most Bible study groups as a set text.[17] Under their influence, prominent SCM leaders began to articulate a new attitude to the Bible.[18] In 1922 Bill McKenzie, the head of the Australian SCM exemplified this more liberal approach:

> The movement recognizes that God's revelation is a progressive one, that only part of the revelation is recorded in the Bible, that

13. Angus, *Truth and Tradition*, 2.
14. Garnsey, "Garnsey."
15. Garnsey, *Arthur Garnsey*, 73.
16. The Freethought society was established at Sydney University by the controversial philosophy professor John Anderson in 1930. Anderson publicly taught that science and Christianity were incompatible and that Jesus was not a historical figure but a myth. See Garnsey, *Arthur Garnsey*, 98; Howe, *Century of Influence*, 189; O'Neil, "Anderson"; Franklin, *Corrupting the Youth*.
17. Howe, *Century of Influence*, 180.
18. This was not only a change in Sydney, but in the SCM internationally. In 1910 the Cambridge InterCollegiate Christian Union (CICCU) broke away from the SCM at Cambridge on account of the SCM's theological liberal view of the Bible and atoning death of Christ. Anon, *Old Paths*. See also Goodhew, "InterCollegiate Christian Union," 65.

> God speaks through his prophets today as He did in other times, and there is no limit to the means whereby men may be drawn to understand the truth of Christianity.[19]

McKenzie argued that while the Bible revealed the purposes of God, God continues to reveal truth through other means, and it is, therefore, the responsibility of intellectual Christians to seek this truth.[20] In the SCM, Bible study groups still met after the Great War as they had since its inception, but Howe notes that these groups were smaller in number and moved away from studying the Bible to "a shift in emphasis to ethics, practical Christianity and the teachings of the human Jesus."[21]

A concrete change reflecting this broader trend in the SCM was the formal modification of its membership basis. To become a member of the SCM, each student had previously been required to affirm that "I acknowledge the Lord Jesus Christ as Saviour and as God." In 1920, the Australian SCM movement wanted to have a more open, inclusive basis for membership, which was finally accepted at the King's School conference of 1923 at which Angus had spoken. Their membership now stated:

> The Australian Student Christian Movement is a fellowship of students, who seek, through prayer, study and service, more fully to know Jesus and His principles of life, and who are willing, as they come to realize His claims and power to follow him in service to God and their fellow-men.[22]

The youth of the SCM were no longer making a creedal commitment but rather a commitment to *seek* to know Jesus and his principles of life.

In the 1920s the university student ministry in Sydney was, therefore, facing challenges to its identity and purpose. The assumptions behind its model of raising up male Christian leaders who would be sent out to Christianize the world were being undermined. It would be a new student organization, the Evangelical Union (EU), that would respond to these challenges by affirming a conservative evangelical theology, reclaiming a model of activist student leadership, and encouraging peer ministry, and the ministry of both genders. These four characteristics led to the foundation of a vibrant youth ministry that would prove fruitful in the long term.

---

19. Quoted in Howe, *Century of Influence*, 164.
20. Howe, *Century of Influence*, 172.
21. Howe, *Century of Influence*, 172.
22. Howe, *Century of Influence*, 165.

Theological Conservatism and the Formation of the Evangelical Union

There were divergent responses in student youth ministry in Sydney to the challenges of liberal thought. The SCM moved away from a focus on missionary service to a concern for social issues, and a new approach to the Bible as it sought to nurture Christian leaders. The EU, by contrast, rejected biblical criticism and a concern for social action, and reasserted old ways of thinking in a new context. Both approaches reflect a struggle to stay faithful to the Christian message while seeking to communicate and apply it in a new context in the modern world. It is not surprising that this contrast was most apparent in the transmission of faith to young people, as the youth needed to articulate and live out their faith in a dramatically different context from their parents and church leaders. The EU sought to follow the lead of the Cambridge Inter-Collegiate Christian Union (CICCU) and look for *Old Paths in Perilous Times*.[23] There was a reactionary conservatism within the EU that was fundamental to its formation and character.

The formation of the EU in 1930 at Sydney University was largely a response by evangelical students and leaders to a perceived movement away from orthodox Christian theology by the Student Christian Movement. From the early 1930s, there was a diverging[24] and hardening of theological views between liberal and conservative evangelicals in Sydney among those with influence in youth ministry.[25] Whereas the SCM responded to the liberal challenge by developing a more open view of Scripture and orthodox belief, and open membership; the new evangelical student group would reject such openness as an unacceptable accommodation to the thinking of the world and instead reaffirm traditional Christian orthodoxy. The formation of the EU can be traced to the 1920s when Sydney Protestant churches began to be concerned about the teaching of modernist theology, particularly arising from the public controversy around Dr. Angus.[26] In the 1920s there had been a spectrum of approaches towards

---

23. This was the name of the book written to tell the story of the CICCU breaking away from the SCM. Anon, *Old Paths*. See also, Goodhew, "Inter-Collegiate Christian Union," 65.

24. It should be noted that Australian historian, G. R. Treloar, has warned readers to beware of the analytical paradigm of polarization within evangelicalism, suggesting that historians have been too ready to shape the narrative on the basis of conflicts and division within the movement rather than conveying the unity and breadth that existed. Treloar, "Some Reflections," 3.

25. In later chapters we will examine the impact of this polarization in the Anglican Board of Education and in the Church of England Fellowship movement.

26. Howe, *Century of Influence*, 165.

modernism in the Protestant churches,[27] but leaders from the Anglican, Baptist, and Methodist Churches were noting the liberalizing influence of Angus on the Presbyterian Church and were concerned that the same could happen to them.[28] They began to withhold funds from the SCM and discouraged young people from becoming too involved. The SCM group at Sydney University was seen by conservatives to be drifting from its foundation, particularly by no longer studying the Bible in small groups, and instead becoming more of a "moral debating society."[29]

While the SCM sought to engage with modern biblical scholarship and new theories of social order, conservatives literally retreated to the tower.[30] In 1919, undergraduate student John Deane posted a notice of a meeting in the Carillon Tower at Sydney University to study the Bible and to pray because, although he was an office bearer of the Christian Union (the SCM group at the university), he claimed that the SCM "no longer stood for a definite Christian witness."[31] This meeting developed into a regular group of more conservative evangelical students who met in the carillon tower to study the Bible and pray. An early participant described the meetings:

> It met at the lunch hour as a kind of Gideon's test to those who were genuinely keen. They either had to go without lunch, as I did, or cut it very short. It was attended by anything up to about thirty.[32]

---

27. For example, in the Anglican Church in Sydney there were some key leaders who in the interwar years had been open to engaging with biblical criticism and other new academic thinking. They were called *liberal evangelicals* by some. They sought to engage, but on the other hand, they were deeply attached to their heritage and would consider themselves to be orthodox Christians. These men included the Anglican Archbishop J. C. Wright 1909–1933, the Dean A. E. Talbot, and the principal of Moore College, D. J. Davies. In the 1930s, these men were replaced with conservative evangelicals who were committed to ensuring the Anglican Church remained conservative theologically. They opposed the liberal evangelicals and sought to have them removed from positions of influence.

28. In 1934 the Presbyterian Church withdrew their theological students from his lectures, and then sought to bring heresy charges against him. See Emilsen, *Whiff of Heresy*.

29. Howe, *Century of Influence*, 167. This was the accusation of the conservative evangelical leaders.

30. The tower was the Carillon Tower in the main quad of the University. See Prince, *Out of the Tower*.

31. Andersen, "A Brief History," in Box 316, SUEU, Correspondence, Box 1 SUEU Minute Books 1930–1946.

32. "SUEU Minute Book, March 20, 1930," Box 1 SUEU Minute Books 1930–1946.

The tower group formally became the Sydney University Bible League in 1927,[33] and in 1930 became the Sydney University Evangelical Union (SUEU). Its membership was open to "all who believe in Jesus Christ as their own personal Saviour" and sought to "encourage prayer and Bible study amongst students."[34] By contrast with the SCM, EU membership represented a restored emphasis on personal allegiance and commitment to Jesus rather than to seeking and openness.

The EU was formed in a context of theological polarization in Sydney, but members also looked to comparable events in Britain to reinforce their understanding of their identity. A conservative evangelical resurgence had begun in England, championed by university students.[35] In 1919, the same year that the Tower Group began, a breakaway group from the Christian Unions at Cambridge and London Universities reacted against the more open approach to membership and wrote a letter to *The Christian*:

> The writers of this letter claim to represent those who do not accept as true either Higher Criticism or Evolution, where they conflict with the facts revealed by the Spirit of God in Genesis and the rest of the Bible.[36]

This stance against theological liberalism was formalized in the founding of the IVF (the IVF of Evangelical Unions, which would be called the IVCF in Australia) in 1928. At the first general meeting of the IVF, one of the Cambridge students, Norman Grubb, set the agenda of establishing a "truly Evangelical witness" throughout the world.[37] It was the IVF that sent Howard Guinness[38] to Sydney in 1930 to establish a new conservative ministry at the university, where he found willing collaborators in the Sydney

---

33. "SUEU Minute Book, March 20, 1930," Box 1 SUEU Minute Books 1930–1946.

34. "SUEU Minute Book, March 20, 1930," Box 1 SUEU Minute Books 1930–1946.

35. Pete Ward has argued that in the early 1930s evangelicals in Britain were a struggling minority, but it was the focus on youth ministry, particularly by interdenominational institutions in universities and public schools, that led to resurgence within evangelicalism. Ward, "Reorganising the Chairs," 33; Griffiths, *East End Youth*, 6; Bebbington, *Evangelicalism*, 259–60.

36. Johnson, *Contending for the Faith*, 120.

37. Guinness, *Journey among Students*, 42. Norman Grubb was one of a group of students who stood against the more liberal leanings of the SCM groups. He later went on to be a missionary in Africa, a popular writer, as well as a leader within the IVF.

38. Guinness was a young graduate of Cambridge who was a founding Vice President of the IVF and had particular gifts in evangelism. He was sent overseas by the IVF to establish evangelical student ministries in Canada, New Zealand, India, and South Africa as well as in Australia. He spent time at Sydney University in 1930 and then again in 1934/5.

University Bible League. Guinness, himself a young man of twenty-six, helped these students establish an official group at the university with a constitution as the Sydney University Evangelical Union. The EU was affiliated with the IVF, the conservative evangelical student movement worldwide. They saw themselves as those who were *for* the Bible and witness and *against* the SCM and its liberal agenda.

The self-understanding of those within the EU was further reinforced by stories of English evangelical student ministry in the past. Donald Coggan's book *Christ and the Colleges* (1934)[39] was particularly influential. It related the tension in the British student ministry at Cambridge, which in 1906 had voted to embrace modern approaches. In 1910, a group of students in the Cambridge Intercollegiate Christian Union (CICCU) including Howard Mowll (who would later become the Anglican Archbishop of Sydney and a key supporter of evangelical youth ministry) broke away from the SCM and established a new evangelical movement that asserted an orthodox, conservative view of the authority of the Scriptures and the atoning death of Christ.[40] Historian Meredith Lake claims that Coggan's account was read by many EU members in the 1930s and subsequent years[41] and that they felt that theirs was a parallel situation to that of the earlier CICCU in Britain.[42] The inspirational stories of C. T. Studd and the Cambridge Seven and the IVF magazine sent from Britain further reinforced an identity that looked to Cambridge.[43] Some EU members felt that they could take a person on a tour of the Cambridge colleges without ever being there, so informed were they of the history.[44] These adversarial and heroic narratives helped define the identity of the EU as a group like the CICCU, which was perceived as having courageously stood up against the forces of theological liberalism to defend the faith for the sake of the Lord, comparable to Martin Luther in his battle against the medieval Catholic Church when he allegedly said: "Here I stand I can do no other, so help me God."[45]

The new student ministry conducted the same activities as the SCM, but with a focus on a public witness in the university and on Bible study. In its first year, there was a group of twenty to thirty young men and women

39. Coggan, *Christ and the Colleges*.
40. Goodhew, "Inter-Collegiate Christian Union."
41. Lake, *Proclaiming Jesus Christ*, 23.
42. Donald Robinson interview. Cambridge was so totemic that Robinson claimed that he could have given you a tour of Cambridge before he had been there, he knew it so well.
43. Jean Porter interview.
44. Donald Robinson interview.
45. Barclay and Horn, *From Cambridge*.

who organized Bible studies, public meetings, house parties in the holidays, picnics on the Woronora River, and other social events.[46] Guinness was used as a speaker during the months that he was with them, giving public evangelistic addresses such as: "The Greatest Fact in the Universe," "The Greatest Fact in Experience," "Victory," and "Can Christ Be Real?"[47] The EU sought to evangelize students, which they believed the SCM was not doing effectively.

The liberal-conservative polarization in Sydney made it necessary to articulate fundamental beliefs and values in greater detail than had previously been customary, and for many young people, the EU helped them to do this for the first time. From 1930 their theological conservatism was unambiguously expressed in the Membership Aim and Doctrinal Basis of the EU, which was intended to define who they were and what they stood for as conservative evangelicals. This approach was useful not only in building a stable organizational foundation but also as a basis for corporate identity formation among young people as they sought to live out their faith in the modern world.[48] The expressed aim of the EU was "to stimulate personal faith and to further evangelistic work among students by upholding the fundamental truths of Christianity." The doctrinal basis consisted of nine affirmations of evangelical doctrine including the infallibility of the Bible and the atoning death of Jesus.

1. The divine inspiration and infallibility of the Holy Scripture as originally given, and its supreme authority.
2. The unity of the Father, the Son and the Holy Spirit in the Godhead.
3. The universal sinfulness of man since the fall, rendering man subject to God's wrath and condemnation.
4. Redemption from the guilt, penalty, and power of sin, only through the sacrificial death, as our representative and substitute, of Jesus Christ, the incarnate Son of God.

---

46. "SUEU Minute Book, March 20, 1930," Box 1 Minute Books 1930–1946.

47. "SUEU Minute Book, March 20, 1930," Box 1 Minute Books 1930–1946.

48. Stuart Lange argues that in New Zealand it was the Evangelical Unions who shaped a new generation of evangelical leaders who were very conscious and clear about their identity as evangelicals and able to communicate this to others. The Evangelical Unions did this through their ethos, name, and doctrinal basis. Through interviews he has discovered that it was at the EU that young New Zealanders first learnt the meaning of "evangelical" and came to identify as such. The New Zealand EUs were formed by Guinness, and the Protestant religious culture was mutually influential, so it is fair to say this was probably also true in Australia in the 1930s. Lange, *Rising Tide*, 42.

5. The conception of Jesus by the Holy Spirit and his birth by the Virgin Mary.
6. The bodily resurrection of Jesus Christ from the dead.
7. The necessity of the work of the Holy Spirit to make the death of Jesus Christ effective to individual sinners, granting each one repentance towards God and faith in Jesus Christ.
8. The indwelling and work of the Holy Spirit in the believer.
9. The expectation of the personal return of the Lord Jesus Christ.[49]

Acceptance of these statements was required of any office holder or speaker to the EU. They were a defensive assertion of orthodox faith against the challenge of the liberal evangelicals in overt contrast to the open membership statement of the SCM. Frank Engel, a student leader of the SCM in the 1930s explained:

> Guinness and the EU were committed to a set of conservative theological propositions which the leadership had to accept and propagate . . . the central ones were the verbal inspiration of the Bible and the substitutionary theory of the Atonement. In contrast, the ASCM focused on loyalty to Jesus Christ and commitment to follow him as Lord in a changing world. One could say it was a difference of allegiance to the theological propositions (dogma) on the one hand, and, on the other, allegiance to a living Lord.[50]

In the theological context of the time, the most prominent doctrines of the EU were the authority of Scripture and a conservative understanding of the atoning death of Jesus. This was reflected in an account of a meeting at Sydney University in the early 1930s between the SCM and the EU. The SCM wanted to work together, believing there was little difference between the two groups: "only EU's attitude to Scripture and the atonement." These two issues remained the sticking point and Paul White from the EU executive responded to them by stating: "Man, they are the two legs IVCF walks on!"[51] Paul White had noted the different approach by the SCM to Scripture

---

49. "SUEU Minutes November 12, 1930," Box 1 Minute Books 1930–1946. This list is similar to the doctrinal beliefs set out by the CICUU defining itself against the SCM. They set out the authority and inspiration of the Bible, the atoning death of Jesus, and the personal return of Jesus to judge. Anon, *Old Paths*.

50. Quoted in Howe, *Century of Influence*, 187.

51. Paul White interview. These two issues were the very same debated by student leaders when the CICUU split from the SCM group in Cambridge. Fielder, *Lord of the Years*, 21.

in his early days at university in 1929 when he attended an SCM study circle. He related:

> When I got up there the one Christian organization that I heard about was the Student Christian Movement. I went along to a study circle, and the leader (a prominent Methodist minister) started to tear leaves out of the Bible, and tell me that I really needed to rethink the whole of my faith; that I had swallowed too much without thinking. I didn't like it, and I told him so. I was at the advanced age of nineteen, and perhaps I was a little bit gauche, because after three or four of those particular Bible studies, it was suggested that perhaps they would go more smoothly if I didn't attend.[52]

White and the EU were committed to an unconditional acceptance of the Bible as an authoritative word, and this shaped their identity as the *Evangelical* Union.

Although the EU stood in reaction to modern liberal theology and sought to reaffirm traditional Christian teachings, the group actively sought to participate in intellectual debate. In this, it was led by Guinness himself, who sought to engage intellectually with the challenges of the modern world. The historian of the SCM, Renate Howe, describes Guinness as "a personable young man who projected an image of reasonable conservative evangelicalism that resonated with the concern of the Bible leagues and Bible Institutes, to move from rabid, extreme Fundamentalism to a more moderate position."[53] He led the fundamentalist-tending evangelical students to a more open form of evangelicalism, yet he insisted that the leaders adhere to key creedal evangelical statements. This desire to defend the faith against modern intellectual attacks can be seen in the EU leaders' choice of public talks that were given in the 1930s such as "Archaeology Confirms Scripture,"[54] and "The Bible and Modern Research."[55]

The formation of the EU alongside the SCM at the University of Sydney is significant for this study as they exemplify the different ways that Christian youth responded to the challenge of new thinking in the modern world. Both groups managed to sustain numbers in the 1930s without spectacular growth in either.[56] It was not until the 1950s that the EU began to expand through campus missions when it grew from a group of 191 at the end of the

---

52. Paul White interview.
53. Howe, *Century of Influence*, 184.
54. "SUEU Minutes June 8, 1936," Box 1 SUEU Minute Books 1930–1946.
55. "SUEU Minutes October 15, 1936," Box 1 SUEU Minute Books 1930–1946.
56. See Lake, *Proclaiming Jesus Christ*, 17; Howe, *Century of Influence*, 194.

Second World War to four hundred and fifty members in 1955 (or 7 percent of all students).[57] The SCM became increasingly radical in its approach to orthodox Christian doctrines, whilst the EU sought to maintain adherence to creeds and a commitment to witness and evangelism. As the EU sought to witness to young people, there was an internal coherence in the worldview and values of the EU that helped it stand against a prevailing culture that was increasingly secularized. The SCM, however, seemed to lack an identifying center; they stood both for being disciples of Jesus and for questioning of the faith handed down to them. After World War II it became harder to attract those returning, and as Christian cultural hegemony broke down, the SCM no longer had a clear agenda or identity.[58]

Steven Bruce in his doctoral research contrasting the SCM and IVF in Britain has sought to explain the resilience of the more conservative group as compared with the more liberal. He argued that liberalism is largely defined by what it is not: liberation from the faith passed down, rather than a belief system that is able to create a cohesive identity for the believer. Bruce argued that the SCM declined because of: first, its reluctance to proselytize; second, an inability to generate action; and third, an inability to maintain commitment.[59] The IVF and similarly the EU at Sydney University were committed to witness, promoted activism, and were able to sustain a young person's faith, all as by-products of dogmatic commitments. Much of the strength of the movement can be attributed to its theological conservatism.

The success of the EU as an effective youth ministry can be traced to its foundation as a theologically conservative organization. It began as a movement that was clear about its identity and core beliefs, enabling it to create a robust subcultural identity. This identity was strengthened by the name *Evangelical Union*, its doctrinal basis and its narrative of origins. The SCM, on the other hand, was clear in communicating who they were *not* (i.e. their parents, evangelicals stuck in the past), yet their very openness and the lack of clarity on who they *were* weakened their ability to form a robust subcultural identity.

---

57. Lake, *Proclaiming Jesus Christ*, 69.

58. It is interesting to consider the work of sociologists who have struggled with the question of the resilience of conservative religious belief. Sociologists of the past had presumed that with the growth of secularism, conservative religious belief would die out; instead, it has in some places flourished. Writers such as Kelley, Kepel, and Tamney have argued that a conservative religious belief can be a potent reaction to secular modernity and a coherent identity-shaper. Kelley, *Conservative Churches*; Kepel, *Revenge of God*; Tamney, *Resilience of Christianity*.

59. Bruce, "Student Christian Movement," 380.

Empowering of Youth in Leadership

The second major characteristic underlying the strength of the new EU youth ministry at the university in addition to its theological conservatism was the empowering of youth in leadership. As has been noted, this was not strictly an innovation of the 1930s; university student ministry was already distinctive for its emphasis on student leadership and engagement. Nevertheless, the 1930s saw renewed emphasis on student leadership in the new EU, particularly under the influence of Howard Guinness. From its foundation, the EU nurtured young leaders, many of whom were later to have significant roles in church and other ministries. Importantly, Guinness emphasized active service and ministry through witness in the university in the present, rather than merely in preparation for future ministry. He mentored and encouraged key leaders of the EU, many of whom went on to have significant roles in other youth ministries, including establishing new organizations such as the Crusader Union, the Inter-School Christian Fellowship (ISCF) and the Teachers' Christian Fellowship (TCF).

Student leadership was a hallmark of the EU. All the formal events of the EU were organized by student leaders: public meetings, prayer meetings, house parties, and Bible study groups. As well as leading the activities of the EU, the young people were encouraged to lead activities beyond the university. They gave talks and led at Crusader Union meetings and house parties, missions, and fellowship groups. Many of the members from the foundation year of the EU went on to become influential leaders within churches and evangelical interdenominational societies. For instance, in the church, Gordon Begbie (son of prominent evangelical minister H. S. Begbie) became a bishop in the Sydney Anglican diocese. A number of EU members, such as Neville Langford-Smith and Paul White, became missionaries with CMS in Tanganyika. Paul White was a particularly influential graduate of the EU. He was student president, and after he returned from missionary service became the General Secretary of the IVCF, and also sat on the council of Scripture Union and of the Crusader Union. He became famous for writing the *Jungle Doctor* books and was an influential leader and speaker within these interdenominational organizations, being a "down to earth fun witness" who could entertain as well as educate.[60] There were women undergraduates too who would become very influential in the evangelical world, particularly in the sphere of education. Anna Hogg, who studied philosophy under John Anderson, was an EU member who was in effect the first female professor at Sydney University. She was

---

60. Ian Holt interview.

head of the Department of Teacher Education from 1948 to 1973 and was influential on the councils of the Scripture Union and Teachers' Christian Fellowship and was the founding editor of the *Journal of Christian Education*.[61] Jean Porter (the daughter of Brethren leader and sometime speaker at the EU, Wilfred Porter) became a field worker for Scripture Union and for ISCF schools and camps work. She was an accomplished teacher and became the headmistress of Macarthur Girls High School. Heather Drummond became a staff worker for Crusaders schools and camps ministry, and later a senior mistress at PLC Croydon.

Guinness self-consciously saw his role as raising up new leaders for the movement amongst students and he actively mentored the gifted students who were part of the fledgling EU. When he returned to England at the end of 1930, he left a team of motivated and charismatic leaders behind at the university.[62] Former EU President, Allan Bryson claimed:

> Howard Guinness was very important. He could take a small group and give them a sense of this united strength as a body. This was his strength. He taught that however ineffective we were as individuals, as a group we had strength.[63]

On his second tour around Australia in 1933/34, he took with him three Australian students in order to train and mentor them. These leaders were Lindsay Grant (who was later employed as a staff worker of the IVCF and Crusader Union), Bob Haines, and Stafford Young. Guinness was quite deliberate in training young leaders and he would encourage them to consider ministry as their vocation. In his prayer letter of October to November 1933, he stated that he had read Roland Allen's *Missionary Methods: St Pauls or Ours?* and was convicted that "the rank and file of the movement should be pushed onto their feet and made to take responsibility."[64] In 1934, he wrote that youth needed to be pushed into self-sacrificial service and responsibility: "we must force our young Christians out into a life of direct dependence upon the Holy Spirit and the Word of God."[65] He was concerned that the groups formed in schools and universities should not

---

61. King, "Alumni Remembered."
62. Donald Robinson interview.
63. Allan and Elsie Bryson interview.
64. Guinness, "Prayer Letter 7, October–November 1933," Samuel Marsden Archives. In 1912, Allen wrote a popular book that argued that missionaries must use the same method as the apostle Paul. They should seek converts, but then trust in the Spirit to be at work in groups of new indigenous believers who will establish and lead their own ministries. Allen, *Missionary Methods*.
65. Guinness, "Prayer Letter 26, January 1934," Samuel Marsden Archives.

be dependent on his leadership, but self-sustaining with their own youth leaders. Guinness believed that he was "handing on the torch."[66] The students responded positively to Guinness's approach, even to his genteel bearing and attire. The men imitated his dress, wearing conservative grey slacks and Harris Tweed sports coats, despite the Depression. Guinness was what they all aspired to be.[67]

Apart from his direct personal influence, Guinness shaped an ethos, restoring to the movement a commitment to consecration and self-sacrifice, which was crucial for raising up leaders. In his very popular 1936 pamphlet, *Sacrifice*, he rebuked the church and modern Christians for losing their willingness to give up all in their discipleship of Jesus.[68] In the last few paragraphs, he reminds the reader of the call of C. T. Studd to enlist young men in service of the Lord:

> Where are the young men and women of this generation who will hold their lives cheap, and be faithful even unto death? . . . Where are those who will live dangerously, and be reckless in His service? Where are His lovers—those who love Him and the souls of men more than their own reputations or comfort, or very life? . . . Where are the men who say "no" to self, who take up Christ's Cross to bear it after Him; who are willing to be nailed to it in college or office, home or mission field; who are willing, if need be, to bleed, to suffer, and to die on it? . . . Where are the men who are willing to pay the price of vision?[69]

At the end of his pamphlet, he encourages the reader to sign below a prayer of consecration with a determination for change and action. The decisive commitment to having one's whole life shaped by one's faith was a key reason why the EU approach was attractive to youth.[70] Allan Bryson explained that the:

> Message was to aim for full commitment to Christ and put all other considerations aside and if necessary jettison your career

66. Dr. Paul White interview.
67. Allan Bryson interview.
68. A book that was widely read and reprinted eleven times. Guinness, *Sacrifice*.
69. Guinness, *Sacrifice*, 76–77.
70. Princeton Prof. Kendra Creasy Dean has argued that a call for radical commitment is in fact what young people are looking for and that at their developmental age youth are passionate and desirous of someone to lay down their life for. She argues that the evangelical message of the atonement, of Christ laying down his life for us, still has the power today to challenge young people to a life of radical commitment. She argues that easy religion is actually less attractive to the passionate young person than the demands of a conservative, high commitment religion. Dean, *Practicing Passion*, 32.

for the sake of Christian commitment . . . It's very hard for idealistic young people to resist that type of thing.[71]

Guinness inspired young students with this call to sacrifice to become leaders ready to suffer for their Lord.

After the departure of Guinness in 1934, the EU continued to raise up effective leaders who would go on to influence Sydney evangelicalism. Interestingly, in the years up to the war, all but one of the presidents was training to be a doctor.[72] Dr. Lindsay Grant (President 1933–34) was a travelling secretary for IVCF for a year, founding General Secretary of the IVCF and continued to influence the EU for a decade.[73] Dr. Ian Holt (President 1935) was very prominent in Crusaders on the council and as the Chairman for many years.[74] Dr. Allan Bryson (President 1936) became a doctor and continued to have an influence on CMS council, and in the Anglican Diocese as a lay leader and member of synod. Prof. Harvey Carey (President 1940) became a professor of gynecology and helped pioneer the contraceptive pill and ultrasonic scanning in the 1960s.[75] Dr. John Hercus (President 1941) was to become a leading ophthalmologist as well as a founder of the IVCF graduates Fellowship and the Christian Medical Fellowship.[76] He was also a well-loved writer and Christian speaker. Donald Robinson (Vice President 1941)[77] was the son of an archdeacon. He was chairman of the Australian IVCF Council and was involved with the IVCF all his life, a lecturer and vice-principal at Moore Theological College, and later the Anglican Archbishop of Sydney.

Many of the young women given responsibility in the EU became influential leaders after university as well. Some of them married male leaders and exercised influence as key supporters in the ministry of their husbands.[78] Many of the female graduates were beneficiaries of government teacher's scholarships that were introduced to supply enough teachers for the new and growing government secondary schools. Women like Gwen

71. Allan Bryson interview.

72. This was partly because medical students were at university for six years, so they had more maturity and experience. It may have also been the modelling of Guinness who was trained as a doctor and according to Jean Porter, "loved the med students." Jean Porter interview.

73. Millikin's book has a full biography of his life. Millikan, *Imperfect Company*.

74. Braga, "Holt."

75. "Harvey M. Carey interviewed by Hazel de Berg," Hazel de Berg Collection.

76. Burnard, "Hercus."

77. Cameron, "Donald William Bradley Robinson," xi–xvi.

78. For example, Marie Taubman, Elsie Taubman, Audrey Delbridge, and Dorrie Finkh.

Wilkinson and Win Dunkley, along with Anna Hogg and Heather Drummond, were leaders who had a vision for teaching and who helped establish both the TCF (Teachers Christian Fellowship) and the ISCF (Inter-School Christian Fellowship). They, along with other EU leaders, initiated the formation of the ISCF when they were at the Katoomba Convention in January 1935. Many of those present were already involved in Scripture Union camps and beach mission in their holidays. People like Win Dunkley saw schools as a mission field and were burdened by a desire to serve God in their prospective careers as teachers.[79] Lindsay Grant called a meeting and suggested that a ministry in high schools should be started, the Inter-School Christian Fellowship (ISCF), taking its name from the schools ministry in Canada established by Guinness.[80]

Older evangelicals nurtured the EU students as leaders, and they were careful to help but not take over. Key clergymen from various denominations led Bible studies in the EU and gave talks at public meetings and house parties, including W. Porter (Brethren), Mr. M. McOmish (Presbyterian from the Open Air Campaigners), the Reverend G. Begbie (Anglican), and the Reverend G. Morling (Baptist). In 1934, the Anglican Archbishop Howard Mowll came to Sydney and he became the patron of the EU. He spoke at most of the annual general meetings and the students found him to be a tremendous man, "Big in stature, big in vision, big in experience."[81] Another mentor was T. C. Hammond, principal of Moore Theological College, who taught at public meetings, house parties, and at "squashes,"[82] in his own house. Hammond's book *In Understanding Be Men* (1936) effectively

---

79. Win Dunkley interview.
80. Bill Andersen interview.
81. Ian Holt interview.
82. A squash was an informal meeting held in a living room, where young people were *squashed* together. Noel Palmer, the General Secretary of the IVF described the general pattern of the squash. "[P]rivate invitations are given out, usually by word of mouth, and when the day arrives each guest is introduced to the hostess, while the company get mutually acquainted and so on. Refreshments are often served, first if the hour is afternoon, or last if it is evening. Quite naturally and without any appearance of being forced, choruses and hymns are introduced, and a brief pointed testimony and message are given by some professional man or other suitable speaker. This may lead to other *ex tempore* testimonies, or discussion, or prayer. Always prayer. The meeting breaks up as informally as it began, gradually slipping back into a pleasant social occasion, while the guests take their leave in the usual way. But it may frequently happen that a few will have been deeply touched, and opportunity should be unobtrusively given for such to remain and talk things over seriously with some of the leaders." As quoted in Schmidt, "Crossing the Great Divide," 104.

became the textbook of the IVCF movement, giving students a more coherent and theological understanding of their faith.[83]

Along with clergymen and speakers, there was also a wealth of experience within key families in Sydney who supported the EU as their children took up leadership within it. Many were associated with the South Sea Evangelical Mission, the CSSM (Children's Special Service Mission), and with the Katoomba Convention.[84] Families would offer their homes for house parties, for tennis parties, and squashes on Saturday nights. Some would come to house parties as houseparents.[85] Bryson claims that notwithstanding the help of adults, "actual leadership, however, in the universities and schools was considered best left to the initiatives of the young leaders, but there was advice and guidance aplenty if sought."[86] The EU was very much a student-led body, and excessive outside interference would have been resented.[87] Adults supported and nurtured the EU, but they never tried to run things.

Student leadership was not simply a matter of decision-making but extended to students taking direct responsibility for the exercise of ministry on campus. A conspicuous example can be seen in the account of the famous 1935 EU mission. It was the first large-scale mission that the EU had organized, bringing out the fiery Irish evangelist W. P. Nicholson. When Nicholson became ill after the first talk, student leaders accepted the challenge of substituting for him in the public evangelistic meetings.[88] The student Lindsay Grant received a poor response in his talk so that at one stage he asked all the Christians in the room to stand up, in order to make them take a stand for Christ. The next day the EU president, Ian Holt, spoke to a very rowdy audience. Some members of the audience let off noisy throwdowns and sneezing powder and began coughing and stamping their feet as Holt spoke. When he finished and asked for silence so he could close in prayer, some of the students tugged at a carpet runner to sweep Holt off his feet. They were forcibly removed by an enraged clergyman and later given suspensions from the university.[89] The experience of the mission confirmed the capacity of students to lead the EU themselves, even in the face of unexpected and unfavorable circumstances.

83. Donald Robinson interview.
84. Notably, the Young, Deck, and Grant families. See Donald Robinson interview.
85. For example, Mrs. Deck, Mrs. Hercus, Mrs. Porter, and Mrs. Begbie.
86. "Letter from Allan Bryson to Margaret Lamb, December 12, 1989."
87. Donald Robinson interview.
88. "SUEU Minutes Report of Mission July 28 to August 2, 1935," Box 1 SUEU Minute Books 1930–1946.
89. *Honi Soit*, August 5, 1935, Box 1 SUEU Minute Books 1930–1946.

These young leaders were charismatic and committed to youth ministry and they remained so after they left the university. Many moved into vocational ministry. Others worked for or sat on the councils of the IVCF or Crusaders or Scripture Union or were involved as teachers and in the Teachers' Christian Fellowship. In other words, there was a pool of gifted leaders in youth ministry that had been mentored in the university and were committed to supporting the movement. The empowering of youth to lead ministries is important in understanding the effectiveness and vitality of youth ministry in the 1930s.

Peer Ministry

As well as theological conservatism and the empowering of young leaders, a third characteristic contributing to the effectiveness of the new university ministry was the appeal of peer ministry. In the 1930s, youth ministry was shaped by the increasing importance of peer groups rather than adult instruction and intervention. Peer groups were strengthened by a theological appeal to the importance of fellowship. Ministry to one's peers was encouraged in the form of witness or personal work. This reflected a broader shift from ministry *for* youth to ministry *of* youth.

Fellowship was not a concept unique to conservative evangelicals in the 1930s. Liberal evangelicals had rejected an individualistic focus for a more corporate view of the meaning and purpose of the Christian life, and *fellowship* was seen as a key reason for their meeting. The historian Ian Randall argues that after the First World War, ideas of comradeship in the trenches may have helped lead to this focus on fellowship and deep relationships in small groups.[90] In 1927, the SCM produced *The Book of Fellowship*.[91] Helen Balfour recounts the first singing of the song *Lo, Here is Felawschippe* at the SCM national conference in 1931 as the students held hands.

> Lo, here is Felawschippe
>
> One faith to hold
>
> One troth to speke
>
> One wrong to wreke
>
> One loving cuppe to suppe
>
> And to dip in one dyshe

---

90. Randall, *Evangelical Experiences*, 113.
91. Randall, *Evangelical Experiences*, 126.

> Faithfullisch
>
> As lambkins of one fold:
>
> Either for other to suffer all thing,
>
> One song to sing in sweet accord,
>
> And maken melodye.
>
> Lo, here is felawshippe. (Anon)[92]

This song was sung at SCM conferences and weddings and was known as the "song of the SCM." It represents the idealism of those students whose generation faced the Depression and war, and their joy in experiencing spiritual unity with their friends. This vision of spiritual unity was embraced by conservative evangelicals as well as liberal evangelicals.

The focus on fellowship was further encouraged in the 1930s by a university ministry in England called the Oxford Group. This was a student organization set up by Frank Buchman at Oxford in 1920 based on small cell groups for Bible study and prayer. These groups focused more on Christian living than doctrine and saw personal relationships and conversations in groups as "life-changing." Buchman's vision was for groups of Christians to be living the kind of fellowship evident in the first-century church of Acts. He encouraged "the law of fellowship"[93] which was made up of four absolutes: honesty, purity, unselfishness, and love. In the groups, he also encouraged members to share confessions of sin, which led to some concern that the group had an unhealthy obsession with sexual sin.[94]

In 1932, Howard Guinness went to an Oxford Group house party because he had heard that many people were being converted. He stated that despite the lack of theological orthodoxy (particularly the absence of teaching on the atonement), he loved the idea of organizing house parties, and the focus on fellowship and deep sharing they facilitated.[95] His conclusion was that the:

> Most important problem in almost every union was that of fellowship. How could we avoid misunderstanding, jealousy, pride, and egotism? How could we improve our teamwork? How could we love each other? That was the crunch! . . . But sharing on a

---

92. Howe, *Century of Influence*, 224.
93. Randall, *Evangelical Experiences*, 246.
94. Randall, *Evangelical Experiences*, 252.
95. Guinness, *Journey among Students*, 76.

deeper level between members was a help towards this love and was also one of its continuing results.[96]

Guinness went on to regard house parties as a key to evangelism as well as for effective decision making.

In the EU, fellowship inspired by the example of the early church was an important theme. For them, fellowship involved a unity with God through the Holy Spirit as well as a unity with other believers who shared the one Spirit and met together like the early Christians for prayer and worship. This fellowship emphasis was expressed and nurtured in the different activities of the EU, particularly house parties and prayer meetings, as well as in the way that decisions were made in the group. On the house parties, groups of EU members went on holidays together and listened to a speaker, shared testimonies, sang, and socialized together. For example, at a house party in 1934:

> Nearly all had to tell of some new experience of Christ's reality and of a fuller and more detailed surrender of the life to him. ... There have been definite and lasting results from this house-party. Several can look back on it as the time when Christ first became real to them, and all of us learnt more about the meaning of fellowship, of detailed surrender, and of God's plan for and claims upon our lives.[97]

Fellowship was both an experience of the spirit of Christ as well as a surrender of one's individual will. Prayer meetings were also times of fellowship when small groups met together to pray, with much open sharing and examining of their motives every day. This experience for many was life changing.

> Many of us look back on those meetings as our first real glimpse of the vital fellowship of the early Christians whose witness to the Resurrection of Jesus Christ turned the world upside down. The keynote at these meetings was the thought of complete abandon to Jesus Christ.[98]

In 1935, a motion to change the name of the group from the Evangelical Union to Christian *Fellowship* was only narrowly defeated.[99]

---

96. Guinness, *Journey among Students*, 76.
97. "SUEU Minutes August 10, 1934," Box 1 SUEU Minute Books 1930–1946.
98. "SUEU Minutes October 12, 1934," Box 1 SUEU Minute Books 1930–1946.
99. "SUEU Minutes October 12, 1934," Box 1 SUEU Minute Books 1930–1946.

The focus on fellowship did bring with it certain challenges. There were times when there was tension in the EU as it struggled to remain concerned about evangelism and not be too inward focused. In 1934:

> It was pointed out that members of the EU were liable to form cliques, and while gaining a great deal from the fellowship, miss the best which was to be found in opportunities for service and witness amongst those outside their intimate circle.[100]

Moreover, there was occasionally a sense of elitism amongst the privileged members that at times threatened to weaken the fellowship of the EU. There were students who felt excluded because they came from a less privileged background and a public high school rather than a private school.[101]

The emphasis on fellowship influenced the approach to evangelism promoted within the EU during the 1930s. Peer witness, whether in one-to-one conversations or in structured meetings, was encouraged. Guinness believed that the heart of Christian service was to present the Christian message to one's friends and convert them to the Christian faith; what he called "personal work." He himself became a Christian this way, and his autobiography is full of conversations that he had with students as he did personal work.[102] He believed that witness was most effective in one-to-one conversations that challenged the listener to make some kind of commitment. This was not at the expense of witnessing in formal settings, however. In conversation with Paul White in 1930, Guinness asked him what his abilities were, and on finding out that he was a champion runner he said: "you ought to be on your feet witnessing to school boys because they are interested in sport."[103] His encouragement to White to be actively engaged in ministry is evident in the way that he soon organized the young student to give his testimony at St. Hilda's Church of England, Katoomba. White claims that:

> Howard really motivated us, to witness, to pray, to get on with the job for God. And really, he put into my mind the verse that the Lord brought out on the Sermon on the Mount, to seek first the kingdom and righteousness.[104]

Other students like Jean Porter were taught that they should be a visible witness at university, even as they walked from lunch to Bible study.

100. "SUEU Minutes October 12, 1934," Box 1 SUEU Minute Books 1930–1946.
101. For example, Jean Porter interview.
102. Guinness, *Journey among Students*.
103. Paul White interview.
104. Paul White interview.

> Now the natural thing was for me to take my books through from Manning and you always put your Bible on top, I was taught that, and it cost me personally to carry my Bible at five to two, through the quad and right up.[105]

The EU continued to stress the importance of students witnessing to their young peers after Guinness had left. Teams of four students went to different churches every three weeks where they led youth services, preached evangelistic sermons, or gave their testimony. There are accounts of some being converted at these meetings[106] and that the church fellowship groups that were just beginning in Sydney were inspired and built up by the EU teams.[107] Teams of students were also involved with the *Life with a Capital L* missions, combined events with the CSSM and Scripture Union. At these missions, EU students gave talks and led children's services as well as squashes for young people at night. EU office-bearer Rob McBeth spoke at a Salvation Army service of the mission in 1936 to Goulburn, where he claimed seventy-five people were converted.[108]

Witnessing to peers was so much a part of the ministry of the EU, that it was possible to feel excluded if you were not able to be public about your faith in the same way. The student Agnes Earl wrote to the President of EU in 1938 to explain why she was going to resign her membership. She explained that she had never brought anyone to Christ and felt like a hypocrite. "'The Evangelical Union' if it is for anything, is for the conversion of those around by its members. In the Union, I am 'less use than a piece of furniture.'"[109] In this subcultural group, if a young person was not committed to witness they felt they were not quite part of the group and did not belong.

The peer group was equated with an understanding of the meaning of fellowship. As such, it became the determinative context for spiritual experience, shared beliefs, and a commitment to surrendering to the will of God. The idea of fellowship encouraged a peer ministry that was both empowering and joyful. Moreover, during the 1930s, the peer group became the primary context for transmitting the Christian faith, which proved more effective than older methods of religious education. Students were mobilized to conduct ministry amongst other youth, with a focus on witness and self-surrender.

---

105. Jean Porter interview.
106. Ian Holt interview.
107. Andersen, "EU: A Brief History," "Correspondence," Box 316, SUEU Archives.
108. "Life with a Capital L Campaign Closes," *Goulburn Evening Penny Post*, June 5, 1936, 1.
109. "Agnes Earl Letter to President of EU," October 17, 1938, Box 314, SUEU Archives.

The evangelistic mission field was no longer primarily the non-Christian lands of the East, but friends and neighbors; one's peers.

Increasing Acceptance of Coeducational Ministry

The last characteristic to be considered in the university ministry is the increasing acceptance of coeducational ministry as the EU responded to changing attitudes towards women and sexuality. By the 1930s there were increasing numbers of women entering the university in various faculties[110] and many who were training to be teachers in the new government high schools. At the same time, there was a new awareness of the sexuality of youth in society, partly influenced by psychologist Stanley Hall. Intellectuals such as Margaret Mead were asserting the right for women (as well as men) to express and experiment with their sexuality.[111] The cinemas and dance halls were also reflecting sexual mores not always in keeping with conservative middle class values which frowned upon unchaperoned dancing, fraternizing with the opposite sex, drinking alcohol in public, and dressing in a way that was different from their parents. Changing attitudes in society towards sexuality posed a challenge to evangelical Christians, who sought to accept sexual desire as natural, but at the same time encouraged young people to suppress this natural urge until marriage. Evangelicals did encourage socializing of young Christians in a morally safe context, with the possibility of finding an appropriate marriage partner. The EU created a subculture where there was equal involvement of women and men in most leadership and ministry activities, as well as a commitment to speaking candidly about issues of sexuality and reasserting conservative values. The response of the EU was influenced by Howard Guinness, who encouraged social mixing of both sexes and taught candidly about the benefits of mixed fellowship, but also of the need for Christian sexual self-restraint.

The EU responded to the social changes of the 1930s by including women on an equal footing with men. During the 1930s, the EU included women among the office-bearers on its General Council as vice-presidents, women's secretaries, and prayer and mission secretaries. The only office reserved for men was the presidency.[112] Charismatic women such as Alice

---

110. In 1936 in Arts there were about two hundred male students and three hundred women. In Science, there were 202 men and 166 women and in medicine, there were 735 men and 137 women. Barcan, *Radical Students*, 100.

111. Shelley-Sireci, *Developmental Psychology*, 95.

112. More could be said here about the different roles of men and women within the EU and the way this reflects a particular theological or cultural view current at that

Smith and Jean Porter held leadership roles in the EU and went on to be leaders within the Crusader Union and Scripture Union. Youth ministry had become coeducational. Activities of the EU such as prayer meetings, public meetings, and Bible studies were mixed. Even the house parties were mixed, though the men and women stayed at different houses and came together for the daily program.

As well as the inclusion of women in leadership and ministry activities, the EU sought to be frank in its teaching on sexuality and the temptations faced in a mixed-sex group. In his very first public talk at the university, Howard Guinness spoke of "Man, Woman and God." According to a report of the talk in *The Union Recorder*, three hundred students attended and heard Guinness speak on the "sex problem":

> That the sex instinct provides temptations of no ordinary magnitude is a known fact, but powerful as are the temptations of the world, there is a mightier power, that of the indwelling Christ.[113]

Despite the temptation, Guinness saw coeducational youth ministry as healthy and enriching within Christian fellowship. In his book *Sacrifice*, he stated that segregation was "both unnatural and harmful; each sex has something to give and receive from the other"[114] and that friendship with the opposite sex should be cultivated. Guinness was candid about relationships and sexuality but urged his readers to suppress this natural urge until marriage. He argued that there should be natural boundaries (he probably meant the socially acceptable boundaries of physical contact and polite behaviour to the opposite sex) kept within these relationships in order to guard the young person against becoming sexualized.

> Let us keep them, however, on a high intellectual and spiritual plane (avoiding silliness and mere frivolity, for each is worth more and can give more than that) and let us observe the usual healthy barriers which God has appointed between the sexes. Let us neither become too distant nor too familiar in our

---

time. Historians have noted a "masculinism" that has shaped male/female relationships. See for example: O'Brien, "Church Full of Men"; Lake, "Historical Reconsiderations," 116–31. What is noted here, however, is the acceptance of the leadership of women within the EU as a response to changes in culture. In fact, the EU seems to be ahead of the times in an Australian society that was very conservative in its views on gender roles.

113. "Union Recorder No. 4, Thursday April 10, 1930," Box 1 SUEU Minute Books 1930–1946.

114. Guinness, *Sacrifice*, 31.

friendships, and this happy balance God will help us achieve if we ask him.[115]

Within these friendships, it was then possible to seek a marriage partner that was compatible and would share the Christian values of the young person. As relationships developed, Guinness warned young people of the dangers of sexual desire, and the importance of not feeding desire but directing this passion to other areas. He claimed that this was not repression, which is a psychological illness (responding to the claims of psychologists like Freud), but a deliberate and self-conscious decision.

> Such an attitude demands deliberate and planned avoidance of all that leads to sexual excitement. This is not repression, will not lead to harmful consequences, it is suppression.[116]

Guinness believed that the decision to control one's sexuality may involve surrender to the Holy Spirit, a taking up of the cross of Christ which says no to one's own desires in order to obey the will of God. In his autobiography, he even describes his own struggle with "Eros" and sense of overcoming this desire through the help of the Spirit in surrendering and presenting his body as a living sacrifice.[117]

The teaching of the EU on sexuality was open and certain standards of behaviour were encouraged in the group when romantic relationships developed. Allan Bryson, for example, sought to be a model to others when he kept his attachment to a fellow EU member a secret until he finished his degree, believing that his behaviour was countercultural. He recounted:

> . . . at the time things were loosening up at a pace that we felt was unbecoming to Christians, especially in the student environment where marriage was, financially speaking, virtually impossible until graduation was over.[118]

Such principles had been accepted moral standards within their subculture, along with no drinking, no smoking, no makeup, no dancing, and no kissing before engagement.[119] But by the late 1930s, some of these were to come under discussion and challenge. When John Prince claimed during a talk on "Girl/Boy relationships" that they should not hold hands before engagement, the students responded with much debate and even dissent.[120]

---

115. Guinness, *Sacrifice*, 31.
116. Guinness, *Sacrifice*, 32.
117. Guinness, *Journey among Students*, 37.
118. Quoted in Lake, *Proclaiming Jesus Christ*, 22. Bryson and his fiancé Elsie Taubman were the EU President and Vice President in 1936.
119. Allan Bryson interview.
120. Bill Andersen interview.

In reflecting and responding to wider social changes, the EU therefore, encouraged a model of ministry that was coeducational and in which women were encouraged to participate and lead in the ministry on an equal footing with the men. The danger of transgressing sexual mores was recognized as a risk, and so there was an encouragement to avoid cultural practices such as dancing and makeup and to socialize with a clear awareness of sexual boundaries. Over time, this approach to ministry facilitated marriages between likeminded Christians, which helped to ensure the strength of evangelical Christian families and therefore the transmission of faith to their own children and mutual encouragement to service and witness. The success of the university ministry is in part due to its acceptance of the mixing of the sexes, responding to the changes within culture among young men and women in the 1930s.

Conclusion

As stated earlier, one of the key factors producing the new ministry *of* youth ministry paradigm in the 1930s was the establishment of new institutions which applied new methodologies. In this regard, the university ministry was seminal, with consequential changes for schools and parish ministry. It drew elements from older models of youth mobilization, but with important differences. It was characterized from the first by a commitment to the conservative Christian faith that led to the establishment of the EU in 1930 and then continued to shape the identity of the group and of individuals within it. This conservatism proved resilient in the face of secularism, and with the help of leaders and teachers, such as Howard Guinness and T. C. Hammond, the EU was able to build a theological foundation that would withstand liberalism. In a departure from models heavily reliant on the direction of older adults, the EU recruited young leaders from within its own membership for the ministry who were charismatic and effective both in the EU itself and then later in other youth ministries. A belief in the value of peer ministry was also critical to the vitality of the new organization, with young people assuming responsibility for witnessing to their peers, and being inspired to build strong fellowship relationships within a like-minded group of Christians. Finally, the university ministry brought into youth ministry a model of coeducation that reflected changes within society and the place of women within it. How these changes to youth ministry thinking and practice which were pioneered on campus subsequently led to new movements and vitality within youth ministry in schools and parishes is the subject of the next two chapters.

4

Protestant Youth Ministry at Schools

The Beginnings of Crusaders and the Inter-School Christian Fellowship in the 1930s

THIS STUDY HAS ARGUED that changes in secondary education constituted one of the key social forces that led to a new methodology of youth ministry. In the 1930s there was a significant increase in the number of high schools in NSW, which created strong peer groups and the beginnings of a youth culture that was different from the parental generation. It is therefore valuable to examine the extracurricular youth ministry at secondary schools that was pioneered in the 1930s. It moved beyond classroom-based religious education to provide a ministry that was characterized by student leadership and peer ministry. This model is portrayed in accounts of the formation and activities of the Crusader Union (CU) and the Inter-School Christian Fellowship (ISCF) in NSW. This model was similar in many ways to that of the university ministry. A key difference, however, was the continued segregation of the sexes, as most of the secondary schools were still single sex.

These new institutions began as a response to changes in secondary education, but there were also other key factors. The conservative theological resurgence was important: it led to the sending of Howard Guinness to Australia and the nurturing of key leaders such as Paul White and Vincent Craven. The Crusader Union and ISCF were both strongly conservative in theology and believed in the importance of defending the authority of the Bible from attack. The leaders in the EU were also integral to the flourishing of this new ministry and were directly involved in the formation and leadership of the new institutions as well as leading and speaking at camps and meetings. The university ministry fueled the schools ministry.

Characteristics of Schools Ministry Before the 1930s

Ministry in both state schools and church schools before the 1930s was largely limited to religious education. This involved basic instruction in the beliefs and practices of the Christian faith. It constituted part of the school curriculum and was typically taught by an adult to children who were fairly passive. The methodology relied on rote learning and catechesis and the students were given examinations and prizes.[1] In effect, religious education was the means by which adults (particularly ministers and teachers) would socialize the next generation of young citizens into the Christian faith.

In secondary state schools, religious education was fulfilled in part by the regular curriculum and in part by some denominational Christian teaching. The curriculum taught by classroom teachers included a General Religious Education (GRE) that included common Protestant teaching about the Christian faith. The new state education was not intended to be "secular" in the sense of free from religion, as the term is sometimes misunderstood today, but rather non-sectarian.[2] In addition, an hour every day was to be set aside for Special Religious Instruction (SRI) taught by a denominational minister. This time was not fully utilized by busy ministers, but the Church of England did seek to do its best by sending ministers, paid workers, and volunteers into schools once a week.[3]

1. Warren, "Instructing Them," 37, 84.

2. Piggin, *Spirit, Word and World*, 50. The first schools in Australia were all church schools and despite the growth of a national state school system, religious education was seen as vitally important in both the church *and* the government schools. When the colony was started in NSW in 1788, there was a presumption that the church (and in particular the Church of England) should give primary education to the young. In 1826 the clergy and School Lands Corporation was established and one-seventh of all New South Wales land was given for the maintenance of the Anglican Church and "the education of the Youth in New South Wales." A new kind of system was envisioned by Governor Bourke in the 1830s who argued that a common public school system (as he had seen in the Irish National System) would bring together children from different denominations and end sectarianism. It was not until 1880, however, that the state took back responsibility for schooling from the church. In the Public Instruction Act of 1880, state aid to church schools ended, and the majority of the small parochial schools closed or were taken over by the state. See NSW Government, "Government Schools from 1848"; and Barcan, *Short History*.

3. The Church of England reached at most 80 percent of the school children in public schools. Judd and Cable, *Sydney Anglicans*, 130.

A similar approach to religious education was used in the elite church secondary schools. These schools were established for the children of the growing Protestant middle class, to give them "sound religious training" and the grounding needed for entry into the University of Sydney and the professions.[4] The churches sought to establish schools that would nurture young Christian leaders by means of the curriculum, the weekly services and the ministry of a chaplain. For example, in 1913, the Headmaster of Trinity Grammar School, the Reverend George Chambers, stated it was essential:

> ... to have a school where the environment and atmosphere of the teaching would be that of the Church, the vision that rose before us ten years ago, with the prospect of great possibilities for the training of Christian men who would be true citizens of the Commonwealth.[5]

The purpose of these church schools was that young people would be given a Protestant religious education in order to be good Christian citizens.

There had been earlier attempts to establish cocurricular Christian groups at schools modelled on the university ministry in addition to timetabled religious education. The SCM movement under Mott had allowed school students over fifteen years to join the movement from 1896,[6] and Christian Unions (CUs) were established at a few of the Sydney church schools.[7] During the war years, however, the groups had virtually died out. There was more success in the CU groups in the state high schools where graduates of the SCM were now teachers.[8] These teachers were not always sympathetically received by students from conservative evangelical stock. Students like Win Dunkley in the 1930s remembered her teacher telling her stories of the saints in her CU, and claimed that CUs had gone "very Liberal." "I would tear what she said to pieces on the way home in the train."[9] The CUs were "fairly intellectual affairs" and not flourishing and soon they were to disappear from the records.[10]

---

4. "A Report of the Opening of Trinity Grammar School at Dulwich Hill," January 1913, *Sydney Diocesan Magazine*.

5. Harris, *Trinity Grammar School*, 13.

6. Howe, *Century of Influence*, 44.

7. For example, there were small CUs at PLC, Riviere College, Newington College, Scots College, and Sydney Grammar School, but not at Sydney Church of England Grammar School or Kings. Howe, *Century of Influence*, 46.

8. Such as North Sydney Boys, North Sydney Girls, Fort Street Boys High, and Sydney Girls High School. Howe, *Century of Influence*, 139.

9. Win Dunkley interview.

10. Howe, *Century of Influence*, 172.

The Development of a New Kind of Schools Ministry in the 1930s and Howard Guinness

Religious education had been the only method of ministry to young people in schools before the 1930s, but after this time a new kind of extracurricular ministry began to develop based on student mobilization and leadership. The reasons for such a change must be understood in the historical context. It has already been noted in chapter two that modernism, war, and the Depression were shaping a new generation of youth in the 1930s. As well as these social forces, there are two other significant reasons for change to be considered: developments in secondary education, and the impact of Howard Guinness and the evangelical university ministry.

The rapid growth in numbers of young people entering secondary education rather than work led to a reassessment of methods of nurturing faith in young people. The *Sydney Church of England Board of Education* minutes noted in 1937 that classes of SRI were too large and that many classes were not being taught.[11] Two years later it was noted that Archbishop Mowll was concerned that Protestant ministers could not cope with the load of SRI.[12] Even with the help of volunteers, there were not enough teachers, and ministers chose to prioritize the work in primary rather than secondary schools. The old methodology of ministry to youth through religious education was not able to cope with the growth in secondary schools.

Howard Guinness more than any other individual was responsible for the development of a more effective approach to ministry in NSW schools. His method prioritized empowerment of young people in ministry to peers, the model that had proved so effective in university ministry. Guinness's own early religious experience and his later methodology in ministry were shaped by the Crusader Union in England. It was an interdenominational movement that sought to evangelize young people, particularly those of upper middle-class background who were not reached by the Sunday schools. Its method was simply to encourage boys to form small groups for Bible reading and prayer. The Crusader Union at Guinness's school had met for ten minutes every day after lunch for a devotion. The groups were organized by the boys themselves, and the boys took turns to lead.[13]

Along with the Crusader Union, the Varsities and Public Schools Camps (VPSC) in England had been a crucial influence on Guinness. At

---

11. Mason, "History of the Board."

12. "Board of Education of the Diocese of Sydney Minutes 1934–1958," June 2, 1939, Youthworks Archives.

13. Guinness, *Swords Drawn*, 26.

these camps, school students were taken away to a country house for a holiday called a house party. At the house party, there were biblical talks, as well as lots of outdoor activities and sports. The VPSC had become influential in England under the leadership of Eric Nash in the 1930s, and through it, he trained a whole generation of evangelical lay people and clergymen.[14] Nash invoked the theory of the British missionary Alexander Duff who in the mid nineteenth century had sought to educate and Christianize upper caste Indians, believing that the knowledge of Christianity would eventually filter down the social ladder. This came to be known as the "downward filtration" theory of evangelism.[15] Nash called the English public schools (the elite private schools) the "multiplication tables" that would spread a revival in England.[16]

Crucially, the VPSC model linked the schools ministry to the university ministry and also focused on the social elite. This was the model brought by Guinness to Sydney in 1930. Guinness believed that deploying leaders from the university ministry in strategic ministry in private schools would produce the greatest results. After the first Crusader camp in NSW, Guinness explained:

> Our first camp was held at Katoomba and run by the newly formed Evangelical Union. The boys who attended and were either blessed or converted have since risen to high positions in Church and State and have exercised a profound influence on their generation.[17]

Guinness replicated the English VPSC preferential focus on the elite by focusing on students at the Greater Public Schools (GPS): "key boys from key schools."[18] This was a strategic decision, as he believed that these stu-

---

14. Eric Nash was employed by the CSSM to run the VPSC ministry. He personally mentored many of the future evangelical leaders of the Church of England, for example, John Stott. Eddison, "Bash."

15. Kalapati, "Early Educational Mission."

16. Chapman, *Godly Ambition*, 17. Although this did not eventuate, there have been historians who have argued that Nash, along with other youth and student ministers, helped revitalize the evangelical movement in England and a "new breed of Evangelical clergy learnt how to preach, how to do evangelism, how to run groups and how to express theology as they had become involved in student and youth ministry." Percy and Markham, *Liberal Churches*, 33. "In an English context there is a good deal of agreement that modern day Evangelicalism has emerged as a powerful force within the Church and that this resurgence is in no small way due to the efforts of those engaged in work among young people and students." Griffiths, *East End Youth Ministry*, 14. See also, Ward, *Growing up Evangelical*, 6.

17. Guinness, *Journey among Students*, 67.

18. This was the unofficial motto of the VPSC and of Eric Nash, who argued that

dents would become the future leaders of Australian church and society.[19] Guinness had been trained at VPSC camps in the basics of Christian leadership which he believed to be "the essentials of Bible study" and "personal work."[20] That is, how to run a small group Bible study and how to "witness" or evangelize one's friends. These priorities of English evangelical youth ministry, imported by Guinness, would lead to the establishment of both the Crusader Union NSW and the ISCF.

Along with his methodology, Guinness's charisma and ability to inspire young leaders helped in the formation of the new institutions. His influence was personal, and not just structural. When Guinness was brought to Australia by J. B. Nicholson,[21] one of the first events organized was a tennis party with some boys from the private schools who had a strong evangelical heritage. These boys included the young Ian Holt, Alan Bryson, Bruce Bryson, and Lindsay Grant. They would become key leaders in the Australian Crusader Union. At this tennis party, one of the boys had "grazed" his white trousers and subsequently turned up in greys. When Guinness arrived to meet the crew, he saw the boys, disappeared for a while and then came back changed from whites to greys. This consideration was remembered fifty years later by Ian Holt: "That went down very well to schoolboys. A Christian chap to notice that and put him at ease. Bang on."[22] These young Christian leaders were inspired by the person and example of Guinness.

---

this was a strategy for the evangelical conversion of English society, not elitism. Yet many have accused the movement of snobbery.

19. There is also some indication that Guinness was influenced by Roland Allen, another influential thinker on the methodology of mission. In a Guinness prayer letter of 1933 from Australia to supporters back at home, he claimed that he had been reading Allen and asked the question: "[A]re we tending to produce indigenous groups in the schools which will go forward independently of outside leadership?" He concluded: "we must force our young Christians out into a life of direct dependence upon the Holy Spirit and the Word of God." Howard Guinness, January 26, 1934, "Prayer Letter," Papers of Howard Guinness.

20. Guinness, *Journey among Students*, 28. Although Guinness was not mentored himself by Nash but by other CSSM workers, he was influenced by his methods and writings. Guinness includes in his book *Swords Drawn* (1934) a chapter on "Personal work" made up of extracts from a book written by Nash called *Effective Witness*.

21. Nicholson was the chairman of Standard Waygoods Managing Electrical Engineers. His leadership and financial generosity had already been an important influence in the revival of the CSSM in NSW as well as the Sydney City Mission and the CIM (China Inland Mission). He and his wife and daughter Mary continued to be influential elders within the IVF and Crusader movement. Thornton, "Crusader Union of NSW," 2.

22. Ian Holt Interview.

The Formation and Character of the Crusader Union in NSW

The Australian tour of Howard Guinness in 1930 was integral to the formation of the Crusader Union. Early in the year, J. B. Nicholson organized a meeting at his house of twenty-five young men and women from the Sydney University Bible League and from prominent private schools. At this meeting, he cast a vision for ministry in schools similar to that of the Crusader Union Bible classes in England. One of the school students at the meeting, Ian Holt, later a key Crusader leader, remembered Nicholson pointing out that:

> Whilst most independent schools have chaplains, chapel and divinity [classes], there was little opportunity for boys and girls to "witness" to their peer-groups to the faith that gave them a very real experience in their own lives.[23]

Nicholson knew that Dr. Howard Guinness of the English IVF could build this kind of ministry.

In practice, Guinness had a strategy that was concerned primarily with university ministry and only secondarily with school students. Ministry in church schools would be a "feeder" to the IVF work to raise up evangelical leaders for the future. It was for this reason that on his tour, he went to schools to establish Crusader Bible classes. Moreover, he believed that young people were more open to the Christian gospel in secondary school, so it was strategic to evangelize school students. He explained that:

> Our first target was the schools, for we believed that a Christian witness in any university was largely dependent on the Christians who joined it from school. School was then the place in which to confront students with the living Christ before their attitudes hardened and spiritual truths were rejected in the name of reason or expediency.[24]

This would multiply the numbers of evangelical Christians entering university to be trained as the future leaders of church and state.

Guinness inspired Christian students at private schools to join together and form Christian Bible clubs that were to be called *Crusaders* like their English counterparts. In Sydney, the schools meetings in the girls' schools began well and by February 1931 there were Crusader groups at the Sydney Church of England Girls' Grammar School, Darlinghurst (SCEGGS), the Presbyterian Ladies' College, Pymble (PLC), Abbotsleigh, Wenona, and

---

23. Thornton, "Crusader Union of NSW," 2.
24. Guinness, *Journey among Students*, 67.

Normanhurst.[25] In the boys' schools, Crusader groups were started at Shore, Trinity Grammar, Scots College, and Barker College.[26] There were five "Drawing Room Meeting" locations where groups met on alternate Saturdays.[27] The new institution, the NSW Crusader Union, was formed in September 1930 with separate divisions for boys and girls.[28] The Crusader Union shared an office with the IVF, and the first President of the Crusader boys' division, Paul White, also became the General Secretary of the IVF.[29] The close ties between the university ministry and schools ministry were therefore encouraged through proximity as well as common personnel.

It has been argued that part of the success of the EU was in its ability to create a strong subcultural identity shaped by its name, doctrinal basis, and narrative of origins. Acquiring membership in the Crusader Union similarly involved affiliating with a particular subcultural group through which a strong subcultural identity was formed. Sociologists explain that this identity is how a group establishes a "morally orienting collective identity."[30] That is, the self-understanding of the group that shapes an individual's presuppositions of *what is* and *what ought to be*. It gives those within the group a sense of meaning and belonging. The subcultural identity is formed and maintained by identity boundary markers. These markers help distinguish who is *in* and who is *out* of the group.

To become a member of the Crusader Union involved agreeing to the aims, motto, and basis of belief. The Crusader Union aligned itself by name with the English movement that was committed to the study of the Bible. The name *Crusader* represented an assertive evangelistic stance. A Crusader was someone committed to God's word and to the battle of winning souls. Students who were members called themselves *Crusaders*, by this they meant those willing to stand up and be counted despite the cost. When Judith Young from SCEGGS sought membership, she claimed: "I want a Crusader badge so that I may have some visible sign that I belong to Crusaders and that I am a real Crusader."[31] To become a member of the Crusader Union, a student had to sign a card that stated: "I declare my faith in the Lord Jesus

---

25. Parker, *Vision of Eagles*, 9. Normanhurst was an Anglican girl's school at Ashfield that closed down in 1941.

26. "4th Annual Report 1933–34, The Crusader Union of NSW Boys' Division," Crusader Union NSW Archives.

27. "4th Annual Report 1933–34, The Crusader Union of NSW Boys' Division," Crusader Union NSW Archives.

28. Parker, *Vision of Eagles*, 8.

29. Thornton, "Crusader Union of NSW," 13.

30. Smith, *American Evangelicalism*, 91.

31. "Membership Application of Judith Young," Crusader Union NSW Archives.

Christ as my personal Saviour and my desire to witness for him, not only with my lips but with my life." This card was then given to the school leader and then ratified by the Boys' or Girls' Division council. On the back of the card was printed the basis of belief which had been borrowed from the IVF and written by Guinness. To become a member an applicant had to be associated with Crusaders for six months and had to answer six questions that represented conservative evangelical beliefs, spiritual experience, and practices.[32] The student had to recount a conversion experience, explain why they thought they were "saved," and agree to two mandated practices: to read the Bible each day and to witness to others. The final question asked the student whether they were able to support the work of the Crusader Union itself. A badge was then issued to the member that they might wear to school as an outer sign of their allegiance.

The Crusader Union badge was very important as both an identity marker and an artefact.[33] It was a reminder of affiliation and fellowship within the group and also their identity as a Christian believer. It was a

---

32. The questions were:

Why do you want a Crusader badge?

Have you taken the Lord Jesus Christ to be your savior and have you surrendered yourself to him? Try to tell what led you to do this.

Can you say that you know your sins are forgiven, and that you have eternal life? Try to give reasons for your answer and the promises of Scripture on which you base your faith.

Do you realize that every true Crusader tries to meet his Master each morning for a quiet time of Bible Reading and Prayer, and are you prepared to do this day by day as He helps you?

Do you realize that every true Crusader is called to be a witness to the Lord Jesus Christ both by his life and with his lips? Are you prepared to tell others of your faith in Him as your savior?

Do you mean to back up the Crusader Union in all its activities in your school and Drawing Room Meetings? Have you gone out of your way to bring someone else from your school to a Crusader meeting?

"Crusader Union of NSW Application for the Unions Badge," Crusader Union of NSW Archives.

33. Sociologists have been helpful in alerting historians of religion of the use of artefacts or objects within religious experience and faith. Colleen McDannell claims that the artefact is an object that is given meaning by the religious person and can help shape religious identity of young people. McDannell, *Material Christianity*. Pete Ward has analyzed objects as part of evangelical style which generates a sense of belonging for young people "defining themselves within the wider culture by difference." Ward, *Participation and Meditation*, 148. He looks at modern examples such as the WWJD (what would Jesus do?) bracelet, which reminds young people that they are to love as a disciple of Jesus, and the silver ring a sign of commitment to chastity before marriage.

conspicuous reminder to members that they belonged to the group and also that they were distinct from others. Guinness explained that the badge itself was a witness to other students, that they "constantly remind people of your faith"[34] and may lead to opportunities to invite a friend to Crusaders. Furthermore, they were to be taken away if the student was not living in a way that "tells for Christ,"[35] in line with the practices and beliefs of the group (though there is no documentary evidence of this exclusion being carried out). The Crusader badge depicted the armor of God, representing the battle of the Crusader as a soldier for Christ. The symbolism of the badge is explained in the membership application form:

> The badge is a bond between all true Crusaders throughout the world. It is the privilege of those to wear it to be witnesses to their Lord and Saviour Jesus Christ (Acts 1:8) and its symbol speaks of their equipment as soldiers of the cross (Ephesians 6:10–18).[36]

Membership continued even after the student left school through the senior Crusader fellowship, and the badge continued to be worn as an outward marker of the young person's commitment.[37] The badge was therefore expressive of the subcultural identity of those within Crusaders.

---

34. Guinness, *Swords Drawn*, 36.

35. "56th Annual Report Scripture Union & CSSM, 1938." Scripture Union and CSSM Council Minutes Vol. IV, 1933–1941.

36. "Membership Application to Crusader Union NSW," Crusader Union NSW Archives.

37. It is interesting to note that the Crusader badge was also important to those who were involved in the Crusader Union in England. Roy Hession was a famous English writer converted through the Crusader Union in the late 1920s. His reflections on the badge give us an insight into the way this identity marker shaped how young people saw themselves. "As I began to work in a London bank, the little Crusader badge I wore in the lapel of my jacket was especially precious to me. Although the world did not know what that little badge meant, I knew, and God knew. It meant that I was marked out by Jesus to be separated from the world, part of a special people unto Himself... Crusader badges proliferated in the city of London as young people came from the surrounding suburbs to work and we knew we were all in possession of the same secret joy." Hession, *My Calvary Road*, 29.

102 FROM A MINISTRY *FOR* YOUTH TO A MINISTRY *OF* YOUTH

The Southern Cross distinguishes Australian Crusaders.

The red central Cross is the empty cross, the symbol of Christ's death and resurrection. Jn. 3:14-18.

The Crown shows the Crusader is serving a King. The crown is that of the Lord Jesus Christ, the King of Kings. The crown is also what the faithful soldier of Christ hopes to attain, it is the Crown of Life. Rev. 2:10.

The shield: the red cross shows faith in Christ; the white of the shield is to emphasise the purity of life in Christ. The shield itself is a guard against temptation. 1 Tim. 6:12.

The helmet is the helmet of salvation. The helmet is in the centre of the Cross to show that our salvation is centred in the Cross of Christ. 1 Thess. 5:8.

The heart and scroll remind us that we are given a new heart and in that heart must be hidden the Word of God that we might not sin against God. Ps. 119:11.

The sword is the sword of the Spirit which is the Word of God. Matt. 4:1-11.

Figure 2: The Crusader Union badge[38]

38. In 1946, a card was issued explaining the different symbols of the badge and what they each meant. Some of the symbols are taken from Ephesians 6:10–18 and the idea of a Christian needing the "Armor of God," spiritual defenses in a spiritual battle against the devil and temptation. The title *Crusader* itself evokes someone who has taken up arms for the sake of the Lord and is willing to sacrifice their life in his service.

The Activities of the Crusader Union

There were three basic activities of the Crusader Union: small groups, Drawing Room Meetings (DRMs) and camps. In combination, these activities were the ways that the goals of evangelism and the raising up of student leaders were achieved.

Small groups or Bible clubs were the basic units of the Crusader Union. They were generally held at lunchtime when Christian students could read the Bible together and give testimonies and talks. In order to encourage students to form new small groups, Guinness wrote a booklet, *Swords Drawn*, in 1934. In this booklet, Guinness explained the steps for a young student to start a Crusader group at their school. They were to find other Christians (perhaps by looking for those that are wearing church or Scripture Union badges), meet in order to pray and read the Bible,[39] and then finally ask for permission from the headmaster to start a public meeting. The group was typically led by a senior student or a university student who returned to her old school to help, or occasionally by young Christian teachers. The high level of student leadership in small groups is noteworthy.[40]

As well as reading through the Bible and discussing it, small groups were also a setting where students could witness to friends. A popular way of witnessing was to tell one's testimony of conversion to the group and invite friends to come and hear it. This kind of activity was encouraged by Guinness in *Swords Drawn* to stimulate the formation of Crusader Unions in schools.

> Let us take a glance at their meeting because it is just typical of those about which we have spoken. The room is soon filled with boys. A word of welcome to the visiting team is given by their leader. One of the visitor's replies and then leads them simply in prayer, asking God to bless their meeting and help them as they speak of the Lord Jesus. Two of the team, one a member of his school football team, then speak, telling how they came to know Jesus Christ as a personal Saviour from the penalty and power of sin, and how he has given them a new impetus to life and a new meaning to their sport, recreation and even their studies. The concluding speaker, a member of the crew and an honours

---

39. The systematic reading of books of the Bible, followed by discussion, was typical of Crusader meetings. For example, in the Normanhurst Crusader Group logbook, the records show that the girls slowly worked their way through the books of John, Acts, Ruth, and Mark, generally reading through a different book of the Bible each year. "Log of Normanhurst Crusader Group 1931–1938," Crusader Union NSW Archives.

40. Guinness, *Swords Drawn*, 27.

fellow, then appeals to all to respond to the call of Jesus Christ and surrender their lives to him.[41]

Of note here is the reference to prominent students, for example, "a member of the crew and an honours fellow." It is these leaders whom Guinness believed would be "key boys" who would become leaders of the church and society.

As well as Crusader Union Bible studies in schools, student leadership was encouraged through the additional structure of Drawing Room Meetings (DRMs). The DRMs were held in private homes every second Saturday night with the goal of gathering girls or boys from different schools. The meeting consisted of a time of shared worship, a talk, feedback about how the Crusader groups were going, and lots of time for relaxed socializing. These meetings were primarily for training leaders. It was here that older statesmen (school graduates who were now involved in the EU), and other adults, such as those in the senior Crusader fellowship, could guide the student leaders and encourage them to take a lead.[42] This concern for training can be seen in the actions of the young graduate staff worker, Lindsay Grant. Grant complained that younger Crusaders were "being a little pampered, and were not sufficiently encouraged to stand on their own two feet."[43] In 1934, he established school student regional *teams* to run the DRMs and give the talks.

Along with the small groups and DRMs, the third key activity of the Crusader Union was camping. The model of the VPSC camps and their success in England had excited Guinness.[44] It was at camps that he believed significant "personal work" could be done, that is, personal conversations about spiritual matters in a context of fun and fellowship. The camps were held at Easter and in the summer, usually in the Blue Mountains or on the South Coast of NSW. The boys often camped out, whereas the girls generally rented a holiday house and had someone to come and cook for them.[45] The camps were a fun place to bring friends for a holiday, particularly in the days of the Depression when there was little extra money for family

---

41. Guinness, *Swords Drawn*, iv.

42. Thornton, "Crusader Union of NSW," 15. Thornton describes the influence of the fellowship to be a "pressure group," so that the network of key adult leaders was actually very influential on the movement.

43. "The Crusader Union of NSW Boys Division 5th Annual Report 1934–1935," Minutes of the Crusader Union of NSW Boys Division.

44. On his way to Australia, Guinness had toured Canada to establish the IVF and encourage school groups and there he had established the Pioneer Camps under the IVF.

45. Parker, *Vision of Eagles*, 19.

holidays, but outdoor fun and sport were national pastimes.⁴⁶ In part, the object of the camp was to have a "real holiday" and through fellowship and fun to "explode the idea that Christianity is something to be avoided."⁴⁷ A report from a boys' Crusader camp held at Lawson in 1933 describes the experience of the boys:

> We found an ideal place in Stratford Grammar School at Lawson, what with tennis, basham, bumble-puppy, swimming, puddox, and hiking. The one hundred and fifteen odd, who attended these ten days of bliss, found them slip by all too rapidly. Not a few were brought to know and love the Lord Jesus Christ as their personal saviour during this time, and under the inspiring leadership of Dr Guinness, the community singing and informal talks on the vital things of life, held each evening, were entered into with great zest. The camp concert was once again a roaring success.⁴⁸

As well as fun, camps were considered to be the reaping ground for the sowing that went on during the year within the Crusader Bible study groups. Camp "counsellors" were found from the EU or the senior Crusader fellowship, counsellors who were older than the school students, but still of the same generation.

The Crusader model of ministry to youth through Bible study groups, DRMs, and camps that Howard Guinness helped establish in 1930 proved effective in reaching and empowering for ministry a generation of young Christians at private schools. We have noted, however, the deliberate elitism of Howard Guinness and the Crusader movement in targeting "key boys from key schools" and hoping for a "downward filtration" of Christian faith. A different institution would be required to reach youth within the growing state high schools who were not from the upper middle class: the Inter-School Christian Fellowship (ISCF).

The Formation of the Inter-School Christian Fellowship

The ISCF grew out of the ministry of Scripture Union (SU) which had long been at work in Sydney conducting beach missions, parish missions, and

---

46. Ward, *Nation for a Continent*, 191.
47. "Crusader Union Boys Division Camp Brochure 1937," Donald Robinson Archives.
48. Quoted in Parker, *Vision of Eagles*, 28.

encouraging Bible reading clubs for children. Many children had been converted and nurtured in the conservative evangelical faith through these activities. In the 1930s, it was felt that SU should attempt new methods of doing ministry similar to that of the Crusader Union. The new institution, the ISCF, was begun through the inspiration of key leaders from the EU under the leadership of Vincent Craven.

Vincent Craven, like Guinness, was a charismatic and energetic leader. Unlike Guinness, he inspired young leaders not through his gentility but through his typical Australian masculinity. He was seen as a "man's man," solid in build and attractive to clever young men,[49] even though he never finished his secondary education.[50] He had been mentored by an English CSSM worker Edmund Clark and as a young man had gained experience helping Clark run beach missions, inner-city missions, and camps. In the early 1930s, with his friend Stacey Woods, he led popular weekly Bible studies for boys that grew into the hundreds.[51] Craven's leadership gifts were recognized when he was appointed the national secretary of SU at the age of twenty-two. He remained in this position for fourteen years, financially supported by J. B. Nicholson who paid his salary and provided a car.[52]

Craven's work in the growing high schools of the 1930s began to bear fruit. He was particularly gifted in ministry to teenage boys whom he reached mainly through teaching Scripture classes and leading SU camps. By 1934, there were small groups of students meeting for prayer and fellowship at Fort Street High and Drummoyne Intermediate,[53] and reports of boys being converted. In the SU annual report of 1934, Craven's time spent with high school boys was acknowledged:

> Many have been definitely won for the Saviour through his all-important ministry . . . Groups are meeting in some of the schools for prayer and Bible study week by week, and who knows the results of such a testimony being given by the boys themselves.[54]

---

49. Win Dunkley interview.
50. MacLeod, *C. Stacey Woods*, 36.
51. MacLeod, *C. Stacey Woods*, 38.
52. Lamb, "Nicholson, James 1863–1954," Australian Dictionary of Evangelical Biography.
53. Prince, *Tuned In to Change*, 105.
54. "Scripture Union and CSSM 54th Annual Report 1934," Scripture Union Council Meetings Vol. III, 1930–1934, Scripture Union NSW Archives.

Among those who were converted were some later to become important leaders within the evangelical churches.[55]

The need for a new coordinated schools ministry was accentuated as it became clear that the Crusader movement was not going to extend its ministry to government schools. As early as October 1930 the Crusader Union executive had considered whether to include the state high schools but instead wrote to the EU asking it to assume responsibility for the work. The EU answered that the task was too large and that this work should be left until a capable leader could be found.[56] The EU, however, continued to be concerned about this opportunity and eventually, it was individual EU leaders who took the initiative. In 1934 Gwen Wilkinson claimed that:

> By the end of that year, some of us who were about to go out into schools were very conscious of the need for an evangelical emphasis in work amongst school boys and girls, we were aware of some of them wanting it because of our involvement with camps [i.e. the Varsity and Public Schools camps].[57]

These students were studying to become secondary school teachers and included Win Dunkley, Gwen Wilkinson, Heather Drummond, and Jean Porter. In January of 1935, they held a meeting at the Katoomba convention under the leadership of Lindsay Grant and committed themselves to starting this new ministry, naming it the Inter-School Christian Fellowship (ISCF).[58] Vincent Craven then brought the new group under the umbrella of the SU to give it a firm theological foundation and senior advisors.[59] Craven was appointed to lead the ISCF boys' ministry and Miss Heather Drummond was appointed to the SU staff in order to build up ministry in school for girls.[60]

Using a similar methodology to Guinness, the ISCF grew quickly in the first decade to outstrip the reach of the Crusader Union. According to the annual report of 1935, there were five groups meeting at schools as

---

55. For example, the Reverend Bill Ostling who was converted during Vincent Craven's scripture lesson at Sydney Tech High. Win Dunkley claims that there were fifty or more "important" people who were nurtured by Craven. Win Dunkley interview.

56. "October 1930, Minute Book Crusader Union of NSW (Girls Division) 1930–1933," Crusader Union NSW Archives.

57. Win Dunkley interview.

58. Win Dunkley interview. This was the name of the schools ministry begun in Canada by Guinness. Bill Andersen interview.

59. Win Dunkley interview.

60. "December 4, 1934 Scripture Union NSW Committee Meeting," Scripture Union Council Meetings Vol. III, 1930–1934, Scripture Union NSW Archives.

well as thirteen Drawing Room Meetings (DRMs). There were also twelve Varsity and All Schools Camps for high school students led by university students.[61] Social events became very popular, including hikes and picnics, with more than two hundred attending. The figures bear witness to the rapid growth. Five years later, there were forty ISCF groups at different high schools and thirty-eight DRMs each week.[62] The ISCF also ran twenty-one camps with six hundred and ten young people attending. In all, there were two thousand young people on the roll in the ISCF.[63] This growth in numbers reflected the growth in numbers at state high schools and far surpassed the numbers within the Crusader Union.[64]

Like the Crusader Union, the ISCF had a badge that symbolized a strong subcultural identity. It was the badge of the Scripture Union. It bore the image of an oil lamp which symbolized the light of God's word. In order to become a member, a student had to pledge to seek to read God's word daily and was sent a series of Bible passages to study. This expressed the conservative evangelical commitment to the authority and centrality of God's word. For those in the ISCF, the badges were significant reminders of who they were and that they were to witness and live distinctive lives.

The Activities of the ISCF

The methodology and activities of the ISCF were largely the same as the Crusader Union. The key activity was the running of small Bible study groups in schools by student leaders with the support of Christian teachers and ISCF staff. There were also DRMs and many different camps. But there were three distinguishing marks of the ISCF: their connection to the beach missions, the development of the Teachers Christian Fellowship, and the leaders' training camps.

The beach missions were an early ministry of the CSSM, with the first mission at Manly in 1888. They were evangelistic services on the beach aimed

---

61. "Scripture Union & CSSM 55th Annual Report July 1935," Scripture Union Council Meetings Vol. III, 1930–1934.

62. This is a high proportion of the high schools as there were only sixty-six in NSW in 1940. Wilkinson, "Education in Country."

63. "61st Anniversary of Scripture Union," Scripture Union and CSSM Council Minutes Vol. IV, 1933–1941.

64. The Crusader Union at around the same time had about twelve school groups and ten DRMS. They had one annual camp for girls and one for boys with a combined total of about 120 students. "Crusader Union of NSW Boys Division Annual Reports 1933–1946," Crusader Union NSW Archives.

at children.[65] Along with the services, there were often camps for boys and girls that followed the beach mission. In 1935 there were sixteen active beach missions as well as missions in the parks of Camperdown and Balmain.[66] The students of the EU were often leaders at these missions, as well as young people who had come through the ISCF groups and camps. These young leaders gave Bible talks, organized, gave testimonies, and gained a variety of leadership skills by being involved in the beach missions.[67]

Another distinctive of the ISCF ministry was the Teachers Christian Fellowship (TCF). The TCF was founded in June 1935 by the SU staff worker Heather Drummond, with the aim of supporting isolated Christian teachers and encouraging teachers to establish ISCF groups in their schools. Initially, there was great support for the new organization; by the end of 1935 there were already two hundred members.[68] Many of these teachers, especially keen graduates from the EU, went on to establish ISCF groups within the schools to which they were appointed. In the Annual Report of 1940, it was stated that: "to many of the teachers in the fellowship we are indebted for the formation of Scripture Union branches and leading ISCF groups."[69] For those within the TCF, teaching was seen as a vocation, doing the "Lord's business," and schools were viewed as a "tremendous mission field."[70] This new organization established a cycle of regeneration, of teachers encouraging the ministry of students, who would then grow up to do the same for the next generation.

Another ISCF distinctive was the deliberate approach undertaken to leadership training. The ISCF movement saw itself from very early on as committed to training leaders for the ministry amongst young people. School students, university students and young teachers were enlisted as the key leaders for their camps and beach mission and lunchtime groups. In 1935, a CSSM annual camp was held in the Blue Mountains with about one

---

65. For more on beach missions in Australia see Prince, *Tuned In to Change*, and Dunk, "Atmosphere of Joy."

66. "56th Annual Report, Scripture Union and CSSM, July 28, 1935," Scripture Union and CSSM Council Minutes Vol. IV, 1933–1941, Scripture Union NSW Archives.

67. "SUEU Minutes December 17, 1935," Box 1 Minute Books 1930–1946, Fisher Library Archives.

68. "56th Annual Report, Scripture Union and CSSM, 1935," Scripture Union and CSSM Council Minutes Vol. IV, 1933–1941.

69. "61st Annual Report, August 1940, Scripture Union and CSSM," Scripture Union and CSSM Council Minutes Vol. IV, 1933–1941.

70. Win Dunkley interview. Dunkley went on to be a significant leader within the TCF.

hundred attending, leaders who "labour for the master among the young."[71] This became an annual training and encouragement conference, and in 1940, 115 members attended. The commitment of the movement to training its leaders has led the historian John Pollock to remark that the "CSSM should go down in history not only as a nursery of the church, winning the children, but as a training ground of Christian workers."[72] This was certainly reflected in the work of the ISCF.

Notwithstanding the distinctives considered above, the ISCF and Crusader Union worked alongside each other doing similar ministries with much the same methodology and often even the same clientele and supporters. They cooperated in large-scale missions such as the united campaign in Goulburn of the SUEU, CU, ISCF, and CSSM, led by Alex Brown in 1935 in a caravan trailer.[73] Brown reported that the mission was a grand success and that there were "Scores won to the saviour."[74] More than once the Crusader and ISCF movements came close to amalgamating. In the end, the hesitation came from the Crusader side with their commitment to reaching a particular cultural/demographic group within Sydney.[75] There was some bitterness expressed by those who were in the ISCF rather than Crusaders, who felt they were not part of the elite. Jean Porter, who was to become the ISCF girls' division worker, recalled that: "If you were not Crusaders it was very, very, bitter. They've forgotten it now, but if you'd been to a (government) high school you were nobody."[76] Nevertheless, the two youth movements were united in ethos and theology and in particular, there was an "unbreakable circle" between the IVF and Scripture Union.[77] Mark Hutchinson has noted the interrelatedness of the interdenominational youth organizations and the:

> ... mutual supportiveness and even organizational continuity between members of the institutional evangelical family. Scripture Union, CSSM on the beaches, and ISCF at high School level fed directly into Evangelical Unions at university and Christian

---

71. "57th Annual Report Scripture Union and CSSM, 1936," Scripture Union and CSSM Council Minutes Vol. IV, 1933–1941.

72. Cited in Sylvester, *God's Word*, 45.

73. Brown was a staff worker and children's evangelist with the CSSM.

74. "57th Annual Report Scripture Union and CSSM, 1936," Scripture Union and CSSM Council Minutes Vol. LV, 1933–1941, Scripture Union NSW Archives.

75. Bill Andersen interview.

76. Jean Porter interview.

77. It was Paul White and Charles Troutman who spoke of the "unbreakable circle" between the EU and Scripture Union. "Charles Troutman Notes to Mark Hutchinson," June 30, 1990, Moore College collection.

Fellowships at College, and these fed into and were supported by the Graduate Fellowships and professionally-related fellowships like the ACTF (Australian Teachers Christian Fellowship).[78]

This cycle generated a vibrant ministry *of* youth that went beyond denominational ministry and produced key leaders, resources, and a great concern for youth ministry for the next generation.

There were clear factors that account for changes in methodology in the youth ministry in schools, and for the rise of new institutions. The impact of Howard Guinness as the instigator of the movement, his encouragement of leaders, and his guidance in forming the model cannot be over-emphasized. Along with Guinness, there must also be an acknowledgement of the initiatives and financial support of J. B. Nicholson. The students mentored and encouraged into ministry in the EU became key figures in both the Crusader Union and ISCF schools ministry—people such as Lindsay Grant, Paul White, Jean Porter, and Alice Smith. The university ministry was therefore vital to the development of a different kind of schools ministry in the 1930s. The model was based on the Crusader and IVF model Guinness brought from England. It was strategic in its focus on training key leaders, it emphasized small groups that studied the Bible, and stressed the importance of students witnessing to their friends.

Theological Conservatism

This study argues that part of the impetus for change in youth ministry methodology was a worldwide resurgence in conservative evangelicalism, which was in itself a response to social forces. The EU was formed in the context of a perceived need to assert conservative theological views in contrast with those of the SCM. The sense of threat from liberalism was not as apparent within the Crusader Union and the ISCF, particularly because there were no opposing liberal groups in schools. Indeed, the key challenges for the schools ministry seemed to be nominalism or institutional Christianity represented by school principals who did not want to allow the student groups for fear of trouble, and other students who may persecute earnest Christians for being too "enthusiastic" in their religious convictions. The religious identity of the students nonetheless was shaped by conservative evangelical theology expressed in a strong commitment to the authority and centrality of God's word.

78. Hutchinson, "American Evangelical," 5.

Although there was no opposition from rival student groups, there was a perception that the new modern world could undermine evangelical faith. Young people at high school in the 1930s were facing challenges in their thinking. The Christian faith and the Bible were no longer the unquestioned foundation for worldview. In Sydney in the 1930s, there was a polarizing of views between the conservative and liberal evangelicals. John Prince claims that the visits of Guinness:

> ... took place at a time when evangelical life was at its lowest point in the century. Liberal theology dominated church life to a degree which made evangelicalism almost disreputable; habitual church-goers resented the religious enthusiasm which carried Sunday observance into weekday living. Yet this is precisely what Howard challenged people to do.[79]

At high school, children were taught about evolution and were developing a critical mind that did not simply accept the views of their parents. There is evidence that some school Christian groups were struggling with the challenge of theological liberalism and particularly higher criticism of the Bible.[80] In the logbook of the Normanhurst Crusader group in 1937 it was observed that the girls had doubts over "the inspiration of the Bible and also its truth." In response, it was decided that a study should be done on the issue for the following week.[81]

Howard Guinness, the force behind the schools ministry, was shaped by the polarization experienced in the university ministry. His book for school students, *Swords Drawn*, is a defensive response to liberalism. Guinness wrote that what it meant to be a Christian was to surrender all your life to the Lord, even your thought life. So that:

---

79. Prince, *Tuned In to Change*, 103.

80. Higher criticism or biblical criticism is an academic discipline that concerns itself with the sources and methods used in the study of the Bible. It was associated with liberal evangelicalism. Some school students would have had liberal evangelical ministers. For example, Bill Andersen went to the Anglican Church at Mortdale in the 1930s where he claimed the minister was "broad church." He invited his friend Marcus Loane to come and speak at the church about the "Inspiration of Scripture." Bill Andersen interview. As mentioned in the previous chapter, liberal theology was being taught to those aspiring to be Presbyterian and Methodist ordinands at Sydney University. In the Anglican Church there had been key leaders in the 1920s and early 1930s, including the Principal of Moore College, D. J. Davies, who considered themselves liberal evangelical and were influencing rectors in parishes.

81. "September 1937, Log of Normanhurst Crusader Group 1931–1938," Crusader Union NSW Archives.

> ... if previously I was broad and modern in my thinking, believing large portions of the Bible out of date and untrustworthy, I must be willing to become the narrowest of the narrow in my conceptions of God and the Universe should he say so.[82]

Guinness also argued for the trustworthiness of the Bible against the challenge of higher criticism, appealing to unspecified evangelical Bible scholars:

> Fortunately higher criticism which would try and point out to us which parts are unreliable or untrue is divided against itself and has been proven inaccurate and wrong so often that we may go forward without fear believing this book to be what it claims to be—the Oracles of God.[83]

Guinness instead directed young people to daily study of the Bible and application to their life, particularly in the area of personal holiness.

The Crusader Union and ISCF remained very conservative theologically. Those that led the movement continued to articulate the beliefs of conservative evangelicalism and obliged their staff to sign the same doctrinal basis that had been written by Guinness for the EU. There was a prevailing theological conservatism, yet small groups were a place where genuine questions could be raised in a context of discussion. In the end, however, the Bible was seen as the ultimate answer and authority and it set the agenda. As reported in 1935 at an annual meeting of the Crusader Union: "The Bible is our textbook and we seek to make these meetings as informal and attractive as possible with a view to encouraging the girls to read and study the Bible which has, we believe, a message for school girls today."[84]

Empowering of Youth in Leadership

As is plain from the account of the formation and activities of the Crusader Union and ISCF, a key characteristic of the schools ministry was the empowerment of youth in leadership. It was the methodology used in the EU at university, and EU students were leaders in the formation and leadership of both organizations. As well as the leadership of university students, the

---

82. Guinness, *Swords Drawn*, 14, 15.

83. Guinness, *Swords Drawn*, 28.

84. "Girls Division 5th Annual Meeting July 1933," Girls Division Crusader Union Minutes. Or as the travelling secretary Alice Smith reported in 1935: "Our desire is that the girls will have an individual and positive faith in the Bible, and that it may become the foundation of their faith before they leave school." "Sydney Morning Herald Report of the Girls' Division Annual Report 1938," Girls' Division Crusader Union minutes.

initiative and energy of school students themselves are striking. They were expected to lead small groups, witness to their friends, and give talks and testimonies. The link between the Crusader Union and the EU in empowering young leaders can be seen in the early staff workers and the office-bearers. The first Crusader Union schools staff workers, Paul White, and subsequently Lindsay Grant and Alice Smith, came to that ministry after graduating from the EU. Conversely, many of the EU leaders in the 1930s came to the EU after having been Crusader leaders at their schools, such as Allan Bryson (EU President 1936) and Ian Holt (EU President 1935), both from Trinity Grammar, Donald Robinson (EU Vice President 1941) from Shore, and Elsie Bryson (EU Vice President 1936) from Abbotsleigh. Once at university, many continued to return to their school to lead Bible studies, such as Elsie Bryson who ran the Crusader group at Abbotsleigh.[85] Many of the EU leaders were also leaders at the Crusader camps.[86] Those leaders who had come through Crusaders and the EU continued to have a concern for ministry and leadership within schools.[87]

In the account of the formation of the ISCF, we have seen that EU leaders were the instigators for the forming of the ISCF and they continued to have an important influence in the ISCF. Heather Drummond (involved in the EU in the early 1930s) became the first staff worker for girls to work alongside Vincent Craven. After she left, Jean Porter (EU women's secretary 1931) continued in her role. These women were regarded as "marvellous leaders"[88] and many girls became Christians at their camps.[89] They continued to exercise leadership within girl's schools after they left the ISCF.

In the Crusader and ISCF groups, older students were expected to take leadership of the group. John Prince notes that: "All the workers were clear that the initiative of the boys and girls themselves was essential for a group to begin at a school."[90] The formation of the ISCF at Fort Street is a case in point.[91] Anglican scripture had been led at the school by an earnest Brethren teacher called Mr. Wilfred Porter. He began a Bible class in the hat room for six or seven boys in 1935 and under his ministry, Dr. Bill Andersen

85. Allan and Elsie Bryson interview.
86. Donald Robinson interview.
87 Ian Holt claims that there were at least six headmasters/headmistresses of Sydney independent schools who were former Crusader leaders, for example, David Grant who became the headmaster at Shore. Ian Holt interview.
88. Donald Robinson interview.
89. Bill Andersen interview.
90. Prince, *Tuned In to Change*, 109.
91. Bill Andersen interview.

was converted as a young boy.[92] In 1937 this group was usurped, largely through the initiative of a student, David Stewart. Stewart was a very clever and rebellious boy. He went to a Christian teacher for help and decided to become a Christian, praying "Oh God, help me out of this terrible mess."[93] After praying this prayer, his behavior changed in an astonishing way, so that other boys noticed and asked what had happened to him. Stewart, with other Christian students who had gathered around him, had heard of ISCF but were not optimistic about the effectiveness of Porter's Bible class. They took a presentation Bible to Mr. Porter and thanked him for his ministry and told him that they knew that he would want the boys to take more responsibility for the group. The senior boys, with David Stewart at the helm, led the new ISCF group and it began to flourish. In 1938, there were twenty to thirty boys at the weekly lunchtime meetings who listened to a Christian talk, largely given by the senior boys. They also organized social activities such as camps and hikes on the weekends. For the camp, they would hire a house near the beach or in the mountains, or sometimes camp under canvas. After David Stewart left for university in 1939, he returned to help lead these camps and other activities.[94]

As well as initiating new groups and leading them, young leaders were also inspired and encouraged by older mentors such as university students, young teachers, staff workers and, of course, Guinness himself. The writings of Guinness for Crusader members encouraged the same kind of consecration and spirit of sacrifice that we have seen in the university ministry. In *Swords Drawn* Guinness uses the language of war to encourage this self-sacrificial commitment and enlist new students for the fight. The booklet called on students to be willing to give up all for the sake of following Jesus as Lord and to be ready to lay down your life as he had given up his life for you. Guinness challenged students to think about their future:

> Be ready either to leave home and friends and bury myself in a far-away mission field or, on the other hand, stay just where I am, however prosaic that may seem at the moment.[95]

In the Crusader and ISCF movement, the emphasis on personal commitment and sacrifice appeared to be a message that mobilized many young people for Christian leadership. The task of adult leaders and teachers was to empower this student-led leadership. In Guinness's instructions in *Swords*

92. He would later become a prominent leader in the Scripture Union and IVF movement.
93. Bill Andersen interview.
94. Bill Andersen interview.
95. Guinness, *Swords Drawn*, 16.

Drawn, his book written for school students, it is the students who are to initiate new Crusader groups, to speak to the school hierarchy, to invite friends to be members, and to speak and lead at the meetings. He encourages them not to rely too much on outside evangelistic speakers but to "concentrate on doing the job yourselves. You can if you will only try!"[96]

Peer Ministry

The importance placed on peer ministry was another characteristic of the school ministry that was similar to the university ministry. Ministry had been conducted *to* youth in the past by ministers and teachers, but for the first time, there was a real mobilization *of* youth in ministry to their peers. The centrality of peer ministry in the vision of schools ministry has been evident as we have looked at the formation of the Crusader Union and the ISCF. Evangelism or "witnessing" was to be the task of every Christian young person. Along with this was the importance of the small Bible study group run by Christian students for their peers and the focus on fellowship.

The simplest expression of peer ministry was witnessing to friends. This was emphasized in Crusaders and in ISCF. The motto chosen for the Crusader Union was based on Acts 1:8, "Ye shall be witnesses unto me." This witness was named by Guinness as "winning souls," the "combat" of speaking to one's friends about Jesus and calling on them to become Christians. The weapon for the fight was the Bible. Guinness called it the "sword of the Spirit and therefore indispensable to you if you wish to be on the offensive and win others for Christ."[97] Therefore, Crusaders were to read their Bibles daily and have knowledge of the Bible to help them explain the message to others. For example, Judith Young in her conversion story spoke of the importance of witness. One night her minister preached on the prodigal son and she realized that she needed to surrender her life to Christ and that he was her only hope.

> Well, I made many resolutions, some of which I kept at first, but as I got older and left the Christian influences which surrounded me at home, I think that I first started to realize what being a Christian meant. I found that I had to witness before many of my friends who scoffed and scorned against Crusaders.[98]

For Judith, being a Christian meant being prepared to witness.

---

96. Guinness, *Swords Drawn*, 35.
97. Guinness, *Swords Drawn*, 35.
98. "Membership Application of Judith Young," Crusader Union NSW Archives.

Though numbers are difficult to ascertain, there are many accounts of young people involved with the schools ministries who came from non-believing families and were subsequently converted. They were invited by their friends to Crusader or ISCF groups and camps. The camps were seen as the time when the student had an opportunity to commit themselves to the Christian life. In the ISCF Annual Report of 1940, it was claimed that: "Constantly we are meeting grown-up folk who tell us that they were brought to a knowledge of God's salvation at a camp."[99] A case in point is Marjorie Hercus, an Abbotsleigh student who came from a nominal Christian family. She was invited to the Crusader group by a friend, but she initially resisted the challenge to become a devout Christian. In 1932 at the age of fifteen, she was invited by her friends to a Crusader camp at Austinmer, led by Mary Nicholson (the daughter of J. B. Nicholson), who taught them from the Bible.[100] At this camp, Marjorie was challenged to weigh up the cost of becoming a committed Christian. She believed the cost would be to not go to dances, to give up her study time to be a Crusader leader, and to oppose ambitious aspirations of her parents for her future career.[101] She decided that she would take up this challenge, and that future plans for marriage and work had to be shaped by a sense of Christian vocation and service.

Peer ministry was nurtured by the language of *fellowship*. In *Swords Drawn* Guinness spoke of the importance of the relationships within the group, reminding the young people of the fellowship of the early Christians, confessing sin to each other and encouraging them to, "live in the open with people then, for 'Fellowship' means in some very real sense the living together of our common life and the passing of our experiences for the purpose of helping each other in a common fight against a common enemy."[102] Close relationships that reinforced the values and beliefs of the peer group were a hallmark of the school groups. These were formed especially on camps, but also on outings such as picnics, hikes, and tennis parties.[103]

The number and strength of fellowship ties within the Crusader Union and ISCF were noteworthy in the 1930s. The sociologist David Olson has argued that the idea of fellowship within modern evangelical groups is significant in forming religious identity. Fellowship within a group "facilitates interaction among persons who share a religious identity

99. "61st Anniversary of Scripture Union, August 1940," Scripture Union and CSSM Council Minutes Vol. IV, 1933–1941, Scripture Union NSW Archives.

100. Mary Nicholson was very funny and could amaze the girls with her disguises at camp concerts. Marjorie Hercus interview.

101. Marjorie Hercus interview.

102. Guinness, *Swords Drawn*, 50.

103. Marjorie Hercus interview.

and shields many from significant exposure to religious pluralism,"[104] enabling members to sustain and pass on their beliefs to others. If correct, this would help explain why the strength of fellowship and relational networks was a key factor in the vitality and stability of these ministries. The strong personal networks, defined as "fellowship," were understood as a spiritual bond, like being part of the same family. You didn't always like the people within your group, but you belonged to them. Olson concludes that "the ability of religious subcultures to transmit and maintain a real identity will vary with the depth and the number and strength of fellowship ties among participants and the number and strength of subcultural institutions."[105] Adding to the interconnectedness in the Crusader Union were a number of key families that were heavily involved.[106] The immediate families and then extended families through intermarriages created a close interlocking web of intergenerational relationships and fellowship.[107] There truly was a Crusader *family*. In the ISCF and Scripture Union there were close ties of fellowship. At the huge Scripture Union and CSSM reunion of 1949, Alex Brown addressed the meeting and stated:

> The starting of schools work, alongside steadily increasing beach missions, had brought together a substantial body of voluntary workers. Their sense of belonging to a family was strong, for, despite its many strands, the CSSM was small enough to allow people to know each other well. It is not surprising that those involved look back to the decade as the halcyon days of the CSSM.[108]

Despite with the growth in numbers and staff, the 1930s were remarkable for the strong sense of belonging and fellowship. This fellowship reinforced the continuing strong sense of subcultural identity and of mutual dependency in peer ministry.

---

104. Olson, "Fellowship Ties," 35.
105. Olson, "Fellowship Ties," 37.
106. In particular, the Young, Deck, Nicholson, Grant, and Holt families.
107. For more on the dynamic of these family relationships, see Thornton, "Crusader Union of NSW."
108. It was the Diamond Jubilee and 1,500 people attended. Prince, *Tuned In to Change*, 121.

Coeducation and Sexuality

The shared methodology of empowering youth leadership and peer ministry was common to both the university and school ministry. However, one of the key characteristics of the university ministry was bringing the sexes together, whereas the schools ministry did not do this. The schools ministry was separated into boys' and girls' divisions, reflecting the division of boys and girls in both public and private high schools. There was some mixing of the sexes at leaders' camps, beach missions, and the Katoomba convention, and there are accounts of older high school students socializing with mixed-sex groups in more informal ways at tennis parties, picnics, or at an adult's house.[109] In general, however, there was a conservatism in the schools ministry about the way that the sexes interacted, and the most important ministry structures such as Bible study groups, DRMs, and camps were single-sex.

We have seen that the issues of sexuality and gender are significant in understanding the experiences of those young people involved in university ministry. In schools ministry, sexuality was not on the agenda as it was at universities. The cultural norm was that marriage was left until after study was finished. In middle-class Australian culture, and especially in Christian culture, sex was to be experienced only within marriage. Sex was seen as something to be kept from young people until they were older and ready to face these issues.[110]

It was noted earlier that a distinctive feature of the university ministry was its inclusion of women. The schools ministry did not mix the sexes, though interestingly the new groups flourished at girls' schools as much as if not more than at boys' schools. In the Crusader Union ministry the boys' groups struggled, and in 1934 the groups at Sydney Grammar and Scots College were closed, continuing the trend of earlier closures at Newington College, King's School, and Cranbrook.[111] In 1934, Lindsay Grant was employed as a travelling secretary (part-time with the IVF as well) to try and boost the boys' ministry. Meanwhile, the girls' Crusader groups prospered under the "rallying verve and dynamism" of Alice Smith.[112] Within the ISCF too, it was also the girls' groups that flourished. This can be partially attributed to the leadership of Heather Drummond as the girls' division worker and the many

---

109. Marjorie Hercus interview.
110. Fabian and Loh, *Children in Australia*, 228.
111. "The Crusader Union of NSW Boys Division 5th Annual Report 1934-35," Crusader Union Archives.
112. Thornton, "Crusader Union of NSW," 52.

young female teachers (such as Win Dunkley) who viewed teaching in the same way as a religious vocation was viewed by their male peers.[113]

Along with the effective female leaders, another reason for the greater success of schools ministry amongst girls may have been the ongoing impact of the Great War on boys. In the 1930s, the children of men who had fought in the war were young people making their own decisions about faith. The impact of the war on the evangelical church had been dispiriting; churches had sent their best and brightest young men.[114] The impact was varied:

> . . . some came home to resume active roles in their respective churches, others who were not yet Christians during the war were later converted to Christ, others wrestled mightily with their demons and dropped out, yet others never darkened a church door again, and many never came home at all.[115]

Many evangelical fathers never returned home[116] or returned home emotionally scarred, and for many teenage boys, a strong role model and father figure was absent. It seems a reasonable hypothesis that Christian faith may have been more attractive to young girls than to the boys who lacked a male Christian role model in their fathers.

Conclusion

The formation of the Crusader Union and the ISCF represent a methodological shift in Protestant youth ministry with school students in the 1930s. They were in part a response to social changes, most importantly the rise of government secondary education in NSW but were more directly attributable to the influence of key individuals such as Howard Guinness. From the outset, there were methodological parallels, as well as institutional connections, between the new youth ministry in the schools and at the university. The schools ministries were theologically conservative, believing in the importance of defending the authority of the Bible from attack, and setting a

---

113. Along with the impressive female leaders, another reason for the strength of the girls' work may be that the Christian faith was not as attractive to young men in the 1930s. Despite attempts to attract men, the church was often viewed as a place for women and children. See Lake, "Historical Reconsiderations," 117.

114. Piggin and Linder, *National Soul*, 69–76.

115. Piggin and Linder, "Norman Makin," 113.

116. These casualties were particularly felt by evangelicals who had sent so many of their sons. Linder speaks of the "evangelical vacant pew." Linder, *Long Tragedy*, 151. For more on the impact of the Great War on that generation and Christian faith, see Wohl, *Generation of 1914*.

vision of fellowship and surrender that was attractive to young people. They empowered youth in leadership. Adults gave responsibility and encouragement, but there was little intervention. Howard Guinness provided mentoring, a model of small groups, camps, and witnessing, but it was young people themselves who assumed the initiative in setting up and leading new groups, organizing events, witnessing to their friends, and giving talks and testimonies. The groups had a very strong subcultural identity expressed through membership pledges and symbols, and strengthened by the values of peer ministry, witness, and fellowship. Every member was responsible to be a public witness to their faith and every member was part of the fellowship and was bonded to others in the group as to a family. However, whereas in the university ministry the sexes had been brought together in fellowship, in the schools ministry this was not the case. Finally, university students were instrumental in the formation of the Crusader Union and ISCF, and these older youth continued to help lead the movements as well as speaking and leading meetings, camps, and beach missions. The offices of the schools and university organizations were in close proximity, and there was a close relationship between them. Like the university ministry, the new youth ministry in schools represented a movement away from a ministry *for* young people to a ministry *of* young people.

5

The Fellowships

Denominational Youth Ministry in the 1930s

IN THE 1930S, THERE was a change in the way that local churches conducted ministry to the young, similar to the changes noted in the university and schools ministry: from a ministry *for* youth to a ministry *of* youth. Social forces in the interwar years gave rise to a sense of imminent crisis and great anxiety about the *youth problem*. These social forces included the Depression, as many young people faced unemployment. They also included new ideologies such as socialism and fascism which were leading to unrest amongst the young. The world seemed to be lurching towards war. Another social force was the development of secondary education, which created peer groups for young people with a subculture distinct from their parents. Churches were concerned with a youth problem, noting the *leakage of youth*, as young people were absenting themselves from churches. *New methods* of youth ministry were sought to solve this problem, which ultimately led to a change from dependence on the established youth societies, to the rise of a new kind of group: the local church youth fellowship.

The fellowship was a group of young people who met on a Sunday morning or late afternoon and organized their own Bible discussions, social events, house parties and other activities. The fellowship group was not a new innovation in the 1930s; in fact, the Presbyterian Church in Australia established fellowship groups from the 1870s. In the 1930s, however, these groups grew in numbers, became an Australia-wide organization, and spread to the other Protestant denominations. Its popularity as a method was in step with the spread of fellowships worldwide.[1]

Two different theological streams shaped the fellowship groups as they developed. A conservative evangelical resurgence in the university and schools was fundamental to the origins and goals of the new youth ministry. Similarly, many youth fellowships were shaped by the conservative goal of evangelism and revival. They sought to encourage the evangelization *of youth by youth*. This priority can be seen in many of the Church of England fellowships and the Presbyterian fellowships. However, there was another strand which was influenced by liberal evangelicalism. Its adherents believed that the proper response to the crisis of civilization was to form groups of young people worldwide who would work to build a Christian world. In the Presbyterian Church, these two streams achieved a remarkable unity. In the Church of England, there was much conflict until the conservative evangelical stream became dominant. Though they had different ultimate goals, fellowship groups from both streams had very similar methods. Both emphasized the relational over the institutional and promoted the significance of peer groups for spiritual formation. The fellowship groups brought men and women together and encouraged the leadership of the young people. The concept of fellowship was a theological idea that expressed a conviction that being a Christian was more than merely belonging to the church or subscribing to a set of beliefs. Being a Christian was a religion of the heart, lived out in close relationship with God and other believers.

The Presbyterian Fellowship Union

As mentioned in chapter two, the Presbyterian Fellowship Union (PFU) was a forerunner for modern fellowship groups within churches. The PFU was a pioneer as the first denominational youth society in Australia; it was another fifty years until other denominations embraced this method.[2] The

---

1. As mentioned in chapter one, changes in the methods of youth ministry in Australia were part of a transnational change in the Protestant churches. Senter argues that the third cycle moved away from societies to youth organizations that relied on relationships and the peer group as the key means of spiritual formation. He notes that youth fellowships were pioneered by the Congregational City Church in 1936. Senter argues that this reinvention of youth ministry was a response to a time of crisis, secularization, and a loss of Christian moorings. Senter, *When God Shows Up*, 182.

2. In fact, it seems that the PFU was the first fellowship association in the world. Prentis, "Fellowship," 23. In New Zealand, there were already Bible classes that were similar in many ways to the PFU, and in America, there was a concern for this age group in local churches and societies formed.

PFU encouraged the leadership of youth, was coeducational, and was the first to use the name "fellowship." It pointed toward the future of denominational youth church work but also retained a nineteenth-century character. It continued to foster a rather paternalistic posture towards young people and especially a concern to form character by the foursquare principle. The PFU was a transitional organization, sharing the characteristics of both societies and fellowships.

It is striking that local church fellowship groups did not begin in the other Protestant Churches until fifty years later. It was only in the interwar period that social forces provoked churches to consider other methods. The reason that the Presbyterians were pioneers may perhaps be found in their minority status. Presbyterians were a predominantly Scottish cultural minority. They were very aware of the need to retain their young and to nurture in them a sense of Presbyterian identity. They were concerned for the next generation and the need to strengthen them as they navigated the temptations of the new world.[3] This desire for maintaining distinctiveness was, therefore, stronger in Presbyterians than in those within the Church of England who had more confidence in the strength of their own identity as a majority culture. There may have been a sense of mainstream presumption in the Church of England that meant they were less anxious about their youth. The Methodist and Congregational Churches were also minority groups, but the Christian Endeavor groups in which they were involved remained very strong, so there was not as much need for distinctive denominational fellowship groups until after the 1930s.[4]

The Youth Problem

As outlined in chapter two, churches became concerned about the "youth problem" and in response began to look for new methods in ministry to youth in the 1930s. They believed that social forces, such as the Great War, the Depression and the rise of atheist ideologies, demonstrated that there

---

3. Hutchinson argues that there was a level of fear in the late 1920s about the "leakage" of young people from the Sunday schools. "And as an ethnic community, there was the added fear that the Scot roots of many in the congregations would be lost among this 'new generation of Australians,' who were growing up amidst the dangers of secular society, evangelistic science, and expansionary Methodism." Hutchinson, *Iron in Our Blood*, 137.

4. For example, at the Congregational Assembly of May 1933 all State Young People's Departments were encouraged to form local Christian Endeavor groups. "Congregational Union, Work Amongst Young People," *Sydney Morning Herald*, May 6, 1933, 18.

was a "crisis of civilization"[5] and that youth were "in revolt."[6] The development of government high schools also exacerbated the youth problem and fostered a peer culture that at times challenged the culture of their parents.[7] At the same time, there was romanticism about the idealism, sacrifice, and enthusiasm of the young. They were regarded as "Our Greatest Asset,"[8] the hope of the future.

In the Protestant Churches, youth departments were formed and reports were written about the problem. For example, M. C. St. Arnaud, the Chairman of the Australian Church of England General Board of Education, believed that there was an urgent need to focus the churches' mission on the young.

> It is a truism to say that the whole question of Youth today is of overwhelming importance, and without the spiritual inspiration of the Church and the Gospel democracy is in grave danger of losing its way, and falling into chaos.[9]

A subcommittee of the Sydney Church of England Board of Education met in September 1930 to "investigate the best means of dealing with the adolescents of the diocese in their relationship with the church."[10] For many church leaders, the youth problem was evidenced by a decline in numbers involved in Sunday schools and societies. Reports often referred to a "youth leakage": high rates of dropout, particularly at the age of fourteen.[11] Between 1933 and 1936 the Youth Commission of the Methodist church met to discuss reasons for the youth problem. It defined the problem as the decline in numbers in Sunday schools and societies, and the challenges of sex and popular culture. The report stated that the cause of the problem was the cataclysm of war, irreligious families, the increase of cars and Sunday drives, and the rise of new ideologies.[12] In the Presbyterian Church, John Jamieson

---

5. "Spiritual Revival Needed," *Sydney Morning Herald*, July 17, 1937, 12.

6. "The Revolt of Youth," *Sydney Morning Herald*, June 27, 1933, 3.

7. Sara Little argues that the US high schools strengthened peer groups and led to the development of fellowships because "The term fellowship picked up the importance increasingly attached to the peer group, as well as an understanding of the church as community." Little, "Youth Ministry."

8. This was the title of the handbook for Sunday Schools and fellowships written for the Church of England in Australia. Blackwood and Walton, *Our Greatest Asset*.

9. Blackwood and Walton, *Our Greatest Asset*, Preface.

10. Quoted in Mason, "History of the Board," 56.

11. Churches were concerned that confirmation at the age of fourteen was seen as a "graduation service out of Church life." Hicks, *City on a Hill*, 123. Blackwood and Walton, *Our Greatest Asset*, 67.

12. Anon., *Challenge of Youth*, 19–24.

publicly noted in 1936 that there were two challenges that led to the youth problem, the first was external and the second internal. The first challenge was modern social and economic problems and ideology, particularly socialist ideas. The second challenge came from within youth itself:

> Youth needed a spiritual fellowship, brotherhood and an opportunity to exercise leadership in spiritual work... The real issues were the search for peace and a purpose in life. The social and economic problems were often raised to obscure the individual problems of sex, cocktail drinking and bad habits.[13]

Jamieson argued that there was a need for a spiritual fellowship so that young people could withstand these external and internal pressures. He often repeated the popular idea that the energy and leadership of young people were needed because they were the "future of the Church."

> It is to these young people with their fresh outlook on life, with their optimism and unbounded faith in their ability to accomplish those things which they set out to do, that the Church looks to today for that revitalizing force which it needs so much. Today the Church is challenged like never before, but youth has accepted the challenge and as the young men answered their countries call in the days of the great war, so the young men and women are today enlisting in thousands under the banner of the Church to combat the evil and disruptive forces that are seeking to destroy the social and religious fabric.[14]

It was these concerns and reports about the youth problem that led the churches to begin or expand their own fellowship groups in the 1930s.[15]

The church reports concluded that what was needed were *new methods*. Already in the Sunday schools, new methods had been advocated since 1913 amongst children. These methods included dividing children into developmental stages and focusing on the child rather than the content of the curriculum.[16] Many educators in the interwar years had also called

---

13. "Modern Youth and Church," *The Argus*, May 1936, 10.
14. "St Andrew's Church Youth Rally," October 24, 1932, *Riverine Herald*, 2.
15. This concern of a *youth problem* reflected a wider concern in the Western world. Mark Senter has argued that in America the fellowships were a defensive trend to deal with the youth problem. There was a fear of changing cultural values, particularly sexual morality and the influence of these on the young. Senter, *When God Shows Up*, 195. Perhaps this concern for the youth reflected an anxiety about the future in the churches as well as less surety about direction and the future.
16. In 1913 an Australian curriculum was developed in line with graded lessons and Sunday schools were encouraged to develop senior departments and extracurricular

into question old methods of ministry to adolescents and young people.[17] They believed that the Bible class or fellowship group with their own space and time, different from the Sunday school, would be more effective.[18] The new methods, therefore, acknowledged that ministry to youth must take into account the different developmental stages and needs of young people. No longer should youth work be teacher and curriculum centered like the youth societies. Instead, it should give opportunities for young people to lead, and should leave plentiful space for discussion.

The Formation of the Fellowship Groups

The youth problem, therefore, led the churches to reevaluate their methods and embrace the concept of the local denominational youth group: the fellowship. The Protestant churches took up the concept from the PFU and from modern educational writers. This new method was relational, coeducational, and based on the significance of the peer group. It was shaped by a theological understanding of fellowship which empowered young people in leadership. The fellowships were generally made up of the children of congregational members who were zealous in their faith and gathered together in order to enjoy relationships with like-minded youth and to be spiritually challenged and encouraged by talks and singing. Although clergy had an important role speaking in these fellowships and often the young student minister or curate would be called upon to lead the young people's fellowship, the young people themselves were actively involved in leadership in the group, unlike earlier youth societies.

The Presbyterian Fellowship of Australia

A new organization was formed in January 1931 called the *Presbyterian Fellowship of Australia* or PFA, which brought together all the state associations of the PFU and other youth associations that catered for those fourteen years or older. They were to have a "common name, badge and programme."[19]

---

activities. There were some who resisted the new methods and continued a "Bible-centered" course of study with stress upon instruction, catechism, and memory work. Kelley, "Nurseries for Christians," 75, 80, 174.

17. In the US there were also critiques of old methods. For example, Niles, "Survey and Critique," 534.

18. Clover, *Senior Department Handbook*, 5.

19. Prentis, "Fellowship," 14. See also White, *Challenge of the Years*, 245. Peter Boase first became aware of the PFA when he was on a train and bumped into some young

The PFA continued to operate with the same foursquare methodology of the PFU: "The objects of the PFA shall be to unite the young people of the Presbyterian Church of Australia in a fellowship of worship, study, recreation and service."[20] An optimistic campaign was launched to raise the numbers of members in the Association in Australia from two thousand to five thousand.[21] It grew exponentially during the interwar era and by 1939 there were five thousand members.[22]

The PFA badge (like the SU and Crusader Union badge) was very important to PFA members in shaping their identity. The significance of the badge was explained by C. J. R. Price in *The Witness* in 1932. The blue represented loyalty to the Lord, church, ministers, leaders, and fellow PFA members. White represented purity in speech and thought. Silver represented genuineness. P stood for Presbyterian, the glorious church. A stood for Australia, citizens of a great land. Finally, F was bigger than the other letters and represented "vertical fellowship with God and horizontal fellowship with each other."[23]

The activities of the PFA were essentially the same as the old PFU: fellowship teas, social events and camps, but the most important was the study circle. At the study circle on Sunday mornings, the group would gather at church, the members would take turns in giving a paper on a Bible passage or topic, and then there would be a discussion.[24] The syllabus of topics and passages used in the study circle was published in the monthly journal *The Witness* along with daily Bible readings. The study circles in the 1930s were divided into different departments: junior, intermediate, and senior. Each group included twenty to forty members on average, though there were some very large groups, for example, Haberfield Presbyterian PFA had 130 members.[25] At the Northbridge PFA in 1932, seniors met at 10 a.m. on Sunday with about twenty-one members

men who had PFA badges. He asked about the badge and was told that it stood for the Prize Fools Association, then the Prize Fighters Association. Finally, when they confessed the true meaning of the badge, they invited Boase to a fellowship meeting and Easter camp. This began a long and happy association with the PFA. He himself wore the badge whenever he wore a suit, "which was most of the time." Peter Boase interview.

20. *The Witness*, January 1, 1931.

21. *The Witness*, February 18, 1931.

22. Prentis, "Fellowship," 14.

23. *The Witness*, May 18, 1932.

24. The study circle seems to have taken this model of group discussion from the University ministry, and indeed there seems to be an ongoing relationship between the Student Christian Movement and the PFA as there are many mentions of the SCM in the journal *The Witness*.

25. *The Witness*, June 18, 1931.

and juniors met at 8 p.m. Papers were prepared by members on topics such as "The Four-Sided View of Jesus Christ," "Fellowship," and "Adventurers with God." Another PFA group at Ashfield Presbyterian Church had between one hundred and two hundred members in the 1930s. For one of the members, Nessie Aitken, the study circle and social events helped to create a group that offered "great comradeship," which was very important to her. As well as study circles she remembers PFA mock trials, gymnastic displays, picnics, hikes, and tennis club on a Saturday.[26]

One offshoot of the Sunday morning meetings that developed in the 1930s was the fellowship birthday tea. These were annual events when a fellowship group would invite the other regional fellowships and friends to celebrate the fellowship anniversary on a Sunday afternoon. For example, in 1930 the Rose Bay fellowship had a birthday tea with "corned beef, jelly and ice cream and a birthday cake" set on beautiful tables with hibiscus. There were ninety-six guests who enjoyed the food and songs, and a talk by Miss Dulcie Davison on "Human Fellowship."[27]

In the 1930s the PFA extended its camping ministry and also developed a leadership training course. The first camp of the PFU had been held in 1911, inspired by the idea of the Summer Conference by J. R. Mott.[28] Land at Thornleigh was donated in 1911 and finally developed in the 1930s to hold large annual conferences for all PFA members in NSW. Each year there was an Easter Conference and a Summer Conference. At the girls' Easter camp in 1931, a camper wrote of the highlights in *The Witness*. She noted the talks on Psalm 23: "How Can Christianity Meet Present Day Needs?" She also enjoyed the walk to Koala Park, the tennis, and the blackberry pie.

> While the spiritual side of camp was predominant, yet no one could get bored between the various meetings, as there were other activities such as tennis, skipping, bush walks etc., not forgetting the well-patronized tuck shop, which Noel never left unattended. Ha ha![29]

The other significant development in 1931 was the development of the training curriculum for fellowship leaders produced by the Welfare of Youth Department. Lessons were held in the city one evening a week. The curriculum included three sections. The first contained some psychological teaching about children and how to teach. The second was on how to teach the Old

---

26. "Ashfield Presbyterian Church 1876–1976," Presbyterian Church NSW Archives.
27. *The Witness*, February 18, 1930.
28. White, *Challenge of the Years*, 245.
29. *The Witness*, May 18, 1931.

and New Testaments. The third section included sessions on adolescence, the study group, week-night activities, social and personal problems, and the book of Philippians.[30] The PFA had come to recognize the importance of training youth leaders who could both teach and organize events.

The Church of England Fellowship

The first Church of England fellowship groups began in 1929, the first at St. Paul's Chatswood in April. At the instigation of the young man, Alan Begbie,[31] eighteen young men and women began meeting at 10 a.m. on Sundays for worship and discussion. One of these young men, David Stewart, gave the first fellowship talk on the meaning of the word "fellowship" or *koinonia* in Greek.[32] In later meetings, members took turns to lead, and they also organized visiting speakers or ran studies from a book called "The Meaning of Life."[33] By December 1929, there is evidence of another fellowship at Manly as forty-two members of the Chatswood fellowship travelled on the back of a lorry to visit the Manly fellowship on a Friday night.[34]

Archbishop Mowll sought to boost these fellowship groups and encourage more, as he had a particular concern for outreach to young people. He encouraged a subcommittee of the Sydney Church of England Board of Education to meet in September 1930, to "investigate the best means of dealing with the adolescents of the diocese in their relationship with the church."[35] The subcommittee decided to establish a new institution, the Sydney Church of England Fellowship (CEF). The CEF was affiliated with the General Board of Religious Education, Church of England Fellowship,[36] an Australia-wide body. The object of CEF was the "linking of young people more definitely with the work and worship of the Church."[37] Members had to be over the age of thirteen and needed to be willing to sign up to the

---

30. *The Witness*, May 18, 1931.

31. Dickey, "Begbie."

32. A few years later, a junior fellowship at Chatswood was formed with about forty members. Hicks, *City on a Hill*, 124.

33. Hicks, *City on a Hill*, 124.

34. Hicks, *City on a Hill*, 124.

35. Mason, "History of the Board," 56. The three members of this subcommittee were F. A. Walton, the head of the Board of Education, W. G. Coughlan, and A. G. Frazer.

36. Hammond, "History of the Church," 6.

37. *Year Book of the Diocese of Sydney, NSW, Australia* (1932), 184.

"foursquare" way of life. In order to become a member, according to the constitution, the following requirements needed to be met:

1. Attendance at divine worship each week.
2. Faithful attendance at Holy Communion
3. Daily prayer and Bible reading
4. Definite Christian service and practical missionary interest
5. Wholehearted loyalty to the Church
6. Support of the Church through the envelope or other approved system.[38]

These requirements focused on commitment to the church and personal holiness. A badge was given to the new member with a white cross with four arms that symbolized purity and the universal character of the Christian faith.[39] The motto of the CEF was Luke 2:52: "And Jesus grew in wisdom and in stature, and in favour with God and man."[40] Like the PFA, the CEF used the methodology of the foursquare as foundational. New members were initiated in a church service and were asked questions such as:

> Are you prepared to follow the Trail blazed by our Lord Jesus Who 'increased in wisdom and stature and in favour with God and man?' Do you promise to do your best to keep the Rule of Life? In the power of the Holy Spirit to be loyal to Christ and His Church? To keep my Baptismal Vows, to fight against what is wrong, to believe what is true, and to obey Christ's Law of Love?[41]

Members of the CEF were expected to follow the model of Jesus, growing in all areas of their lives to become Christian leaders and citizens.

Although the constitution seems to be focused on piety and service rather than outreach, many of the CEF groups began in the context of evangelistic mission to the young. Archbishop Mowll appointed Alan Begbie to be "missioner to young people" in 1934. Begbie went to local parishes and conducted missions to young people and children after school. Within two and a half years he had conducted fifty-six missions and contacted 17,500

---

38. "Board of Education Minutes 1934–1958," Youthworks Archives.
39. Nobbs, *You Are God's Building*, 132.
40. Hammond, "History of the Church."
41. "Draft of Handbook of Church of England Fellowship of Diocese of Sydney," July 15, 1940, in "Board of Education Minutes 1934–1958," Youthworks Archives, Ingleburn, NSW, 12.

children and after the mission, many fellowships were established.[42] By 1935, there were twenty seven registered CEF branches operating[43] and by 1938, there were forty one.[44] In a Standing Committee report to the Board of Education in 1939, it was stated that alongside the fellowship meetings, there was also a Christmas camp, a combined launch picnic and many fellowship teas.[45] By 1940, many CEF groups ran evening meetings as well as Sunday morning groups. These meetings tended to be more social and committed to the foursquare, leaving the Sunday to focus on the spiritual side. A suggested program for the evening meeting was:

1. Opening devotion and Bible study (twenty minutes)
2. Business: rolls etc.
3. Group activities e.g. debate, tournament (one hour)
4. Recreation (twenty-five minutes)
5. Closing devotions (five minutes).[46]

The activities of the CEF were very similar to the PFA, with weekly Bible studies, social events and fellowship teas. The weekly Bible study or service on Sunday was at the heart of the fellowship. Unlike the PFA, there was no curriculum, so the Church of England groups tended to be more autonomous in deciding the content of the studies and the direction of the group. The CEF fellowship teas soon became a highlight of the movement with a real outreach focus that the PFA did not have. These teas were held once a month on a Sunday afternoon and included a speaker and a light meal. The historian Lesley Hicks argues that the CEF teas began at St. Paul's Chatswood. She quotes a letter written to her by Nora Tress, an early fellowship leader in the early 1930s. Nora claimed that a group of fellowship girls asked the rector whether they could have a tea in the parish hall to save them the long walk home in the afternoon after Sunday school

---

42. Gray, "Thesis Chapter on the Anglican Youth Department," Youthworks Archives.
43. Hammond, "History of the Church."
44. "Standing Committee Report 1938–1939," Board of Education Minutes.
45. "Standing Committee Report 1938–1939," Board of Education Minutes.
46. "Draft of Handbook of Church of England Fellowship of Diocese of Sydney," July 15, 1940, in "Board of Education Minutes," Youthworks Archives. Suggested activities were divided into the foursquare: 1. Spiritual: Sunday fellowship, Bible class, Christian heroes, music, and poetry. 2. Social: indoor games, service for others, thrift, and choral work. 3. Physical: aquatics, indoor athletics, basketball, cricket, football, hikes, camping, and cycling. 4. Intellectual: Essays, home-reading, stamp collecting, debates, economics, astronomy, singing, dramatics, and Arthurian legends.

because they would later return to church for the evening service.[47] These teas flourished under the able leadership of the curate, Alan Begbie, and became a monthly institution. "During the early 30s under Mr Begbie's leadership, the Fellowship at St. Paul's grew in leaps and bounds . . . from then the movement 'took off' and before long fellowship teas sprang up in churches everywhere."[48] At these teas, returned missionaries or young clergymen gave evangelistic talks and members were encouraged to bring their friends who were not yet Christians.

The fellowship house party was also a significant event in shaping the fellowship experience. The first St. Paul's Chatswood fellowship house party was held at a school ground in Mona Vale in 1938. To run the house party, the leaders of the Chatswood fellowship had to hire cutlery and stretchers for forty people. In the minutes the goal of the house party was outlined:

> Such a thing had never been done before in the annals of St Paul's fellowship, and yet we felt that such a venture would deepen the spiritual life of our young people and cement their fellowship with each other more firmly.[49]

The talks at the house party were given by an Arts student, Clive Kerle. On Sunday night he spoke on "Full Surrender" and called for a response.[50] On Saturday night, a concert was held and on the final evening, there was an open time for testimonies from those present of how the Lord had changed their life.[51] Other CEF groups followed the example of St. Paul's and had house parties which became a way to call on regular members to become committed Christians and for newcomers to hear the Christian message. These house parties, however, were not organized and centralized the same way that the PFA camps were, and it was not until the late 1940s that the Church of England camps rivalled the size of the Presbyterians after they had acquired a campsite of their own and organized diocesan CEF camps.

---

47. Hicks, *City on a Hill*, 125–126.
48. Hicks, *City on a Hill*, 126.
49. Hicks, *City on a Hill*, 128.
50. The title of the talk certainly indicates that Keswick-style teaching on holiness had an impact on the local youth fellowships. House parties were likely to be the time of intense spiritual community and teaching that speakers would feel that they could call on the youth to yield to the Lord and allow him to sanctify their lives.
51. Hicks, *City on a Hill*, 129.

Other Protestant Denominations

In the other denominations, the idea of fellowships took a little longer to be embraced. In the early 1930s, Congregational Youth Fellowships (CYFs) were established and in 1933/34 a National Youth Council was appointed to oversee them and a national Easter camp organized.[52] Christian Endeavor, however, continued to be the most popular local church organization in the Congregational Church. The CYF had to work in harmony with Christian Endeavor, providing a social outlet while Christian Endeavor focused on the spiritual dimension. Christian Endeavor was also strong in the Baptist Church. In 1934, the Christian Endeavor groups unified as part of the Young Baptists Union,[53] but it was not until 1961 that the Baptist Youth Fellowship was formed.[54]

The formation of fellowship groups in the Methodist Church took a different path. The Methodist Church in Australia had the largest numbers in Sunday schools and also in its youth societies. In the 1930s, the societies continued to attract young people to their activities,[55] though there was some concern about a decline in numbers and the failure of the societies to bring about firm Christian commitment.[56] There is evidence from 1933 onwards of requests at conference (the basic organizational unit in the denomination) for fellowship groups to be formed that would be like the old Methodist classes and lead to a revival.[57] Young peoples' councils in each circuit were formed to unite the societies and some fellowships were established. In 1944, the director of Methodist Youth Work proposed bringing all the organizations under the one umbrella of the Methodist Youth Fellowship (MYF).[58] Under this scheme, a young person could belong to their own society, but also be part of the fellowship which would unify them and help them realize that " . . . they are Methodist girls or Methodist young men,

---

52. There is little documentation of the fellowships, but there has been a recent reunion which celebrated their influence. "UCA Historical Society."

53. "Young Baptists Union Suggested," *The Courier Mail*, September 20, 1934, 16.

54. Manley, *Woolloomooloo to "Eternity,"* 525.

55. In 1934 in Christian Endeavor there were 9,161 members, Methodist Order of Knights: 4,840 and Girl's Comradeship: 6,650 in Australia. Anon., *Challenge of Youth*, 19.

56. The Reverend A. T. Robens stated that in 1936, 90 percent of Methodist children came through Sunday Schools, but 80 percent were lost to the church in young manhood/womanhood. "The Church and Youth," *Newcastle Morning Herald and Miner's Advocate*, November 5, 1936, 13.

57. "Group and Class," *The Methodist*, January 4, 1933, 4.

58. Gallacher, *Forward*.

linked together in Christian Fellowship by their common loyalty to Christ, and the one desire to extend His kingdom."[59]

The MYF group at the local church was led by the young people themselves. They had the guidance of adults, but they were responsible for their own fellowship services.[60] Groups were formed such as the fellowship at Enfield Methodist Church on a Sunday which had their own decorated fellowship room. At these meetings, activities, discussions, and lectures were organized by the young people on subjects such as "What Are We Here For?," "How to Find Our Work in This World?," and "What is Christianity?"[61]

Liberal Versus Conservative Fellowships

It has been argued that one of the reasons for the change in methodology in the 1930s was the conservative evangelical resurgence. The university and schools ministry that developed in the 1930s was energized by this theology and focused on evangelism. In the fellowship movement, however, there was a breadth of theology with conservative as well as decidedly liberal evangelical groups. These two different strands were both responses to social forces and to the belief that there was a crisis of civilization. The conservative response was expressed in renewed energy for evangelism in order to bring about revival, and the liberal evangelical response was to encourage young people to be engaged in shaping a Christian civilization. The two strands are evident in the different fellowship groups. The CYF and MYF groups tended to be liberal with a focus on political engagement and building a Christian civilization.[62] In the CEF groups, there was a division between liberal and conservative that led to a political battle over the direction and leadership of the organization. In the PFA, the liberal and conservative members succeeded in maintaining their unity. It is instructive to compare the different way that the CEF and PFA were shaped by the theological strands.

The PFA managed to retain a kind of nineteenth century evangelical breadth of opinion. It was influenced by liberal evangelical theology,

59. Gallacher, *Forward*, 10.
60. Gallacher, *Forward*, 12.
61. "Enfield Youth Fellowship," *The Methodist*, August 30, 1947, 12.
62. For example, at the Congregational Youth Easter camp in 1938, discussion centered on "controversial modern problems of world peace, and economic and social reform" and "implications to the economic and social order." The young people stayed awake until 3 a.m. and "it was generally agreed that the purpose of the Church was to establish the Kingdom of God on earth." *The Congregationalist*, May 5, 1938. It could be argued that this broadening of theology was influenced by university students who were active in the SCM.

particularly that of Professor Samuel Angus. Angus caused much controversy in the Presbyterian Church in the 1930s because of his writings and his teaching at the theological college.[63] In 1931, Angus spoke at the PFA Summer Camp on "The New Testament and How It Arose" and on "The New Testament, How Is It to Be Used?"[64] In 1934, *The Witness* positively reviewed Angus's controversial new book, *Truth and Tradition*. Key ideas of Angus were quoted favorably: "I maintain that Christianity is not a system of doctrines but a way of life" and "a Christian man's business is not to talk grandly about dogmas, but to be doing arduous and great things in fellowship with God."[65] The leaders of the PFA organization were influenced by Angus, especially the Reverend E. H. Vines, who wrote the curriculum in *The Witness*.[66] Under the direction of Vines, the syllabus turned more to social issues such as "Under What Conditions is the White Australia Policy Christian?," "What Are the Essentials of Christian Business?," and "What are the Essentials of Christian Citizenship?"[67] Vines also wrote on the kingdom of God in a way which adopted a liberal view of progressive revelation.

> The whole process of evolution and of history has meaning when you see that it leads up first from animal to man, then to Christ; the God-man, then to Christ's Kingdom, which is being more and more realized on earth as man catch His spirit. History is mystery until it is His story, but when you see it as His story, it becomes luminous with meaning and progress.[68]

In *The Witness* a liberal view of the Bible and a concern for creating a Christian civilization was expressed.

> Never in the history of the world was there an age so romantic as ours, so packed with possibilities, with hopes, and fears and golden dreams, with a sense of destiny knocking on its door . . . Never was the Youth of the world so alert, so ready to rally

---

63. Between 1928 and 1933 there was public debate about Professor Angus's theology that made it into the newspapers. There were complaints by students and charges of unorthodox theology by Presbyterian leaders such as the Reverend McGowan (Ashfield Presbyterian Church) were brought to the Presbytery. In 1934, Angus's book *Truth and Tradition* was published which reignited complaints to the Presbytery and National General Assembly. In this book he challenged orthodox "traditions" such as the Trinity, the virgin birth, and the atonement. For more on Angus and the debate, see Piggin and Linder, *National Soul*, 122–31, Emilsen, *Whiff of Heresy*; Garnsey, *Arthur Garnsey*.

64. *The Witness*, December 18, 1931.
65. *The Witness*, May 18, 1934.
66. Vines was mentored by Angus. Prentis, "Fellowship," 14.
67. *The Witness*, June 18, 1931.
68. *The Witness*, June 18, 1931.

behind great leaders, so stirred to active, unselfish planning for the future . . . Youth is on the march, and Christ is the hope of a changing world.[69]

There was a great idealism about the prospect of creating a "youth movement" or fellowship that would change the world.

Despite the influence of this teaching, there were still many local Presbyterian fellowship groups that were decidedly conservative (such as the large Ashfield PFA where Nessie Aitken was a member) but unity was maintained, nevertheless. Fellowship and unity were considered by many to be more important than doctrine. In 1936 at the Daylesford Conference, a variety of speakers spoke on the topic "Is There a New Evangelism?" One of the participants wrote a report in *The Witness* praising the breadth of the conference.

> An ultra-Modernist would have been annoyed to find quite "orthodox" people participating and a Fundamentalist would have been disturbed by the presence of both "broad" churchmen and "high" churchmen. Actually, the conference included both the "old" and "the new" and rose above both in its desire to present a living Christ to the youth today.[70]

Many fellowship members were not overly interested or articulate in theological matters: they were Christian and Presbyterian, and this was not defined in a confessional way. Identity was formed by being part of a group and institution that was bigger than them, not through theology.[71]

In the CEF, rather than a unity between the two strands, there was a real contest over the different theological views. Alan Begbie had facilitated the formation of new fellowship groups after evangelistic missions. The purpose of these groups was to encourage the faith of those converted, and to inspire Christians to witness to their friends, the evangelization "of youth by youth." There were, however, other fellowship groups formed with a different goal: the formation of Christian character. This was in keeping with Christians of a more liberal bent elsewhere in the world who were focusing energy on the education of youth as part of a desire to establish a Christian world order. At St. John's Darlinghurst the fellowship group was influenced by the liberal evangelical strand. It began in 1936 with three objects:

69. *The Witness*, July 18, 1932.
70. *The Witness*, April 18, 1936.
71. For example, the Reverend Peter Boase who claims that he was "Not that crash hot on theological differences" when he was a member of the PFA. He argued that his identity was not defined by the Westminster Confession or Calvinism, but by belonging to the PFA. Peter Boase interview.

1. To take an active part in Church life.
2. Overcome shyness in discussing spiritual things.
3. To study subjects to encourage growth of character.[72]

The focus of these objects was Christian character and service, while in the conservative strand the focus was witness.

The tension between the two strands was most evident in the Sydney Diocesan Board of Education, which provided the governance of the CEF. It was here that some of the most vehement contests between liberal and conservative leaders took place. In 1934, Archbishop Mowll began to replace liberal evangelicals with conservative evangelicals in positions of leadership in the diocese[73] and youth ministry found itself to be caught up in the theological battle lines. The director of the Board of Education F. A. Walton was a liberal evangelical, as were others on the board including a prominent fellowship leader, the Reverend W. G. Coughlan. In 1936, the conservatives began to object to some of the Sunday school material in the manual, *The Trowel*, which was produced by the board. They believed the material to be defective in two ways: "(a) Holy Scripture is not always given its rightful place (b) the atoning nature of Christ's death and the application of this to the individual is seldom, if ever, set forth."[74] To prosecute the matter, Mowll brought T. C. Hammond, the Principal of Moore College, onto the board. In response to objections, an editorial committee was established to draw up a new manual with Sydney-authorized lessons. In protest Walton resigned, and the conservative evangelicals won the battle, though at significant financial cost to the Board of Education[75] which no longer supplied Sunday school material to all of the Australian dioceses, only Sydney.

72. Egan, *St John's Darlinghurst*.

73. Before 1934, the key positions in the diocese were occupied by liberal evangelicals: Archbishop Wright, Dean Talbot and Archdeacon Davies. After Davies' death the Anglican Fellowship was formed with the key liberal evangelicals. Talbot said that those in the fellowship "stand for freedom of inquiry and study. We welcome new knowledge as a gift from God (and) we recognize the progressive nature of the revelation of God in the Bible, but our final thought of him is based on the Person and teaching of Jesus Christ." Judd, "Defenders of Their Faith," 351. Those like Arthur Garnsey who were part of the Anglican Fellowship mourned the conservative take-over: "Alas-poor church!" Garnsey, *Arthur Garnsey*, 152. Judd and Cable use a striking statistic to show the success of the evangelicals, claiming that in 1926 the liberal evangelicals, along with a few broad and high church ministers, held 40 percent of the influential positions in the diocese. In 1936 the figure was less than 20 percent. Judd and Cable, *Sydney Anglicans*, 237.

74. "Board of Education Minutes October 27, 1936," Youthworks Archives.

75. See Mason, "History of the Board."

The second battle on the board was about the fellowships. The CEF was affiliated with an Australia-wide movement: the General Board of Religious Education (GBRE) and the President of the Australia-wide CEF organization was W. G. Coughlan. He was distrusted by the conservatives and seen as a renegade who had unlawfully claimed leadership of the movement. A public debate was led by T. C. Hammond's son, C. K. Hammond, about the illegitimacy of the leadership of Coughlan and the fellowship groups affiliated with him.[76] In November 1939, a meeting was organized between the Church of England Fellowship and the Board of Education. At this meeting, Coughlan expressed his fear that breaking with the national movement would lead to a narrowing of theological perspective and that fellowships would all be of a "decided opinion."[77] This was indeed what Mowll and Hammond intended. Coughlan lost the argument, and in 1940, a new fellowship organization was formed which was a breakaway from the national movement: the Church of England Fellowship of The Diocese of Sydney (CEFDOS). The goal of CEFDOS was to:

a. Win young people to full allegiance to Christ, link with a church and service.

b. Promote daily prayer, Bible study and interest in mission.

c. Promote Christian comradeship.

d. To encourage members to "play their part fulltime in the world of today with their body, mind and spirit."

e. Organize branches.

f. Raise and spend funds.[78]

CEFDOS had a distinctive emphasis on evangelism or "winning young people to Christ" that was different from the CEF emphasis. For almost a decade the two organizations ran as separate fellowship bodies in the Diocese of Sydney until Coughlan resigned in 1948.[79] They had the same badge, except the CEFDOS groups badge was blue (the color of Sydney Diocese), whereas the CEF groups had a red badge (the color of the Australian

---

76. Hammond, "Meeting of the Church of England Fellowship, November 6, 1939," Board of Education of the Diocese of Sydney Minutes, 1934–1958.

77. Hammond, "Meeting of the Church of England Fellowship, November 6, 1939," Board of Education of the Diocese of Sydney Minutes, 1934–1958.

78. "Constitution of CEFDOS," July 15, 1940, in Board of Education of the Diocese of Sydney Minutes, 1934–1958, Youthworks Archives.

79. "South Coast Magazine, Preview and Review, Vol. 1, no. 2," Youthworks Archives.

Church of England). There was a rivalry between the blue groups and the red groups, expressed at sports days when the girls wore either a red or a blue cloak to demonstrate their "tribe." The red groups believed that the blue groups were very conservative, that they didn't dance or wear makeup. The blue groups believed that the red groups were "Liberals."[80] In reality, there was probably little difference in their meetings or activities.

New Methods

Despite the theological differences within the fellowship movement and the tension between the two strands, the different denominations all agreed that new methods were needed. All the fellowship groups were remarkably similar in their methods and activities. These methods included a commitment to peer ministry, to youth leadership and to coeducational ministry.

Peer Ministry

Fellowship

The methodology of the fellowship groups displayed a tension between the old model of religious education and the new paradigm of youth leadership. It has been noted that in the formation of the fellowships, the *Foursquare* was foundational as a method. As the 1930s progressed, however, there was a movement away from this old paradigm of religious education to a methodology that was more relational and focused on the spiritual. In the PFA, this change is evident in the monthly magazine *The Witness*. Up until the 1930s, there were many articles on the foursquare. After 1930, however, there were more articles about fellowship and even some critiques of the foursquare. For example, the Reverend J.H. Ryburn wrote:

> The foursquare ideal finds a place for religion but it is the religion one develops within oneself and that is no religion at all. The only religion worth having is one which kindles God within us. It is the very meaning and purpose and power of life, and cannot be 'developed' as we develop our muscles by 'physical jerks.' The 'Foursquare' ideal places man at the centre of things instead of GOD. It aspires to meet man's need not by God's salvation but by developing man's powers.[81]

---

80. Bryde Beman interview.
81. *The Witness*, May 18, 1932.

The foursquare was critiqued as emphasizing the human will and ideal, rather than God's work in a person's life. Later in the CEF, the foursquare was also challenged because it created groups that were too social and neglected Bible study.[82] This change from foursquare to fellowship was reflected in a change in the key Bible verse used as a motto in fellowship groups. In the early days, the verse was Luke 2:52: "Jesus increased in wisdom and stature and in favour with God and man." As the decade progressed, this verse was increasingly replaced with the new motto, 1 John 1:7: "But if we walk in the light as he is in the light, we have fellowship with one another."[83]

In the contemporary cultural context, the word *fellowship* as well as the related word, *comradeship*, was commonly used. The rise of psychology and consequent emphasis on relationships, as well as the interwar desire for peace and unity among nations (expressed in the League of Nations), ensured that fellowship was a concept that was readily taken up. In Australia, the Protestant Church had struggled with a popular attitude to Christianity that valued "practical religion." Many believed that it didn't matter whether or not a person went to church, but that it was important to send children to Sunday school or a youth society so that they might have Christian values. Ministers sought to convince the population that the Christian faith was not just "a subscription to a set of beliefs" or a "prescribed pattern of conduct," but an "intimate and enduring relationship between those who recognized their need of grace and the One from whom all grace proceeds."[84] In this context, fellowship became a useful concept. The concept of fellowship had been integral to the formation of the PFU (as reflected in its name) and was understood as mutual help and encouragement between peers.[85] In the 1930s, the idea of fellowship was given more depth and a theological basis.[86] Fellowship was understood as a way of speaking about the benefits and implications of the Christian gospel. It was not the gospel message itself, that is, the atoning death and resurrection of Jesus for the sin of the world, but it explained the benefits of the gospel. Being a Christian was not merely one's basic beliefs or behavior but was primarily about relationships. A real, active faith was of the heart, motivated by love for God and for others.

---

82. Hicks, *City on a Hill*, 130.

83. For example, at St. Paul's Chatswood the title of the fellowship magazine in 1945 was this verse. Hicks, *City on a Hill*, 145.

84. Hansen, "Churches and Society," 5–8.

85. As outlined in chapter 2, the name originated in the YMCA in Scotland.

86. The influence of the Oxford Group was important in the development of a theology of fellowship. *The Witness* carried regular articles on the group in the 1930s and *The Congregationalist* and *The Methodist* also contained many positive articles. For example, *The Witness*, February 18, 1936.

The Oxford Group[87] further shaped an understanding of fellowship in the youth fellowship movement, particularly the PFA.[88] This was the same group that had influenced Howard Guinness and members of the EU. The Oxford Group emphasized a faith that was "life-changing," brought about by deep fellowship and sharing. The leader of the movement, Frank Buchman,[89] argued that there was a "law of fellowship" made up of four ideals or absolutes: honesty, purity, unselfishness and love. This emphasis led to a focus on small groups and deep and intimate relationships. The PFA was influenced by this teaching, and in 1935, a team of "life-changers" conducted a house party for them. The PFA members who attended found it a transforming experience: "Frankness and fellowship unsurpassed. Led by the team, the deepest personal experiences were given with the manifest sureness of reconciliation with the Father."[90] Fellowship lay at the heart of Christian identity.

The concept of fellowship in the churches was therefore understood first as a deep relationship with God, created through faith in Jesus and the power of the Spirit. Faith included an initial turning to Christ, but also an ongoing surrender of one's will to him. This passage of faith led to a unity "of nature and purpose" as a young person's life was directed by God.[91] The hymn of the PFA was written in 1931 by Miss McGuiness, a leader within the PFA, who expressed this theology of fellowship.

> We lift our hearts in praise, To our great God above, our voices loud we raise, To him in grateful love, In Fellowship with God adore, And unto him our praises pour
> The precious Word we read, Its message seek to know, Which meets our every need, And guides us here below, In Fellowship we seek to know, The way He wills for us to go
> Then from the world apart, A little space we go, As friends speak heart to heart, Our wants to Him we show, In Fellowship with God above, we know and shelter in His love.

---

87. For more on the Oxford Group, see Jarlert, *Oxford Group*; Randall, *Evangelical Experiences*.

88. The influence of the Oxford Group on the PFA is evident in the magazine *The Witness* which carried articles about the Oxford Group regularly from 1932 until 1939. See Randall, *Evangelical Experiences*, 252, 253, 258. In March 1935, Dr. T. Kagawa who was a leader of the Oxford Group in Japan came to Sydney and spoke to Christian youth about pacifism as well as the Group's work in Japan. *The* Witness, March 18, 1935. In June an Oxford Group "life-changers" team came from Western Australia to conduct a house party in NSW that was praised in *The Witness*, June 18, 1935.

89. For more on Frank Buchman see Boobbyer, *Spiritual Vision*.

90. *The Witness*, June 18, 1935.

91. "What is Fellowship?," *The Witness*, July 18, 1935. Jamieson, *Unique Fellowship*, 3–4.

> Then hear his voice divine, "Lo other sheep have I", That
> they might all be mine, I came on earth to die," In Fellowship we
> bear our part, And lay his last command to heart.[92]

As well as a deep relationship with God, fellowship was also understood as a new relationship with other young Christians. These relationships with Christians in youth groups were vital because being a Christian was not seen as a solitary pursuit.

> It is an active comradeship between men or women or both who unite with one another in a common worship, or battle for a common quest, or play their game for the honour of the team, or pool their separate thoughts into constructing or carrying into effect a single plan, or who simply share the needs and desires of a common humanity . . . In fellowship they pull together like a train tugging the wagon of life forward.[93]

Comradeship here has militaristic connotations, evoking the close relationships that were formed in war and necessary for victory. Christians were interdependent and had a shared purpose that united them. This comradeship was nurtured by small groups and discussions, and also by the social events of the peer group. House parties and camps, in particular, fostered these relationships. This can be seen in a history of Crusader camping in the Methodist Church.[94] The authors of this booklet surveyed young people who had participated in the annual camps since 1929. When asked why the camps were so successful, all respondents mentioned the word "fellowship." The authors asked what the campers meant by this, and the answer was: "being accepted", "being valued," "laughing," "trusting," "wholeness of life," "freedom," and "the atmosphere and being part of the wider church not just your local congregation."[95] Fellowship and relationship defined these young peoples' experience of the Christian life. As one camper wrote, "One learned Christianity by being accepted members of a caring fellowship."[96]

The third aspect of fellowship in addition to relationship with God and with other group members was a global one, the unity of young Christians throughout the world. The PFA, MYF, and CYF came to believe that the fellowships were part of a "movement" around the world that would work towards a new Christian civilization.

---

92. *The Witness*, June 18, 1931.
93. *The Witness*, December 18, 1931.
94. Anon., *Lo! Here Is Fellowship*.
95. Anon., *Lo! Here Is Fellowship*, 45.
96. Anon., *Lo! Here Is Fellowship*, 45.

> It is possible for the Fellowship Movement to lead the whole Church into a deeper and richer experience of Christ's fellowship, of peace and power, of conflict and conquest, until multitudes outside shall be gathered in and found rejoicing with us.[97]

They believed that young Christians needed to change the world: "The work thus divinely planned and shared is the building of a better world by a manhood and womanhood transformed and vitalized by the spirit of Christ."[98] They sought to change the world through creating Christian citizens that were politically engaged as well as Christian in their outlook and values. Fellowship members were encouraged through the curriculum to think through issues such as world peace, racism, and poverty. In 1936, members were encouraged to join the Legion of Christian Youth[99] and in 1939, a Christian Social Order Committee was founded in the PFA.[100]

Fellowship, therefore, came to be understood in a theological way. It was an attractive idea in the modernist society of the 1930s that had been influenced by psychology, and youth were becoming more influenced by peer groups for their values and worldview. This reflected a change throughout the Western world as fellowship groups appeared in the US and England. Sara Little has argued that in the US:

> The term fellowship picked up the importance increasingly attached to the peer group, as well as an understanding of the church as community.[101]

This context helps explain the development and popularity of the fellowship associations.

Witness

Peer ministry, therefore, involved a focus on the group itself and the relationships within the group. It also involved a concern for those outside the group. Members of fellowship groups were encouraged to recruit other members

---

97. *The Witness*, October 18, 1935.
98. *The Witness*, August 18, 1931.
99. *The Witness*, July 18, 1936.
100. Prentis, "Fellowship," 16. The belief that they were part of a worldwide movement was encouraged by the World Conference of Christian Youth held in Amsterdam in 1939. Representatives from Australian youth societies and fellowships attended as well as representatives from seventy other countries. "World Conference of Christian Youth," *The Methodist*, September 23, 1939, 1.
101. Little, "Youth Ministry," 19.

and to evangelize. In the more conservative groups, this meant witnessing to friends and trying to convince them to become Christians. In more liberal groups, this meant enlisting young people in service of God and in the building of a Christian nation. The two different strands of youth ministry both encouraged "witness" but meant different things by this term.

In the PFA fellowships, it was taught that adolescence was the time to make a "definite decision" about Christ. Once young people were attending the groups, they would hear teaching about the Christian life and have an opportunity to surrender to Christ at a camp or a decision day. For example, C. J. Price wrote that:

> . . . youth is the time when the big issues must be faced. It is during the Fellowship age that most people make the Great Decision. One of the reasons is that as we are growing up, our feelings are stirred by all that is finest and best—by fine men and women and by fine movements, and we seem compelled to take up some definite attitude towards them. In the same way Christ makes a bigger appeal as Lord and Master in a more personal sense than in our childhood, and our decision to follow him must be looked on as a very natural expression of our ideals, desires and determinations.[102]

The young people within groups were encouraged to invite their peers to social events where they could hear Christian messages and were exhorted to be "workers not shirkers."[103] Leaders within the movement continued to teach that "the *evangelism of the young* by the *young* is the ideal of such a movement."[104] There were campaigns organized to reach more youth. In 1930 there were two thousand PFA members, and they ambitiously began a "5,000 Campaign" to double the number.[105] In 1937 the PFA launched another drive called the "Bring them in" or BTI campaign. For this campaign, every fellowship member was to see themselves as a missionary.[106]

In the CEF too, evangelism was central to the aims of the movement. For example, at St. Phillip's Eastwood the expressed aim of the group was to attract other young people to the Christian community. The way this

---

102. *The Witness*, April 18, 1931. Price in this article also referred to the work of Starbuck et al. quoting them in claiming that the average age of conversion is 16.4 in girls and 14.8 in boys.

103. *The Witness*, September 18, 1934.

104. *The Witness*, January 18, 1927.

105. *The Witness*, February 18, 1930. This number was achieved by 1944, see White, *Challenge of the Years*, 246.

106. *The Witness*, June 18, 1937.

was done was largely through the fellowship tea on a Sunday afternoon. All were asked to BYOG (bring your own grub!) and at the tea, a speaker gave a talk.[107] At St. Paul's Wahroonga the rector stated that the fellowship was started by "the young people of the parish, to endeavour to rope in other young people in the Kingdom of God" by presenting a "happy, healthy Christianity."[108] Another way that fellowships sought to evangelize friends was by inviting them to house parties. It was expected that fun, friendships, and evangelistic talks could change people's lives.

Youth Leadership

The fellowships also encouraged leadership and ownership by the young people themselves. In many groups, the young curate or a university student was given the leadership of the group (this role was usually reserved for a young man).[109] The group was to be self-directing, with committees to organize the services, activities and games, and both men and women were involved in active leadership.[110] The study circle or discussion on a Sunday morning used the cooperative or "yarn method." All the members were to share ideas and ask questions while the leader would supplement and guide.[111] It was hoped that discussion would strengthen the peer group and make the Bible relevant to the lives of young people.

There were significant older leaders within the fellowship associations. In the PFA, there was a travelling secretary and a council who ran the national organization. In the CEF, there were significant curates such as W. G. Coughlan and Alan Begbie. These "veterans" gave a stability to the movement, but at the local level, it was the young people themselves who made decisions and led the groups. Jamieson advised the youth not to dismiss that which older members could bring:

> Keep the younger and the older working together with mutual understanding. The movement specially needs the viewpoint of youth. It also needs what footholders call a "stiffening of

---

107. The speakers were at times eminent Sydney Anglican preachers, such as Dr. Barton Babbage, Dr. Paul White, and Rev. T. C. Hammond, the Principal of Moore College, so they were not lightweight affairs. Daniels and Mitchell, "St Phillip's Anglican," 132.

108. Nobbs, *God's Building*, 131.

109. Many of the young ordinands who went to Moore College developed their skills in speaking and administration in their local fellowship group. For example, at St. Paul's Chatswood. Hicks, *City on a Hill*, 128.

110. Blackwood and Walton, *Our Greatest Asset*, 81.

111. Blackwood and Walton, *Our Greatest Asset*, 92.

veterans." Give plenty of big jobs to the young, but retain in full activity your older members.[112]

As well as leading in the actual fellowship group, members were also encouraged to lead outside the group in different ministries. At St. Paul's Chatswood, fellowship members were encouraged to disciple those younger than themselves. In an effort to retain the fourteen-year-olds who were confirmed, fellowship members were assigned to individual confirmees to look out for and encourage them.[113] In the Bankstown PFA in 1931, 90 percent of the Sunday school staff were PFA members.[114]

The leadership of young people was also encouraged through training programs. As noted above, in 1931, the Presbyterian Welfare of Youth Department established a teacher and leader training course for fellowship leaders. The course involved a series of lectures on a weeknight including some psychological theory about child development and adolescence, some basic teaching techniques, a study of the Old and New Testaments, how to respond to personal and social problems, and ideas for how to develop good weeknight programs.[115]

This strong youth leadership in the fellowship groups reflected the wider world youth movement which embraced peer ministry and leadership by youth. Mark Senter has written of this new cycle of youth ministry in the US, a movement away from the youth society to the youth fellowship.

> Much more peer-oriented, youth fellowships drew their leadership from fellow high school students, while adults served as sponsors. Gone were the memorization of Scripture and catechism; present were discussions and programs prepared by a rotated leadership. Pioneered by the Congregational City Church in 1936, youth fellowships became the norm of the early days of the third cycle of youth ministry.[116]

Senter writes about the US, but a similar change can also be seen in England in the 1930s. In the Church of England, for example, fellowship groups called the Anglican Young Person's Association were formed. In these groups the parish priest retained control, but the responsibility for leadership fell on members.[117]

112. *The Witness*, February 18, 1936.
113. Hicks, *City on a Hill*, 128.
114. *The Witness*, April 18, 1931.
115. *The Witness*, May 18, 1931.
116. Senter, *When God Shows Up*, 132.
117. Anon., *Youth's Job*, 9–10.

Coeducational

As well as encouraging youth leadership, a distinctive characteristic of the fellowship groups is that they were coeducational, and leadership by young people was extended to young women. In the 1930s there was a fear about the changing relationships between the sexes and the challenge to traditional views of sexual behaviour. More opportunities for women were opening up in occupations outside of the home, as shopgirls, in factories, as nurses, and teachers. This led to a greater appreciation of the equality of men and women and their shared humanity.

> No longer are there two races, male and female, each living separate lives and having separate interests, but they are rapidly becoming one with common interests, common occupations, and common lives. This development involves the acceptance of real equality, greatly helped by co-education.[118]

The response of the fellowship groups to these fears about the sexualized society and the changed relationships between the sexes was to encourage close relationships and coeducation, though also to warn about the dangers of sex. The idea of fellowship included a warm relationship between the sexes, but with certain boundaries enforced.

Young women were encouraged by the fellowship movement to serve alongside the men. They were invited to recognize the wider role and the responsibility they now had to be an influence for good in the world based on their opportunities and gifts.

> Today, wider opportunities are opening to her to do all kinds of practical work in fields that were closed to her in the past. "Woman has gone over the parapet," she has left forever the protections and limitations of her shielded life. New powers are being placed in her hands, new perils are around her feet.[119]

In the PFA, Jamieson taught that men and women must unite together and recognize their "active comradeship" and shared humanity and he exhorted fellowship members to "Encourage girls and young men to work together and bear responsibility together in the spiritual tasks of the kingdom. Each needs the other in religious life."[120] Not only were the sexes brought together in discussion and social activities, women were also expected to lead. In Australia, in both the PFA and CEF fellowships women were encouraged to

---

118. Clover, *Youth Fellowship Handbook*, 31.
119. Parry, *Girls on the Highway*, 8.
120. *The Witness*, February 18, 1936.

take an active leadership role on committees, in leading meetings and discussions.[121] The only role restricted to men was the leader of the fellowship group, though this was by convention rather than any written rule.

Fellowship groups also provided a place to find a romantic partner who would share the same Christian and cultural values. The social events provided a context for friendships with the opposite sex to develop that could become romantic. Close relationships between the sexes were to be encouraged as natural and healthy.[122] The fellowship was seen by some adults as a legitimate "mating" association. For example, in a Youth Fellowship Handbook, it was admitted that:

> We need to cultivate a true comradeship between young men and women that each might find his or her natural desire for friendship with the other sex fulfilled with members of the same department. If two young people have worshipped together, there is not much danger from a walk together; but if they pick up a stranger from a park or street, there is a grave risk. Each forms an ideal of the other sex from this first contact in the mating period.[123]

The fellowship groups sought to build a comradeship between men and women, but at the same time protect them from sexual temptation. It was to be a "safe place" where a young person could find a spouse.

The fellowships, therefore, responded to the new context by affirming more equal relationships between men and women as comrades with a shared goal and opportunity to lead. They emphasized the significance of relationships and the need men and women have for each other. The fellowship was a safe place to find a spouse as men and women came to know each other through discussions and social events, by leading and serving together.

Conclusion

Denominational youth ministry embraced a new model in the 1930s that was similar to methods used within the university and schools ministry: the fellowship group. The churches were responding to social forces including war, the Depression, and the development of secondary education. These

---

121. Parry, *Girls on the Highway*, 124. For example, in the Chatswood fellowship, the leaders were both men and women. Hicks, *City on a Hill*, 124.

122. Blackwood and Walton, *Our Greatest Asset*, 80.

123. Clover, *Youth Fellowship Handbook*, 30.

forces had led to a great fear that there was a "youth problem" and that atheist ideologies and sexual temptation were threatening the transmission of faith to the next generation. The fellowships were in part a response to this fear and a desire to retain and reach youth in the modern world.

The fellowships were influenced by two strands of theology that responded to this "crisis of civilization." The first was liberal evangelicalism. Those influenced by this theology sought to bring young people together to build their Christian character, their allegiance to the church, and to encourage them to be part of a worldwide movement of youth. They believed that youth were the "hope of the future" to build a Christian civilization. The other strand was the conservative evangelical strand. Many fellowships began as an evangelistic outreach, "youth to youth." The fellowship teas and house parties were particularly aimed at the outsider. In the PFA there was a unity between the two strands. Within the Church of England, however, there was conflict which was eventually resolved as the conservative mindset became predominant.

The fellowships nurtured mixed peer groups of men and women, the leadership of young people, and close relationships. The relational model of youth ministry began to grow in popularity over the institutional. The old educational methodology of the Foursquare was being replaced by the idea of fellowship. This was true in both strands as it spoke to the modern world and a concern for deep relationships. The fellowships taught that Christianity was not merely subscribing to certain beliefs, but warm relationship with God and other Christians.

6

Challenges to the New Methodology
Heterodox Theology and World War II

AT THE END OF the 1930s, the fear of a "youth problem" had progressed to a wholesale fear of a "crisis of civilization." The years of depression and the rising tide of ideologies such as socialism and fascism had created social unrest, and young people seemed to be rejecting the Christian values and norms of their parents. In 1939, fears of crisis were realized in the declaration of war, and Australia immediately declared their military support for the allies to protect the values of Christian civilization. Harold McCracken at the Crusader Union Annual Meeting in 1937 expressed this sense of crisis.

> The world was trembling on the verge of a great crisis. Events in Spain, the militant spirit in Europe, where Hitler and Mussolini commanded the blind faith of millions, and the feeling of unrest generally, all pointed to this. The only thing that could save the world was a great spiritual revival.[1]

There was an almost apocalyptic sense of global catastrophe.

Broadly speaking, leaders of youth ministry responded in one of two ways to this crisis. The more conservative response was to pray for spiritual revival and boost outreach, particularly to the young generation. Conservative leaders sought to enlist young Christians in more urgent witness to their friends and encourage them to stop being so focused on "worldly" affairs. The more liberal evangelical response was to enlist young Christians to serve through social activism and to join a worldwide

---

1. "Spiritual Revival Needed," *Sydney Morning Herald*, July 17, 1937, 12.

movement. They attempted to build a civilization based on Christian principles that would bring healing to the world.² Between these two poles, there were also those who sought to encourage young people to evangelize *and* to be involved in social action.

For the youth ministries that had been established in Australia in the 1930s, the war years were challenging. In the university and schools ministry, a heterodox theological strain developed among some key young leaders. This challenged the model of youth-led ministries as adults felt compelled to step into discipline and guide the movements. As well as heterodox theology, World War II challenged the model of leadership after 1941, as many young leaders enlisted or were involved in the war effort at home, so they were not available to serve in youth organizations. During the war, churches began to prepare for postwar reconstruction and to direct resources to youth ministries. In the ministries deeply influenced by liberal evangelical theology, this was a time of transition. Classic liberal theology was characterized by idealism about building the kingdom of God on earth: a "social gospel." The reality of human evil demonstrated by World War II undermined this idealism. Neoorthodox theology influenced some young leaders, and in the PFA there was a coup to replace the ageing leaders of the previous generation. In the more conservative ministries, youth leaders renewed their call for young people to witness and evangelize their friends.

Heterodox Theology

One of the challenges to youth ministries in the war years was the development of a particular form of heterodox theology among some of the leaders in the Evangelical Union, the Crusader Union, and the Scripture Union. This theology focused on a doctrine of "entire sanctification" or "sinless perfectionism." It has been the argument of this study that a large part of the success of the new youth ministry approach was the initiative and leadership of the young people themselves. Young leaders were enthusiastic, idealistic, and committed to self-sacrifice. However, when these same qualities were combined with heterodox theology, they became destructive. They created leaders who were unwilling to take advice or guidance from older mentors and were desperate to live a holy life dedicated to the Lord. But this desire became a force of judgment and exclusion of others who did not seem as

---

2. Treloar argues that a motivating force behind the goals of evangelicals at this time was their sense that there was an opportunity to regain the cultural authority they felt they had lost in the early decades of the twentieth century. Treloar, *Disruption of Evangelicalism*, 174.

spiritual. The close fellowship ties they formed led to a group that became inward focused and exclusive of others. The close relationships between these men and women became distorted and traditional Christian moral boundaries were crossed. In the university and schools ministries, the lack of denominational allegiance had given students freedom, but also failed to create the theological checks and balances provided by prayer books, liturgy, and ordained authority figures. The development of this heterodox theology displayed the need in the student movement for elders who could step in to guide, correct, and mentor when needed.

The sinless perfection movement grew out of a Pietist strain of evangelical faith shaped by Keswick teaching. Keswick holiness conventions began in 1875 in the Lakes District when thousands of evangelicals gathered to be inspired by the Christian teaching. The Keswick teaching was founded on the premise that sanctification, like justification, could be attained through faith, not works.[3] Holiness was obtained through consecration, that is, surrendering one's will to the will of God. At Keswick, speakers taught that through consecration, it was possible to experience the "higher life" or "victorious life." This life would be characterized by wonderful self-sacrificial service and obedience. This teaching inspired many young people to missionary work and other Christian vocations, most famously C. T. Studd and the Cambridge Seven.[4] Keswick holiness teaching understood "the Word of God (to teach) that the *normal* Christian walk is one of sustained victory over known sin."[5] But they denied that entire sanctification was possible.[6] They believed that sin will always be present in a believer's life and there will always be a struggle until the resurrection.[7]

This kind of Keswick holiness was made popular in Australia by George Grubb, by the holiness conventions, and by a series of popular Christian writers. George Grubb was a Keswick evangelist who visited Australia in

---

3. Randall, *Evangelical Experiences*, 14. For more on Keswick see Bebbington, *Evangelicalism in Modern Britain*, 151–80 and Randall, *Evangelical Experiences*, 14–45.

4. Howard Guinness wrote that he read Norman Grubb's biography of Studd in the time he was in Australia. It "stirred me deeply and helped me to put prayer more central and live a little more dangerously." Guinness, "Letter No. 8, January 26, 1934," IVF Archives, Box 8, File 1, Samuel Marsden Archives. In this biography, Grubb describes Studd's experience of consecration after reading *The Christian's Secret of a Happy Life* by Hannah Whitall Smith. In this consecration, he was able to give up an illustrious career in cricket and a sizable fortune to become a missionary for the rest of his life.

5. Griffith Thomas, "Literature of Keswick," 224.

6. See Randall, *Evangelical Experiences*, 14 and Deane, "New Evangelical Movements," 21.

7. For example, Figgis, "Some Characteristics," 107.

1891/92.⁸ In response to his visit, Margaret Young began a gathering at her house at Katoomba each year in January during the summer holidays. This gathering evolved into the Katoomba Convention, an annual spiritual clinic for the "deepening of the Christian life."⁹ There were times when the teaching on holiness at the convention seemed to imply entire sanctification. For example, in 1936 Norman Deck spoke on Romans 6 as a "culmination of Paul's treatise of victory over indwelling sin."¹⁰

The Katoomba Convention was a highlight for student leaders and each year a Crusaders and IVF group organized a house party alongside the convention. As well as the conventions, young leaders were influenced by books that contained holiness teaching.¹¹ Many read the classic works of holiness such *The Christian's Secret of a Happy Life* (1875) by Hannah Whitall Smith,¹² the works of Andrew Murray including *Absolute Surrender* (1895) and *The Deeper Christian Life* (1895), the devotional book by Oswald Chambers, *My Utmost for His Highest* (1924),¹³ and the biography by Norman Grubb, *C. T. Studd: Missionary and Pioneer* (1933).

In the 1930s, a new strain of Methodist holiness teaching also influenced some student leaders including Lindsay Grant, one of the original EU leaders who would become the leader of the sinless perfection movement.¹⁴ This teaching was contained in the writing of Paget Wilkes: *The Dynamic of Service* (1924) and *Sanctification* (1931). These books and the Japanese Evangelistic Band that Wilkes founded espoused a view of holiness that emphasized the victory of the new man over the old. The result of this victory was the possibility of life free from the inward pollution of sin, or as Wilkes explained, "the glorious doctrine of entire sanctification."¹⁵

The Oxford Group would also have an influence on the formation of the sinless perfection movement. It was argued in chapter three that

---

8. Prominent clergymen were converted at this mission including R. B. S. Hammond and H. S. Begbie. Braga, *Century Preaching*, 8.

9. For an analysis of the impact of Keswick and the conventions on Australian evangelicalism see Orchard and Briggs, *Sunday School Movement*, 465–504.

10. Parker, "Fundamentalism," 483.

11. Arthur Deane argued that the holiness movement, Keswick, and the holiness writings were influential particularly in the youth societies in Australia. See Deane, "New Evangelical Movements."

12. This book was given to Lindsay Grant by his mother when he was a teenager. Millikan, *Imperfect Company*, 157.

13. For example, Allan Bryson claimed that "required reading" for students in the EU in the 1930s included *My Utmost for his Highest* and the works of Andrew Murray. Allan Bryson interview.

14. Millikan, *Imperfect Company*, 71, 72, 115. Allan and Elsie Bryson interview.

15. Quoted in Randall, *Evangelical Experiences*, 89.

Howard Guinness had admired the group and its four absolutes: absolute honesty, purity, unselfishness, and love. He also valued the emphasis on absolute surrender of the heart and will—"Everything or nothing!"—and the close fellowship nurtured through the confession of sin and small groups.[16] Lindsay Grant was similarly attracted to the uncompromising ideals and mutual confession in the Oxford Group.[17]

The ideals of the holiness movement and the Oxford Group appealed to young Christians. The idealism of seeking to do "my utmost for his highest" was empowering, implying one could live a "higher life" rather than the commonplace, ordinary Christian life. Allan Bryson, who was involved in the EU at the time, explained:

> The fertile soil is there because you have a crowd of devoted young Christians all straining forward in their Christian pilgrimage. Holiness, that's what they want, and deliverance from temptation and they want the victorious Christian life.[18]

Those influenced spoke of the attraction of jettisoning careers and doing great things for the Lord. They sang hymns with words like, "I'm pressing on the upward way, new heights I'm gaining every day."[19]

The story of the sinless perfection movement in the EU has been told before, but it merits revisiting to understand how the movement went on to spread to the different youth movements through the influence of the young leaders involved.[20] The key leaders of the early sinless perfection movement were Lindsay Grant and Alice Smith. Grant was President of the EU in 1933[21] and in 1938 he was appointed travelling secretary for the IVF (in 1938 the word Christian was dropped from IVCF and it became the IVF) and Crusader Union, and co-opted on the committee of the EU. He was a

---

16. Guinness, "Letter to Prayer Helpers," Letter No. 4, 1932, IVF Archives.

17. "Win Dunkley Letter to Margaret Lamb," August 12, 1990 and Marjorie Hercus interview. Part of the influence must have been through Lindsay's cousin Stafford Young who had been converted after a visit by Frank Buchman (the founder of the Oxford Group) to Australia in 1924/1925. Millikan, *Imperfect Company*, 54.

18. Allan Bryson interview.

19. Donald Robinson interview.

20. Piggin, *Spirit, Word and World*, 105–24; Millikan, *Imperfect Company*.

21. He continued to be a leader within the EU and then IVF. He went on tour around Australia and New Zealand with Howard Guinness in 1933/34, and was seen by Guinness as a future leader of the student ministry. He was the first Australian General Secretary of the Australian movement, the Inter Varsity Christian Fellowship or IVCF in 1936, and Vice President of the EU in 1937. "SUEU Committee Minutes," February 6, 1933, Box 309, Minute Books 1930–1946, Sydney University Archives.

compelling person, with athletic honors (like Paul White)[22] but also part of a distinguished Christian family. His family had been involved in pioneering missionary work, as well as the founding of the Crusader Union and Open Air Campaigners. Alice Smith was also an excellent leader who had been in the PFA before she came to university. She was the prayer and missionary secretary of the EU in 1931, on the committee in 1935, and the women's travelling secretary for Crusaders and IVF in 1938. She was a dynamic leader with whom others found it hard to disagree. Jean Porter who was a friend and fellow early EU leader remarked that "if Alice said white was black, or black was white, then you'd believe it."[23]

As a young man, Lindsay was concerned for the "things of the spirit" and "was restless for the *experience* of Christian faith."[24] Yet it wasn't until late 1937 and early 1938 that a more developed sinless perfection doctrine became apparent in Grant's teaching and Bible studies, influenced by friends and family.[25] Ronald Grant (Lindsay's brother) and Alan Neill were missionaries with South Sea Evangelical Mission (SSEM) in the Solomon Islands. There they experienced a revival amongst the indigenous people where many confessed sins publicly and were released from bondage to practices such as chewing betel nut to ward off evil spirits.[26] In March 1938, Grant and Neill were asked to resign from the SSEM because of their entire sanctification views.[27] But it seems that they influenced other members of the Grant family as well as their cousins the Decks,[28] and Scripture Union (SU) leader Heather Drummond.

The sinless perfectionism expounded by Lindsay Grant took the teaching of the holiness movement to an extreme. He and other leaders taught that not only could one conquer sin within one's life, it was also possible to be entirely free from indwelling sin, that is, to experience entire sanctification. They appealed to Scriptures such as Romans 6 to argue that because of the atoning death of Jesus a Christian is dead to sin, as long as he/she completely surrenders. They claimed that Romans 7 was not about the Christian's ongoing struggle with sin, but rather described

22. Marcus Loane interview.
23. Jean Porter interview.
24. Millikan, *Imperfect Company*, 65.
25. Millikan, *Imperfect Company*, 75.
26. Alison and Ken Griffiths interview.
27. Piggin, *Spirit, Word and World*, 111. They were interviewed by Dr. Northcote Deck and their views found to be incompatible with the SSEM.
28. Humphrey Deck and Philip Deck were supporters of Grant at the EU and part of the sinless perfection group in the election campaign in 1938. Alwyn Prescott interview.

a backsliding Christian falling back to a pre-consecration experience.[29] Other favorite verses were 1 John 3:10, "he who is born of God does not sin," and 1 John 1:7, "If we walk in the light, as He is in the light, we have fellowship with one another, and the blood of Jesus, his Son, cleanses us from all sin." They argued that those in the light had no indwelling sin and all impulses were therefore of the Holy Spirit.[30] Lindsay Grant often stressed that a Christian should "walk in the light." This was a key phrase, by which he meant a Christian should confess their sin, accept the teaching of sinless perfectionism, and be subordinate to his leadership.[31]

The CSSM/SU (Children's Special Service Mission and Scripture Union) moved quickly to put a stop to the sinless perfection teaching and its dissemination by the staff worker Heather Drummond. Drummond was appointed in 1934, responsible for the girls' work in high schools and the formation of the Teachers Christian Fellowship (TCF).[32] She had been converted through friends in the Grant and Deck families[33] and had been a prominent founding member of the EU, along with Alice Smith and Paul White.[34] She was an effective and well-loved leader, earnest and wholehearted, and under her, the girls' work in high schools was flourishing. In 1938 she began teaching entire sanctification at ISCF camps and in school groups. Win Dunkley remembered an ISCF camp in 1938 where she and her friend felt unable to pray because of the teaching and attitudes of those who supported Heather: "it shut us out."[35] In 1939, when Win was a teacher

---

29. For example, Alan Neill wrote an article about Romans 6–8 and argued that in Romans 7:24: "This is where we come to the point of controversy. Is there a complete deliverance from that conflict by an act of God, or must this war go on until death? Does this conflict represent God's highest, or is it merely a transitional stage? No, it is not God's highest—God has a complete and absolute deliverance from sin, not merely a partial one . . . The blood of Jesus Christ can-not only cleanse from the guilt of sin, but take away *all* sin in our life." Neill, "Reality of Entire Sanctification," *The Edifier*, June 10, 1938, 5.

30. Alwyn Prescott interview.

31. Millikan, *Imperfect Company*, 176. The phrase "walking in the light" was also an important one in the revivals in the Solomons and East Africa that encouraged repentance and the public confession of sin to live a "victorious life." See Reed, *Walking in the Light*.

32. "Scripture Union and CSSM Council Minutes," December 4, 1934, Scripture Union NSW Archives.

33. Win Dunkley interview.

34. "Sydney University Bible League Members 1928–1929," Box 309, EU Minute Books 1930–1936, Sydney University Archives.

35. Win Dunkley interview.

at Sydney Girls' High, she recalled Heather visiting the school group and teaching sinless perfectionism.[36]

At the end of 1938, Drummond was interviewed by the SU and CSSM council about her views on "eradication" teaching.[37] To their dismay, she continued to associate freely with those who held such views, even taking her annual leave "at the place where sinless perfectionist teaching emanated."[38] In October 1939, the council wrote a letter to the IVF, Crusader Union, and the EU stating that it publicly disassociated itself from sinless perfectionism.[39] Heather Drummond was spoken to by members of the council and when she refused to renounce her views, Archdeacon Robinson was called in to ask her to step down.[40]

In the Crusader Union, a similar pattern occurred. One of the sinless perfection leaders, Alice Smith, had given up her teaching job to become the travelling secretary for the girls' work.[41] Her leadership, characterized by a "dynamism" and "rallying verve"[42] had led to real advances in the work. Alice Smith was a close friend of the Grant and Deck families and in 1938 she began to teach sinless perfectionism in her school groups and camps. Marjorie Hercus recalled leading on a Crusader camp where Alice was in charge. Leaders took girls into bedrooms to talk about sinless perfection teachings in secret: "the proselytising started, they were after school children." On one occasion, when Marjorie came to the door there was a "deathly hush . . . I knew I wasn't wanted."[43] Alice's activities came to the attention of the council through a teacher at SCEGGS who threatened to go to her school principal if nothing was done to stop it.[44]

---

36. Win Dunkley interview.

37. "Scripture Union and CSSM Council Minutes," December 6, 1938, Scripture Union NSW Archives.

38. "Scripture Union and CSSM Council Minutes," March 7, 1939, Scripture Union NSW Archives. Probably with Ronald Grant and Alan Neill in Melbourne. Win Dunkley interview.

39. "Scripture Union and CSSM Council Minutes," October 10, 1939, Scripture Union NSW Archives.

40. "Scripture Union and CSSM Council Minutes," October 30, 1939, Scripture Union NSW Archives.

41. "Annual Report of the Girls' Division NSW Crusader Union, 1938," Crusader Union NSW Archives.

42. Thornton, "Crusader Union of NSW," 54.

43. Marjorie Hercus interview.

44. Alan and Elsie Bryson interview.

The Crusader Council was split between the sinless perfectionists and those who opposed them.[45] In September 1939, Lindsay Grant suggested to the council that Alan Neil should be the speaker at the Crusader Union Annual Conference, which led to a heated discussion about sinless perfectionism.[46] In October 1939, David Grant (the chair of the boys' division), Philip Deck, and Lindsay Grant were asked to give an undertaking not to teach their views as they were dividing the movement. They refused and consequently were asked to leave the movement of which they were founding members. They were very hurt.[47] This conflict divided families. Roger Deck and Brian Deck took a stand against their brother and cousins.[48] The older generation came back into the council and committees to deal with the conflict, in particular, Mrs. Holt and Mrs. Nicholson (wife of the eminent J. B. Nicholson who had invited Guinness to Australia).

In the Girls' Division Committee, Mrs. Nicholson dealt with the sinless perfection issue quickly and firmly. In October 1939, Alice Smith was asked to resign because of the "division and dissatisfaction" the teaching of entire sanctification was causing.[49] Jean Gardiner and Isabel Sawkins (who had been on the first EU executive with Lindsay Grant in 1934) were also asked to resign.[50] Helen Macbeth, who was also suspected of favoring sinless perfection teaching, was asked by Mrs. Nicholson not to take any more school meetings until she was clear where she stood on the issue. The leadership of the movement was now firmly in the hands of those who opposed sinless perfectionism, though there were still schoolgirls with sinless perfection views.[51] Through a decisive response, particularly

---

45. For example, Roger and Brian Deck were anti sinless perfectionism, and Humphrey and Philip Deck were pro. Marcus Loane interview.

46. "Crusader Union of NSW Council Meeting Minutes," September 27, 1939, Crusader Union NSW Archives.

47. Marjorie Hercus interview.

48. Alwyn Prescott interview.

49. "Girls' Division NSW Crusader Union Minutes," October 1939, Crusader Union NSW Archives.

50. "Girls' Division NSW Crusader Union Minutes," October 1939, Crusader Union NSW Archives.

51. In the Girls' Division minutes of February 1940, it was reported that some of the Crusader girls at Abbotsleigh were not enthusiastic about inviting outsiders to their meetings because of their belief in entire sanctification. There was also a letter from a DRM (Dining Room Meeting) host to the council who no longer wanted to invite Crusader girls to her house who held to a sinless perfection view. The council answered that she should not antagonize these girls by excluding them, but that someone on the council would ask them to keep their views to themselves. "Girls' Division NSW Crusader Union Minutes," February 1940, Crusader Union NSW Archives.

by older mentors in the CSSM/SU and Crusader Union, the sinless perfection influence was eradicated.[52]

One of the impacts of the sinless perfection movement was a realization that young leaders were vulnerable to charismatic unorthodox teachers and that they needed older adults to help guide them. In 1940, Dr. John Laird, who was the General Secretary of the Crusader Union in New Zealand, was invited to come to Australia and advise the Crusader committee. He claimed that the Crusader Union movement had passed through three stages of leadership. In the first stage, groups of students were led by indigenous leaders. In the second, senior "advisor-uncles" had come to lead the movement. He argued that now was the time for adults to exercise a definite leadership in the councils and in school groups.[53] These leaders could target one or two boys and train them up for later service in Crusaders and the church.[54] Laird's encouragement of more adult leadership was probably because of the sinless perfection movement. In the same report, he encouraged a more systematic study of the Bible rather than single verses and "study book padding," because without a depth of biblical understanding, "People fall into false cults because they are untaught as to what the Bible says . . . Their minds are a vacuum and in rushes 'Judge' Rutherford, Mary Baker Eddy . . ."[55] Laird believed that young people were vulnerable to heresy and needed good teaching and guidance.

In the EU, it was more difficult to isolate the teaching and ensure that it did not permeate the movement. Unlike the CSSM/SU and Crusader Union, there were no older members of councils who provided oversight and guidance when needed. The IVF Council was made up of new graduates and students and included Lindsay Grant and Alice Smith. As travelling secretary,

---

52. There *was* one more incident involving sinless perfection teaching after 1940. Although Alice Smith resigned in 1939, in 1946 she wanted to again be involved in the Crusader movement. The committee decided to allow her to be a team leader as long as she promised not to promulgate her views. "Crusader Union of NSW Council Meeting Minutes," October 2, 1946, Crusader Union NSW Archives. A year later, Mrs. Nicholson was sent to speak to Alice and ask her to resign again, presumably for actively teaching sinless perfection. "Crusader Union of NSW Council Meeting Minutes," December 11, 1947, Crusader Union NSW Archives.

53. By this he meant that adults were to be members of the councils and help lead and direct school groups, guiding and mentoring young leaders. This model continues in the Crusader Union today.

54. "Notes on the Conference with Committee," February 8, 1940, Crusader Union NSW Archives.

55. "Notes on the Conference with Committee," February 8, 1940, Crusader Union NSW Archives.
Judge Rutherford was a President of the Jehovah's Witnesses and Mary Baker Eddy the founder of Christian Science.

Grant spent a lot of time with the EU at Sydney University and attended executive meetings, as did Smith. In the late 1930s, Smith, Grant and others who supported sinless perfectionism sought to persuade others to join them. Elsie Bryson recalled a conversation with Alice Smith, her great friend, on the way to a Crusader meeting at Abbotsleigh. Alice told Elsie that she should be part of the sinless perfection group and go along with the teaching. When Elsie refused, Alice said she did not want to argue: "There's no point in trying to discuss it because one is the language of the head and the other is the language of the heart." Elsie believed "this was a warning to me that this was something that just wasn't right."[56]

When it came to the election of the new EU executive at the end of 1939, Grant recommended a group of candidates who agreed with his teaching. The election was in October, in the same month that conflict was at its greatest in the other youth movements, and some of the student leaders of the EU were very concerned. Harvey Carey and Alwyn Prescott ran for president and secretary against sinless perfection candidates, Humphrey Deck and Philip Deck. Carey and Prescott won, but the new committee was mixed, with two in favor of the sinless perfection doctrine, three opposed, and two neutral.[57] At the end of 1940, another election settled the direction of the EU and ended the leadership of the sinless perfectionists. This time, there was a resounding victory for the conservative, orthodox candidates over those who held the contentious doctrine. John Hercus, a formidable leader and thinker, was elected president and Donald Robinson, secretary.[58]

Sinless perfectionism was defeated in the Sydney University EU, but Lindsay Grant and Alice Smith were still influential on the IVF council. In response, Hercus wrote to the IVF in 1940 stating that the EU had lost confidence in the committee and would not support an IVF annual conference.[59] It was proposed that a conference be held in January 1941 in order to discuss sinless perfectionism once and for all and to deal with disunity in the student movement. At this meeting, it was decided that the movement could live with such differences amongst the members as long as they focused on what united them and did not propagate sinless perfection teaching.[60]

56. Allan and Elsie Bryson interview.
57. "SUEU Executive Minutes," October 13, 1939, Samuel Marsden Archives.
58. "Sydney University EU Minute Book," September 18, 25, 1940, Samuel Marsden Archives.
59. "SUEU Executive Minutes," October 14, 1940, Samuel Marsden Archives.
60. Donald Robinson interview.

In 1941, Paul White returned to Australia from the mission field and was keen to support the ministry of the EU and Crusader Union again.[61] After hearing Lindsay Grant speak at an EU meeting, he confronted him about his understanding of the Christian's relationship with Christ. "You cast doubt on our knowing Christ. WE *do* know. What more do we need?" Grant answered, "But this is what we are striving for in the whole of life." At this moment White realized that they were talking about different theologies and that despite his long friendship with Grant, he was determined to oppose him.[62] White also believed that the EU was no longer the outward-focused group it had been when he left for mission in Africa, because of the impact of the sinless perfectionists.[63] The journalist David Millikan, who spent time interviewing Lindsay Grant, argues that White's charismatic leadership and persuasion put an end to the progress of the sinless perfection movement in the IVF.[64] White was elected General Secretary in 1943 and travelling secretary for the IVF at the end of 1944. Lindsay Grant left the executive committee to join the army, and at the end of 1945, Alice Smith left the IVF too.[65] Excluded from the mainstream church, Grant and a young woman called Del Agnew took the members of the sinless perfection group and established a cultlike fellowship that was called Tinker Tailor. For decades they operated from a large house in Burwood.

What can the sinless perfection incident teach us about the methodology of youth ministry that had developed in the 1930s, and particularly its strengths and weaknesses? A strength of the EU and schools ministry was its charismatic young leaders. These leaders were empowered to take initiative and were confident in their abilities and their spiritual competence. This strength became a weakness when young leaders would not accept guidance and were not kept accountable by denominational loyalty and authorities, as they could easily get caught up in heterodox theology. In the Crusader Union and CSSM/SU, unlike the EU, this vulnerability was mitigated by older mentors. In the schools ministry, there were older patrons such as the Nicholsons, Mrs. Holt, and Archdeacon Robinson, who worked as "Aunties and Uncles" with the students and were able to encourage and step in when needed. These were the ones who persuaded those with sinless perfection views to either renounce them or leave. This was more difficult in the EU. Alice Smith and

---

61. Paul was one of the contemporaries of Lindsay Grant whom Guinness had mentored.

62. Millikan, *Imperfect Company*, 76. From an interview with Paul White.

63. Millikan, *Imperfect Company*, 80.

64. Millikan, *Imperfect Company*, 80.

65. Millikan, *Imperfect Company*, 80.

Lindsay Grant believed that they had a "hotline" to God, a superior spiritual knowledge.[66] Although T. C. Hammond (the Principal of Moore Theological College) was something of an elder in the EU and well respected, he had no authority over it. He did his best to convince the students that they were wrong, and had them over to his home for a squash on Saturday night to discuss sinless perfection.[67] But it was easy for Grant to veer away from the influence of Hammond and ignore him.[68]

A great strength of the youth ministry had been the very strong peer groups and fellowship ties that were formed. These same strengths could also manifest as difficulties in the face of heterodox theology. The close ties of family and friendship were used by the sinless perfectionists to pressure others to accept their teachings. For instance, Alan Bryson had spent much time at the Grant household as a child while his parents were on the mission field and Lindsay Grant was his closest friend. In 1939, Bryson had a "blazing row" with Grant on the roof of Sydney Hospital. Bryson claimed that Grant ". . . put his finger on me and said it was time that I submitted to his leadership and came along and joined their coterie."[69] When Bryson refused, Grant was enraged and that was the end of their friendship. The peer group became a form of rigid exclusion and would include only those who had special knowledge and were determined to be "spiritual" (like a gnostic sect).[70] These people were flattered by being the "in-crowd," and believed that some Christians were special, "a cut above the rest."[71] One reason the sinless perfection controversy was so painful was because close friendships were broken and families were torn apart. This exclusive mentality for a time caused the EU to lose its outward focus and concern for witness.

Finally, while the interdenominational nature of the university and schools ministry led to energy and flexibility, it too could prove a weakness. There is little evidence of sinless perfection teaching affecting denominational fellowship groups. The one exception was in the Young Peoples' Fellowship at St. Paul's Chatswood when the young people debated whether one could attain perfect holiness in this life. The Reverend R. C. M. Long wrote an article in the fellowship magazine rejecting the possibility of this doctrine (in Spring 1939) and the topic ceased to be a source of debate amongst the

---

66. "Letter from Alan Bryson to Margaret Lamb," December 12, 1989.
67. Donald Robinson interview.
68. Piggin, *Spirit, Word and World*, 120.
69. Alan Bryson interview.
70. Alwyn Prescott interview.
71. Alan and Elsie Bryson interview.

young people.⁷² Piggin argues that to understand Grant, one must appreciate his lack of accountability to denominational structures. His family was associated with the Brethren church, the Baptist Church, and the Church of England, and Grant himself never seemed to stick with one denomination. Piggin argues that Grant's "personal spiritual liberty free of denominational discipline" was a characteristic which led him into trouble.⁷³

The Loss of Leaders

After the problem of heterodox teaching had been navigated by those involved with youth ministry in Sydney, the next big challenge was World War II. How were young people to respond to the war? How were the ministries to continue when so many young men were enlisting or involved in war-related activities? Despite these challenges, remaining leaders sacrificially stretched themselves and most groups survived. New leaders, including women and younger or older men took up the slack. Although the youth organizations were only comparatively recently established, they managed to maintain their ministries with fewer resources and leadership, and when the war ended and the young men returned, the organizations again grew in numbers.

When war was declared, there was general support for the unhappy necessity of protecting ones' country and civilization from the atheistic regime of Nazism, and many young evangelical Christians enlisted to fight. Some joined as YMCA welfare officers, who acted like chaplains to the forces, including Vincent Craven.⁷⁴ Some were conscientious objectors like Bill Andersen, who joined the ambulance corps.⁷⁵ Those who were fighting were encouraged to keep witnessing to their fellow soldiers and maintain their fellowship with other Christians.

The Crusader Union formed a Crusader Forces Fellowship with a regular magazine, containing articles and news to encourage Crusader members on the front.⁷⁶ Roger Deck, the editor in 1942, wrote: "We, too, can best serve our country by maintaining a manly and sane witness for

---

72. Hicks, *City on a Hill*, 144.
73. Piggin, *Spirit, Word and World*, 113, 119.
74. Alwyn Prescott interview.
75. Piggin and Linder, *National Soul*, 187.
76. In the PFA a personal letter was sent every six months to members in the forces, as well as a copy of *The Witness*. "PFU Executive Minutes," August 3, 1943.

God and for the things that we know are worthwhile in life."[77] The soldiers were reminded of the Crusaders hymn to rally them:

> Comrades in faith and fight—Crusaders!
>
> Pledged to the Cross of CHRIST your LORD,
>
> Sworn to resist His realm's invader,
>
> Grip ye afresh the smiting sword!
>
> Heed not the wounds—love not possessions;
>
> Dread not the world's contempt or frown;
>
> Wounded was HE for our transgressions;
>
> Nought but a cross can win the crown . . .[78]

Men in the Crusader forces were committed to protecting their country, but there was no jingoism or hypernationalism. Those who enlisted did so knowing something of the great hardship before them because in many cases their fathers had fought in the first war; they were not naive idealists. In the midst of war, Crusaders were to confirm their commitment to evangelism, because winning the war was not the ultimate good. The salvation of men's souls was their ultimate goal. They were taught that it was important to be a leader not only in peace when conducting Crusader services but also to be a "forceful and courageous leader" while at war, witnessing to non-believers who would be forced to realize that you can "out-think, out-live, and out-die them."[79] Those involved in youth ministry on the home front were to continue to be active in witness and service, in a hope that revival might come.

It was not long, however, until the ministries began to suffer from the loss of so many leaders. Up until 1941, the minutes of the organizations made little mention of the war, but towards the end of that year, after Japan entered the war and posed a terrible threat to Australia, many young people enlisted. All of the organizations began to report the loss of leaders

---

77. "Crusader Forces Prayer and Newsletter," August 15, 1942, Samuel Marsden Archives.

78. "The Crusader Forces Fellowship of Australia," Circular 6, February 15, 1943, Donald Robinson Archives.

79. "The Crusader Forces Fellowship Circular," June 10, 1942, Samuel Marsden Archives.

as a serious problem and were also concerned about petrol rationing, which made it difficult to get around to meetings and services.[80]

Scripture Union suffered the most from the lack of male leadership, although the girls' work flourished. During the war, beach services on Sunday afternoons ceased and the boys' DRMs collapsed with no one to lead them.[81] The girls' work, however, continued under the leadership of Jean Porter[82] and remained strong. John Prince argues that the "war led directly to the post-war domination of the ISCF by girls to an extent that, on occasion, it became difficult to draw boys into it."[83] The Scripture Union administration was also under a lot of pressure in the war years. Tensions between the two staff workers, Vincent Craven and Alex Brown, plagued the union and were only resolved when Craven left to enlist.[84] Morale in the administration was left very low, and there were meetings with the Crusader Union to discuss merging the organizations.[85]

In the Crusader Union, the situation was not as dire as in the Scripture Union. Many of the young men on the council as well as those who spoke on camps and at DRMs had enlisted which led to a need for younger leaders to step up.[86] Initially, there was optimism:

> Despite prevailing conditions and an uncertain future, we believe that God would have us press forward in our work this year. If, for no other reason, an increasingly pagan world irresistibly challenges us to spare no effort in seeking to win boys and girls for our Lord Jesus Christ.[87]

---

80. For example, "CSSM and Scripture Union Minutes," August 16, 1941, Scripture Union NSW Archives.

81. Prince, *Tuned In to Change*, 132.

82. Jean was one of the members of the Bible League and in 1941, after the resignation of Heather Drummond, Jean was offered the position of staff worker to encourage the girls' work. "SU and CSSM Council Minutes," March 4, 1941, Scripture Union NSW Archives.

83. In 1946, there were twenty-six ISCF girls' groups and only thirteen boys' groups. "CSSM and Scripture Union Annual Report 1946," Scripture Union Archives. Prince, *Tuned In to Change*, 132.

84. Alwyn Prescott interview.

85. "Crusader Union of NSW Council Minutes," September 27, 1943, Crusader Union NSW Archives.

86. "Boys' Division Crusader Union NSW Annual Report 1939–1940," Crusader Union NSW Archives.

87. "Crusader Union of Australia Circular Letter," March 18, 1940, Crusader Union NSW Archives.

Reports became more negative as the war went on. By 1943, war conditions were believed to be dampening the Boys' Division, and speakers as well as leaders were hard to find.[88] The Boys' Division was "greatly hampered through lack of leaders and other difficulties arising out of War and general unrest."[89] The sinless perfection episode had also led to the departure of key Crusader leaders and speakers. While school groups and most DRMs did continue despite the difficulties, and camps continued to be successful despite the rationing of food and chaotic supply,[90] the Crusader leaders who led the camps and served on committees were often overstretched and exhausted.[91]

The fellowship groups in churches had similar problems but lack of leaders also led to opportunities for young women along with some new initiatives and interdenominational cooperation. In the Presbyterian fellowship, a loss of leaders led to a decrease in overall numbers. By 1941 membership was already falling.[92] Many leaders enlisted to fight and by 1944, there were one thousand PFA members in the defense forces; twenty percent of the membership.[93] Despite the leadership challenge, the groups, on the whole, did not collapse, as older men and women took up a greater share of the leadership.[94] The PFA reported that of those enlisted:

> A large number of these young men and women were either leaders or potential leaders and their absence has left many gaps in our ranks and has also placed a great strain on others, who are valiantly endeavouring to hold the fort meantime.[95]

88. "Boys' Division Crusader Union NSW Annual Report 1943–1944," Crusader Union NSW Archives.

89. "Crusader Union NSW, Prayer Circular, June 1943," Crusader Union NSW Archives.

90. "Boys' Division Crusader Union NSW Annual Report 1943–1944," Crusader Union NSW Archives.

91. "The Crusader Forces Fellowship of Australia Circular 6," February 15, 1943, Samuel Marsden Archives.

92. "Presbyterian Fellowship Union of NSW Annual Report 1941," Christ College, Burwood. The number of those within the PFU on the eve of the war was five thousand. Numbers fell and did not return to pre-war numbers until 1950. Prentis, "Fellowship," 16.

93. Prentis, "Fellowship," 16.

94. "Presbyterian Fellowship Union of NSW Annual Report 1943," Christ College, Burwood.

95. "Presbyterian Fellowship Union of NSW Annual Report 1943," Christ College, Burwood.

In the PFA, the war helped to make the leadership of women more equal to that of men. *The Witness* was edited by women throughout the war. The General Treasurer was a woman from 1942 to 1947 and in 1945, the first female General Secretary was elected.[96]

In the Anglican churches, many of the fellowship groups closed down during the war because of the lack of leaders. CEFDOS (Church of England Fellowship Diocese of Sydney) groups were often reliant on the leadership of the young curate or catechist (student minister), but the shortage of clergy meant that few were available for this ministry.[97] A creative solution to the lack of leaders was to collaborate with other churches. For example, at St. James Turramurra, the fellowship group joined together with the Presbyterian and Methodist young people's groups.[98] Another outcome of the lack of young adult leaders was that younger men had to take up leadership. At St. Paul's Chatswood, the fellowship had been run in the past by a curate with a committee and subcommittees made up of the young people. As a result of the war, the fellowship was forced to appoint its key leader from within its own ranks, but there was a continual turnover of leadership as young men who were leading the fellowship were encouraged to go to Moore College or to join the defense forces. Lesley Hicks states that the fellowship was "battling discouragement" in the early years of the war.[99] At the same time, there were new initiatives in the fellowship to build the morale of members, such as a breakfast after Holy Communion on Sunday. In 1942 in the fellowship magazine there was a reminder, "Please bring an egg for yourself—write your name on it in pencil. We will boil it."[100] The lack of leadership was resolved midway through 1943 when David Warren at the age of eighteen became the new fellowship leader. Under him, there was new enthusiasm and numbers grew. He helped to organize annual fellowship services that were run entirely by young people[101] and fellowship house parties in 1943 and 1944, and then two in 1945.[102]

The shortage of male leaders during the war led to the increasing significance of the leadership of women in the youth movement. It was the

96. Prentis, "Fellowship," 17.

97. Mason, "History of the Board," 62.

98. Braga, "St James Turramurra, A History of the Church and District," Samuel Marsden Archives.

99. Hicks, *City on a Hill*, 129.

100. Quoted in Hicks, *City on a Hill*, 129.

101. Hicks, *City on a Hill*, 44.

102. Indeed, the last house party was "greatly blessed" and at the end of the year the numbers stood at an all-time high, and the fellowship tea had a record number of 130. Hicks, *City on a Hill*, 130.

women who kept many of the groups going. A history of the St. Andrew's Presbyterian Fellowship Eastwood states that during the war: "senior girls did a sterling job of leadership and the younger fellowshippers responded to the demands for increased responsibility placed upon their shoulders."[103] The shortage of young Christian men at times also opened doors for women in areas that were normally closed. Jean Porter recounted that in 1941, the lack of male preachers meant that she was given an opportunity. One Saturday her father answered the telephone and it was a local church asking him if he knew of a preacher to speak at the service on Sunday. Mr. Porter had no one to recommend because of the shortage of leaders. Jean told him, "I wish I was a man . . . I think it's dreadful." So, her father rang back the church to volunteer her services and she preached the next day.[104]

Unlike the general slowing down of ministry in the schools ministry and fellowships, in the EU it seems that the war did not dampen the number of members or the availability of leaders. The membership in the EU was fairly constant throughout the war years, at about ninety to one hundred, or about 3 percent of the university population.[105] There *was* an increased proportion of women to men at the university so that when Marie Taubman began her Arts degree in 1943 she noted, "there were very few men around the university, it was almost empty of men."[106] There is also some evidence that in 1944, the EU reduced the number of activities because of the need to be involved in the war effort.[107]

Throughout the war years, the EU continued to stress that their primary task was to witness. This was in contrast to the SCM whose agenda was dominated by social issues such as peace, poverty, and work conditions.[108] For the EU, an individual's salvation was far more important than a more just social order.[109] Not only did the EU have no policy on social issues, the EU believed that to have such a political stance was beyond its constitutional goals.[110] As a result, the EU had no public position on the war, though most members

---

103. Anon., "St Andrew's."
104. Jean Porter interview.
105. Andersen, "EU: A Brief History," Fisher Library Archives.
106. Quoted in Lake, *Proclaiming Jesus Christ*, 32.
107. "SUEU Committee Minutes," July 1, 1944, Samuel Marsden Archives.
108. Lake, "Faith in Crisis," 452.
109. The EU's counterpart in England, the CICCU had a similar response to the war. Goodhew claims that it carried on almost as if the war did not exist. The CICCU President in 1944 declared: "Your nation's greatest need is your personal holiness." Goodhew, "Inter-Collegiate Christian Union," 75.
110. Lake, *Proclaiming Jesus Christ*, 34.

supported the war as a just war. There was a minority who argued that any killing was unethical and that it was not right to enlist.[111]

The schools ministries and the fellowships in schools were tested by the lack of male leaders, particularly during the years from 1941 to 1945. As young men enlisted, the organizations asked young women and even younger boys to step up and lead. Some activities were curtailed and some leaders were overstretched because of the ongoing demands. In the EU, however, there was a high proportion of young men who continued their studies and were therefore available for leadership in the movement.

Postwar Reconstruction

During the war Christians and world leaders were concerned with *reconstruction*: how should they shape state and society after World War II? Those with an interest in ministry to youth saw this as an opportunity for young people to lead the way. For example, Neville Harner, an American professor of Christian Education[112] wrote an article on "A Decade of Youth Work in the Churches" in 1943. He voiced the anxiety felt for young people following the war, the youth leaders who would not return home and the emotional damage of those who would:

> What can we do now to salvage as much as possible for youth out of the fearful chaos into which we have fallen? And what ought we prepare to do when the painful days of reconstruction are upon us? To questions such as these, we may well address ourselves with all the devotion and wisdom we can muster.[113]

In Australia, the concern to reconstruct society on Christian principles was shared by church and secular organizations. A National Youth Parliament was assembled in 1941 with many representatives of Christian youth organizations including the CEF and the SCM. At the conference, there were discussions and bills passed in relation to youth and postwar reconstruction. Parliament members believed they were part of a worldwide movement: "all over the world the youth are meeting and deciding that never again will such wars be allowed."[114] Building a new world was the

---

111. Lake, "Faith in Crisis," 450.
112. He was an associate of the Religious Education Association.
113. Harner, "Decade of Youth Work," 30.
114. Anon, "Verbatim Report," 63.

task of the next generation, "a new, happy and prosperous new world where hunger and war shall be unknown,"[115] a new social order.[116]

Australian historians have noted that in the churches there was a new focus on youth and the future of civilization. Hutchinson argues that:

> This shift in focus on life was reflected by a shift in focus within the church, with a particular emphasis on youth issues: the war not only obliterated the past with bombs and tank tracks, it focused the church increasingly on the future.[117]

Treloar argues that the church had a renewed sense of the supremacy of a Christian civilization. The war had helped awaken the churches to the danger of atheistic totalitarianism and showed them where the world without the Christian gospel was heading. It had also shown them the kind of dedication, organization, and resources that were required to build a Christian society.[118]

A Christian Social Order

One of the responses by youth leaders was to embrace the Christian Social Order Movement. They believed that there was a crisis of civilization and were convinced that young people must act and seek the good of the world. Many within the PFA embraced a social gospel based upon a belief in the "Fatherhood of God and the Brotherhood of Man, as revealed by Jesus Christ," that "may be applied to every aspect of life."[119] They sought to look at social issues from a Christian perspective and lobby for peace.[120] They

---

115. Anon, "Verbatim Report," 78.

116. This is the impulse behind the ecumenical movement too, that the restoration of true peace will only be achieved through Christian union. Treloar, *Disruption of Evangelicalism*, 219.

117. Hutchinson, *Iron in Our Blood*, 271.

118. Treloar argues that the "hope for the restoration of Christian civilization soon proved to be unwarranted but was never really relinquished. While support for the churches seemed to have held, the people of the English-speaking world did not come flocking back to evangelical Christianity and there was no great revival." Treloar, *Disruption of Evangelicalism*, 283.

119. "Movement Toward Christian Social Order," *The Witness*, July 18, 1934.

120. In 1927 the PFA had joined the League of Nations to further the ends of peace. *The Witness*, April 18, 1927. In 1936 PFU members were encouraged to join the League of Christian Youth. "Youth Building a New World," *The Witness*, July 18, 1936. Led by the Anglican Bishop E. H. Burgman, it had no creed and the basis of membership was the acceptance of the "Fatherhood of God and the brotherhood of man." Hansen, "Churches and Society," 117.

believed they were part of a worldwide movement, that "youth was on the march" and that the kingdom of God was "being more and more realized on earth as men catch His Spirit."[121] Those within the movement believed it was "the task of the Christian youth to build a social and international order more in harmony with the mind of Christ."[122] Despite the failure of the movement to bring about peace, it continued to be idealistic about establishing a Christian Social Order during and immediately after the war.[123] In the PFA a Christian Social Order Committee (CSO) was formed in 1939.[124] The committee attempted to educate members and to encourage them to act on social issues such as poverty, juvenile delinquency, gambling and alcohol, and international peace.[125]

This social gospel was challenged by neoorthodox theology that was being articulated in the US and in Europe. The World Conference of Christian Youth, *Christus Victor*, was held in Amsterdam in July and August of 1939,[126] and it was here that young Australian youth leaders were introduced to the new theology. There were 1,500 young attendees from seventy nations, including twenty-eight Australian delegates.[127] At the conference, Australian delegates were introduced to Christian thinkers from around the

---

121. *The Witness*, June 18, 1931.

122. Beatty, "The Kingdom of God," *The Witness*, July 18, 1938.

123. For more on the Christian Social Order in NSW see Mansfield, "Christian Social Order," 109–27; Mansfield, "Social Gospel," 432–33.

124. Prentis, "Fellowship," 16.

125. The fellowship magazine, *The Witness*, was edited largely by those connected with Roseville Presbyterian Church and its minister, A. E. Brice. Brice was the CSO Convener of the Presbyterian State General Assembly and taught a version of the social gospel. His teaching and influence on *The Witness*, and therefore over the PFA as a whole, was significant. For example: "The gospel of the 'inner life' says that religion is between God and man, and the gospel of the 'whole man' says that religion is a relationship between God and man, and also man and man." "God and His Kingdom," *The Witness*, June 18, 1937; Prentis, "Fellowship," 16–17.

126. The name of the conference is interesting as it must be a reference to the Swedish theologian Gustave Aulen who wrote *Christus Victor* in 1930. In it he argued that the atonement of Christ was fundamentally about the defeat of evil achieved in the incarnation as Christ enters into human misery and wickedness. His view was in reaction to classic liberal theology's subjective view of the atonement. He argued that the atonement was objectively God's work. He is best seen as a neoorthodox theologian. Schwarz, *Global Context*, 254.

127. "Christus Victor, Report of the World Conference of Christian Youth in Amsterdam," *The Witness*, December 18, 1939.

CHALLENGES TO THE NEW METHODOLOGY 173

world such as William Temple,[128] Reinhold Niebuhr,[129] and Dr. Koo[130] of China. The conference program included many hours of Bible study and talks about the relevance of the gospel in the world today. For example, "Youth in a World of Nations," "Youth and the Economic Order," "Youth and Race," and "Christian Marriage and Family Life." One member spoke of the lasting impression on young delegates who were inspired by such a vision of unity and Christian fellowship.

> The forces of evil may hold sway for a time being but eventually the Church—the fellowship of those who seek first the Kingdom of God—will triumph. The delegates who attended the historic conference will never rest until the fellowship which they knew and felt to be real encompasses the world. They will carry on the high adventure of cooperation and fellowship with Christ as their strength for He is "CHRISTUS VICTOR."[131]

The neoorthodox theology that was to be an influence on the young leaders in the PFA and other youth organizations was a different response to the crisis of civilization, it was a *theology of crisis*. In part, it was a reaffirmation of the reality of sin and the inability of men to save themselves. It emphasized the redeeming work and transcendence of God and the importance of the Bible being preached and enacted in people's lives.[132] The older liberal evangelicals like Angus and Vines had been optimistic about creating a new world and were inspired by the incarnation of Christ. The neoorthodox theologians instead called for a "Christian realism,"[133] a Christian theology and life that

---

128. William Temple was an English Anglican Bishop and theologian who became the Archbishop of Canterbury in 1942. He wrote an influential book, *Christianity and Social Order*, in 1942. Hastings, "Temple, William (1881–1944)," in *Oxford Dictionary of National Biography*. He was also an influential leader of the ecumenical movement.

129. Niebuhr was an influential American theologian who critiqued liberal theology and helped to found neoorthodox theology. In his early years, he taught a social gospel, but in about 1939 he began to move away from the idealism and utopianism in the social gospel. He claimed that liberal Christians were naive. Instead, he encouraged a realistic view of human sin and the reality of corrupt tendencies in society. Edwards, "Can Christianity Save Civilisation?," 51–67.

130. Koo was acting Prime Minister of China from 1926 to 1927. He was an ambassador to France, Great Britain, and the United States. He was a founding member of the United Nations. "C250 Celebrates," *Columbia 250*.

131. Osumi, "Christian Youth—The Hope of the World," *The Friend*, Volume CIX, Number 11, November 1939.

132. Hutchinson, *Iron in Our Blood*, 289.

133. For more on Christian realism see Edwards, "Can Christianity Save Civilisation?," 51–67.

recognized the ongoing nature of injustice and evil but continued to act for righteousness and to seek the welfare of others.[134]

A group of younger leaders who were influenced by this kind of theology plotted a change in generational leadership in the executive of the PFA. Although fellowship group leaders may have been young, the executive was ageing and consisted of "admirable people" who were nevertheless strongly attached to old patterns.[135] When the war was over, a secret group of university students called themselves the "Young Turks"[136] and plotted to overthrow the leadership. At the Annual Conference at Thornleigh, the older members were turned out of their positions in a coup. It was a "clumsily managed" change of generations,[137] however, this is evidence that the fellowship was capable of being revitalized and remaining in the hands of young people as a ministry *of* youth.

Evangelizing the Young

While all the churches were planning to play their part in reconstruction after the war and to rebuild the ministry through and for youth, this reconstruction took different forms. In the PFA, the emphasis was on building a new social order, whereas, in the more conservative Church of England, the goal was to evangelize the young. Conservative evangelical leaders believed that the only way to transform society was to preach the gospel and pray for reformation and revival akin to the days of Cranmer and Wesley. The Anglican Archbishop Howard Mowll preached in 1941 that:

> As we think of the religious revival which swept over the English people in an hour of national peril, in the sixteenth century and again in a similar hour in the eighteenth century, we eagerly look forward to the recurrence of a similar experience today in answer to many prayers.[138]

Mowll believed as individuals responded to the gospel message that they would seek to do good to those around them.

---

134. For more on the influence of the social gospel and of neoorthodox theology see Terracini, *John Stoward Moyes*.

135. Bruce Mansfield interview.

136. Prentis, "Fellowship," 16. These men were Rob Macarthur, Alec Watt, and Bill Webster, apparently helped by the Reverend H. Peak, the Director of the Welfare of Youth Department.

137. Bruce Mansfield interview. Mansfield, *Summer Is Almost Over*, 9.

138. Mowll, "Presidential Address," *Year Book of the Diocese of Sydney, NSW, Australia* (1942), 52.

Mowll and other conservatives showed particular concern for evangelizing the young after the war. He was aware that the younger generation would not automatically have the faith of their parents. He was concerned for Australia to continue to be a Christian country and to uphold Christian values and felt this was to be done through the religious education and evangelism of the young. Mowll, therefore, promoted a strong evangelistic push in local parishes to youth. In 1939, he supported a Young Peoples' Mission run by H. A. Brown of the CSSM "to strengthen Christians and to reach the unborn in Christ."[139] Mowll also held an annual service in the cathedral for those who had been confirmed. In 1942, he spoke of the dangers of non-Christian values, of alcohol abuse, and the use of contraceptives. He argued that the diocese needed to recall people back to a Christian foundation and that,

> Of paramount importance is our work amongst children and youth. Here we have a most receptive and responsive field in which to plant that ideal of life which is best for humanity. Are we giving them as faithfully and as effectively as we should a sound foundation of Christian knowledge and inspiring them to practise it in their daily lives?[140]

In this same speech, he announced his appointment of Graham Delbridge as chaplain to youth.

Mowll's choice was excellent. Delbridge was a charismatic pragmatist who inspired the confidence of young people.[141] Only twenty-four years old, he was a man of "warmth, enthusiasm and unbounding energy."[142] In 1942, Delbridge went to Mowll to ask him whether he could become a chaplain to the forces. Mowll's reply was no, and instead, he asked Delbridge to:

> ... come in and take over youth work and you must get the youth ready for when the war is over ... I don't know what you are going to do or where you are going to do it, and I don't know how we are going to pay for you, but you must begin.[143]

Mowll found funds to pay for Delbridge from the Home Mission Society (HMS) despite the fact that many were critical of this appointment because of the lack of resources during wartime.[144] Delbridge began work

---

139. Cameron, *Living Stones*, 75.
140. *Sydney Diocesan Magazine*, December 1, 1942, 6–7.
141. Don Andersen interview.
142. Harris et al., *Delbridge Years*, 47.
143. "Letter from Graham Delbridge to Mark Rogers," October 13, 1977, Youthworks Archives.
144. Loane, *Mark These Men*, 92.

in the basement of Church House with a table, a couple of chairs, and a telephone. He gathered around him a close group of young adults to act as an executive, to give direction and passion to the denominational youth ministry; they were to become the Youth Department.

Delbridge's role was not to take away responsibility from the local groups or the young people but to create a center in the city that would give overall direction to the ministry, train leaders, and organize big events. Delbridge began by speaking at various events such as fellowship teas and CEBS (The Church of England Boys Society) evangelistic events. He also set up a service bureau to help find jobs for young people after the war and ran a coaching college that would help young people matriculate.[145] Delbridge quickly initiated new activities such as the quarterly tea or rally for all members of fellowships. This tea was held in the city at the Chapter House and each person was to bring half a teaspoon of tea and something to eat.[146] These meetings were well attended, and by the following year, a larger location was needed. A magazine was launched for CEFDOS named *The Venturer*.[147] Delbridge organized a launch picnic and an outing to the national park that 350 young people attended. By 1945, he also ran annual CEFDOS topic nights, sports days, a tennis competition, and the first CEFDOS house party to train fellowship leaders.[148] All this central activity helped to give new energy to the fellowships and by May 1946, there were forty-nine branches of CEFDOS in Sydney.[149]

Another way that the Church of England sought to build up the ministry of young people was by providing them with facilities for house parties. Mowll dreamed of establishing a campsite, perhaps inspired by hearing about the camping ministries established by Guinness in Canada. In 1944,

---

145. Delbridge, *My Life*. He found about five hundred jobs a year for young people There was a concern in the US too, for directing the lives and careers of young people so that they best serve God, a Christian vocational guidance. For example, Harner, "They need assistance when the months go by and no jobs are found," and "The church has something to say to youth as they face their life careers which the public school or guidance bureau cannot say explicitly and fully. It has a divine plan of life to hold before their eyes. It has the Christian ideal of service to throw into their calculations, as they try to find the niche in which they will spend their lives. It has all the needs of all mankind the world around to bring home to them." Harner, *Youth Work*, 43, 44.

146. This reflects war-time frugality. "Report of the CEFDOS," July 15, 1942, in "Board of Education, Diocese of Sydney, Minutes," Youthworks Archives.

147. "Board of Education, Diocese of Sydney, Minutes," May 22, 1943, Youthworks Archives.

148. "Report of CEFDOS to Annual Conference," May 25, 1945, in "Board of Education, Diocese of Sydney, Minutes," Youthworks Archives.

149. "Report of CEFDOS to Annual Conference," May 31, 1946, in "Board of Education, Diocese of Sydney, Minutes," Youthworks Archives.

he discovered that a beautiful property in the Royal National Park facing the Port Hacking River had come on the market and the Home Mission Society (HMS) was again persuaded to pay the cost.[150] House parties began that year with very basic facilities and the personal service of Delbridge who rowed supplies across the river. Weekends were booked by all kinds of youth organizations: ISCF, Fellowship groups, CEBS, CMS League of Youth, GFS, Teachers' College, the Evangelical Union, and on long weekends camps were conducted by the Youth Department.[151] In the next few years, nearby properties were bought (Chaldercot and Rathane) and were used almost every weekend and every holiday.[152] The properties needed extensive repairs, but Delbridge was able to recruit a group of young people who were able to paint, renovate, repair, and at the same time had lots of fun.[153] Food for the camps had to be picked up by rowing a boat over the river to Mr. Daley's store at Lilli Pilli, and campers had to arrive by rowing a boat too.

The sense of ownership of the young people in the ministry of the early Anglican Youth Department was remarkable. Gathered around Delbridge (whose camp nickname was Grimey Dilpickle),[154] and buoyed by his contagious enthusiasm, the youth not only did the work on the properties themselves but also contributed to the ongoing cost of the ministries. The salary of Delbridge was covered by HMS but otherwise, the ministry had to be self-financing. Young people were given little boxes to collect their coins, "powerhouse missionary boxes."[155]

There were two incentives for investing in camping ministries. First, they were flourishing during the war when other ministries struggled, and second, there was a belief that the young were most effectively evangelized at camps or house parties. The success of camp ministry can be seen in the Scripture Union. In the early years of war, numbers at camps doubled[156] and in 1941 there were sixteen VASC camps (Varsity and Schools Camps)

150. "Letter from Norman Fox to Rex Harris," June 13, 1984, Youthworks Archives.

151. "Home Mission Society Port Hacking Management Committee Minutes," November 3, 1944, Youthworks Archives.

152. "Home Mission Society Port Hacking Management Committee Minutes," November 3, 1944.

153. Harris at al., *Delbridge Years*, 19.

154. From a script: "The Early Years," March 19, 2012, anecdotes given by those involved in the camping ministry in its early days at the 70th anniversary celebration at Port Hacking, Youthworks.

155. "Letter from Bishop Graham Delbridge to Mark Rogers," October 13, 1977, Youthworks Archives.

156. "SU and CSSM Council Meeting," October 16, 1941, Scripture Union NSW Archives.

with 688 children involved.[157] In October 1940, the Grange in the Blue Mountains was purchased for SU camps with a capacity for eighty persons and was dedicated by Archbishop Mowll.[158] The petrol rationing that began at the end of 1940 meant that Sunday drives and family holidays were no longer possible, so youth camps were a way to distract and entertain children during years of deprivation. Youth leaders came to see that study groups, fellowship nights and Bible study groups were not the most successful way to witness. It was easy to invite friends to camps or to house parties, and the community created there was warm, joyful, and accepting. Having a series of talks with an evangelistic address on the last night became an effective means of encouraging young people to make a commitment to the Christian faith.[159]

In the other youth organizations, there was also a new interest in camping ministries and a desire to use their scarce resources to invest in properties for camps and house parties. In the Methodist Church, the camping ministry was called *Crusaders,* and it too was flourishing. The records for 1939 show seven camps with seven hundred to eight hundred campers, with these catering to young people seventeen years or older. As the war progressed numbers did decrease a little, possibly because the older age meant many of the potential campers were involved in the war. A twenty-acre property at Otford was bought in 1937 and funds raised for building in 1939, and like the Anglican site, "hard voluntary work by Crusaders and their friends" helped set up the property ready for its first camp. They renovated the grounds and a large house and set up a marquee for camping style accommodation.[160]

As the war progressed, the youth organizations looked forward to young leaders returning to take up positions and resource the ministries. The Crusader Union communicated to members at war of the needs back home and the burden that the few leaders left had been shouldering.

> We need Christian tradesmen—urgently: leaders for drawing room meetings and Senior Fellowships, planners of camps and house-parties, quartermasters to oversee them, writers of

---

157. "SU and CSSM Council Meeting," October 16, 1941, Scripture Union NSW Archives.

158. "CSSM and SU Council Minutes," October 1, 1940, Scripture Union NSW Archives.

159. Donald Robinson recalled that house parties were where people got converted. They encountered "authentic fellowship" and asked, "What have you got that I haven't got?" Donald Robinson interview.

160. "Crusaders' Camps," *The Methodist,* April 15, 1939. Anon., "Lo! Here Is Fellowship."

prospectuses and pamphlets, speakers, pianists, people who will lend their homes... There are all kinds of "positions vacant."[161]

One leader who was also the Crusader Union secretary ran two DRMs, coached a hockey team, spoke at school meetings, and led on the camps subcommittee.[162] If the Crusader Union was to effectively evangelize the young after the war and help rebuild their nation, then many Christian leaders were needed—urgently!

This chapter has contrasted the differences in responses to the challenge of war, particularly the differences in approach between the PFA and CEFDOS. There is a danger of imposing a binary view of either social issues or evangelism.[163] Of course, there were many young people in the middle ground and many who believed that evangelism and social action were both aspects of living out the Christian life.[164] Indeed, the PFA was effective, as we have seen in chapter five, in encompassing both liberal and conservative fellowships within the one organization. The Church of England in Sydney tended to be more theologically adversarial and concerned to prioritize evangelism. Joan Mansfield, an Australian historian, has described a change in 1945 after a report in England commissioned by Archbishop Temple. This document *Towards the Conversion of England* reported a movement away from belief and was widely read in NSW. It argued that the church was a *field* for evangelism rather than a *force* for evangelism. Although the Church of England in Australia had been more open to considering the call to transform the world through a new Christian social order during the war years, after 1945 there was a:

> Swing towards evangelism as the Church's most urgent task. Occasionally social witness was related to evangelism as an essential part of the Gospel; but the stronger tendency was to see the social gospel as a rival to, rather than a necessary component of, evangelism.[165]

161. "The Crusader Forces Fellowship of Australia Circular, Circular 20, November 1945," Samuel Marsden Archives.

162. "The Crusader Forces Fellowship of Australia Circular, Circular 20, November 1945."

163. Treloar warns historians to be careful about creating a dualistic/polarized situation which distorts the "diversity, breadth and complexity," of the evangelical movement. Treloar, "Some Reflections," 3.

164. Stuart Piggin argues that evangelical faith is most effective when it can keep together different "strands" of the evangelical belief and experience. Piggin, *Spirit, Word and World*. It could be argued that at this time, the liberal evangelicals were stressing *the world* and the conservative evangelicals, *the word*. Piggin, *Spirit, Word and World*, i–x.

165. Mansfield, "Christian Social Order," 120.

Those who were conservative evangelicals believed that what was needed was the building up of Christians to share their faith, not social change.[166]

Conclusion

During the war years, the fledgling Christian youth organizations faced challenges that threatened the new model of youth leadership. In the EU and the schools ministries, this challenge took the form of heterodox theology in key leaders. Student leadership with the self-sacrifice and enthusiasm it engendered had been a strength, but this challenge showed the need for adult guidance and denominational allegiance. Denominational youth work and schools ministry also faced the challenge of a loss of leaders because of the war. The number of youth involved and the number of events organized necessarily contracted. At the same time, the lack of leaders boosted the leadership of young women and younger boys, which was foundational for growth in postwar years.

The church continued to believe itself to be facing a crisis of civilization during the war. If it was to continue to be a force for good in Australian society, a cultural authority, then more needed to be done to secure the next generation for Christ. The youth organizations faced the question of the future: what was to be done after the war to ensure Christian civilization? Some emphasized the need for young people to be involved in creating a Christian Social Order, and the PFA exemplified this movement as it sought to inspire young people with this vision. As the war progressed, a neoorthodox theology brought a Christian realism to this goal, and at the end of the war, there was a young group of new leaders ready to take the PFA into the modern world. The members of more conservative youth ministries believed that a renewed witness to friends was needed, which would then lead to revival. Camping ministries were seen as the ideal means of doing this. All the denominations responded to the war years by investing resources into their youth organizations, youth departments, and campsites.

---

166. Mansfield, "Christian Social Order." Mansfield also argues that this change happened due to a fear of Communism, another idea worth pursuing, as after the war the world moved towards a Cold War.

7

Witness and Mission

Postwar 1945–1959

IN THIS STUDY, THE development of a model of modern youth ministry has been traced between 1930 and 1945 at university, in schools and in parishes. The model faced the challenges of World War II and of heterodox theology and survived, still strong though a little bruised. After the war, four trends in youth ministry were still evident. First was the commitment to a ministry *of* youth rather than a ministry *for* youth, expressed in youth organizations with a high level of student leadership and engagement. Second, youth ministry moved away from religious education by adults of young people, to a ministry that facilitated peer ministry and fellowship amongst the young. The third trend was theological and contested, a trend from the dominance of theological liberalism in shaping youth ministry towards the dominance of conservative evangelicalism. The final trend was empowering young people to witness, and this was evident in the years of the 1950s. Rather than focusing on nurturing Christian citizens, the churches and youth organizations emphasized the responsibility of every Christian to witness to their friends and to be involved in mission.

An important question is whether this new model was proving effective. That is, was there a growing recruitment of young people into the church? Was there spiritual vitality and growth within the youth ministries in the university, schools, and local churches? The answer is a qualified yes. Particularly amongst the more conservative evangelical youth ministries, numbers grew, and new believers were brought in. There was a "mini-revival" within churches that included growth within the youth ministries too. In the university ministry, some of the youth who had been mentored to be leaders in the 1930s, and then served in the war, continued to invest in organizing and resourcing ministry to youth. The EU continued to empower young leaders and to encourage fellowship and witness. After the war, many campus outreach missions sought to engage every member and train young people in witness. The challenge posed by greater numbers to the ideal of close fellowship was answered by the creation of faculty groups and cell groups. In the schools ministry, there was sustained growth in numbers and witness by the young. Camping ministry was embraced as the key way to witness to friends. In the local churches, youth ministry was recognized as important for the growth of the church and resources were applied to build campsites, youth departments in churches, and facilities for training. As well as local and denominational ministries, interdenominational youth rallies became popular as a way for young people to witness to their friends.

In the midst of growth and mission, theological distinctions between different youth organizations remained. Amongst the conservative evangelical ministries such as the EU, the Crusader Union, and Scripture Union, and in conservative churches, numbers grew and there was a consequent growth in confidence in the intellectual respectability of the Christian faith and a hope of revival. The more liberal evangelical ministries continued their call to postwar reconstruction. This included a challenge to the status quo and push for new social organizations based on Christian principles. There was also a demand for a "new evangelism" that sought to bring out the relevance of the gospel to the modern world and the needs of young people. Some youth leaders managed to hold the two evangelical concerns together—evangelism and social justice or "witness and service"—notably, Alan Walker[1] and the PFA. Others seemed to lose their spiritual vitality, and some fellowships became mere social groups. The SCM and the Methodist and Congregational church fellowships did not grow and flourish like the more conservative youth ministries.

Social and Religious Context

After the war, Australia entered a new era as a modern nation. It was more confident in its independence, yet there were underlying fears for the future.[2] The diminished power of the British Empire and alliance with the US

---

1. Alan Walker (1911–2003) was a Methodist minister and evangelist. He led the Mission to the Nation from 1953 to 1957 and the Wesley Mission in Sydney from 1958 to 1978. See Walker, *Australia Finding God*.

2. For more on Australian society and religion after the war see Murphy, *Imagining*

in the Pacific meant that Australia was able to "cut the apron strings" of the mother country and feel herself an independent nation rather than a colony. Increased population due to a postwar baby boom and immigration began the "suburban sprawl" in Sydney.[3] The economy was ready to expand, and state government investment in new housing and public works helped lead to full employment. Servicemen returned, bringing with them a desire to build homes and families to create security and stability. The government sought to encourage in its citizens a strong sense of responsibility and a readiness to play one's part in nation building, which included building homes and communities.[4] Australian families had a strong sense of duty to nurture citizenship in young people. At the same time as this growth in confidence as a nation, there was anxiety and fear fueled by high inflation and the Korean War. The possibility of another depression or World War III seemed real. This fear was interpreted in the media as a "crisis of civilization," and the perceived need to build a *Christian* civilization.[5]

For young people in the late 1940s and 1950s, there were many changes. The "Youth Welfare Act" of 1946 further raised the school leaving age from fourteen to fifteen years.[6] This led to an expansion of secondary education and the extension of the "in-between" time of adolescence. The government offered free tertiary education for returned servicemen and servicewomen to build skills needed for a modern society. The Commonwealth Scholarship Scheme enabled thousands of bright children who did not have the funds to attend university with financial help from the government.[7] New universities were established and Sydney University grew exponentially.[8] A youth culture developed as young people had more disposable income to consume clothes, records, comics, and cinema, and those who were wealthier even purchased motorbikes and cars. Young

---

the Fifties; "Cold War Family"; Brett, *Forgotten People*; Hilliard, "God in the Suburbs," 133–46; Hilliard, "Church, Family and Sexuality," 137–46; Curthoys and Merritt, *Australia's First Cold War*.

3. From 1947 to 1961, the population increased from about 7.5 million to 10.5 million. About half of this increase was the result of childbirth and half postwar immigration. Murphy, *Imagining the Fifties*, 155.

4. This was expressed by the Prime Minister Robert Menzies, especially in his famous "Forgotten People" speech of 1942. In it he appealed to those of the middle class and aspiring working class who longed for, "homes, material, human, spiritual," that is, for security and stability. Brett, *Forgotten People*, 22.

5. For more on the anxieties of the Cold War in the 1950s, see Murphy, *Imagining the Fifties*, 5; Hilliard, "God in the Suburbs," 410.

6. Barcan, *Short History*, 277.

7. Ward, *Nation for a Continent*, 272.

8. Barcan, *Radical Students*, 260.

people were influenced by styles from America, particularly Hollywood. Many members of the older generation responded with panic to "youth culture," especially the culture expressed by the *bodgies* and *widgies*.[9] To counter juvenile delinquency, many argued that youth should be recruited into Sunday schools and youth organizations.[10] Many adults embraced conservative family values and traditional beliefs that were conducive to the growth of conservative youth ministry.

There was also a widespread desire for revival in both church and society in Australia.[11] In 1953, an Australian poll asked the question, did "Australia need a religious revival?" The majority of Australians answered, "yes."[12] The churches were generally viewed as a constructive "frame of moral reference" for values concerning family, society, and sexuality.[13] Within the churches, this desire for revival was fueled by a report published on the state of the church in England, "Towards the Conversion of England" (1945). This report was a wake-up call to Protestants in both England and Australia, arguing that the general population was far more indifferent to the Christian faith than previously believed. It created an anxiety that the church was losing some of its cultural influence, although Christian identification and even church attendance were actually very high.[14]

The historian Brian Stanley argues that the response by Western evangelical Christians was twofold. First, to argue for fresh energy in proclaiming the traditional gospel, a "new Evangelicalism."[15] For example, Archbishop Mowll argued:

9. The bodgies and widgies were young people who dressed in a certain way that was associated with American popular culture, music, and dancing. They were portrayed by the media as rebellious young people. Stratton, "Bodgies and Widgies," 3.

10. Hilliard, "Church, Family and Sexuality," 152.

11. The desire for revival can be seen in the 1951 "Call to Australia." Church leaders from the four largest denominations as well as all the chief justices of the Supreme Court issued a public statement which was broadcast widely on radio stations and published in all the major newspapers. It called Australia to a revival of Christian faith and values. It reflected the continued fear that Christian civilization was under great threat and that Australian citizens needed to reaffirm their commitment to Christian values. For more on the call, see Chilton, "Evangelicals," 43; Hilliard, "God in the Suburbs."

12. Murphy, *Imagining the Fifties*, 61.

13. Murphy, *Imagining the Fifties*, 65.

14. Evangelical historians, Treloar and J. Carpenter talk about this fear amongst evangelicals in the Western world. Treloar, *Disruption of Evangelicalism*; Carpenter, *Revive Us Again*.

15. Stanley, *Global Diffusion*, 12–13. In the transnational theological context after the war there was resurgence within conservative evangelicalism and the formation of what has been called, particularly in America, the "new evangelicalism." This strengthened the Australian conservative evangelical leaders by allowing them to distance

The Evangelical still maintains that a renewed heart is the source of a renewed life and that it is idle to press for a recognition of God in the world politic if we neglect to enforce a recognition of God in the heart and mind of an individual. Converted men and women will carry the banner of Christ into every avenue of our social life.[16]

Second, those who were more liberal in their theology called for a "new evangelism"; a radical rethinking in communicating the gospel message in the modern age.[17] An example of this was Alan Walker, who sought to communicate a Christian message that was "socially aware and intellectually respectable."[18] Motivated by a desire for revival, churches seemed to have a new energy in the 1950s to attempt more optimistic outreach. A report in the *Sydney Morning Herald* in 1950 claimed that:

> ... with a rediscovered sense of mission, and new methods, bold attempts are being made to confront the Australian people with the claims of the Christian Gospel. No one who watches trends in our society will deny the presence of a revived spirit amongst Christians. Crusades for Christ, missions to the nation, new life campaigns are the order of the day.[19]

All the Protestant churches engaged in missions with combative militaristic language that expressed a new assertiveness in their proclamation. The Methodists began the "Commonwealth Crusade for Christ," the Presbyterians launched a "New Life Movement," and the Congregationalists organized a "Forward Movement." In the Anglican Church, the mission was

---

themselves from fundamentalism, and gave them a new confidence. In the US, younger conservatives such as Billy Graham, Carl Henry, and Edmund Carnell wanted to be less aggressive in their disputes with liberal Christians and were committed to developing evangelical scholarship that engaged with the mind. In Britain, evangelical preachers and scholars such as F. F. Bruce, Martin Lloyd Jones, and John Stott were concerned to develop a biblical mind. They were committed to scholarship and helped established the Tyndale Fellowship, the Biblical Research Committee of the IVF, and Tyndale House. They were committed to a "believing criticism" and to rejuvenate reformed evangelical thought. They were linked to Sydney through the influence of D. B. Knox. See Carpenter, *Revive Us Again*; Stanley, *Global Diffusion*, 13. British evangelicalism was more influential on Australia than American and it was particularly the British IVF books that came to Australia that encouraged a conservative intellectual confidence. Many IVF books came to Australia and were enthusiastically read by students.

16. Mowll, "Presidential Address," *Year Book of the Diocese of Sydney, NSW, Australia* (1948), 12.

17. Stanley, *Global Diffusion*, 12–13.

18. Piggin, *Spirit, Word and World*, 152.

19. "Evangelism Has New Vigour," *Sydney Morning Herald*, October 9, 1950.

focused on young people with a "Youth to Youth Campaign" and various parish missions.[20] In these missions, denominations organized rallies, evangelistic speakers in public spaces, processions of witness, children's parish missions, and/or house to house visitation. Capturing this spirit, the Australian Council for the World Council of Churches designated 1951 as the "Year of Evangelism."[21]

As a result, there was a "modest revival" in the 1950s.[22] In Australia since the census of 1901, around 90 percent of the population had identified with a Christian denomination. But during the period from 1947 to 1954, this proportion actually increased.[23] Around three in ten Australians indicated in opinion polls that they were regular attenders at church services and these numbers remained fairly steady between 1947 and 1954.[24] In Morgan Gallup polls in 1950, 23 percent of those surveyed over the age of twenty one years claimed to have attended church in the last seven days, and between 1950 and 1960, this percentage grew to 30 percent.[25] Sunday schools and membership of youth societies and fellowships grew, and in the early 1960s, Sunday school enrolments were numerically at their historic peak.[26]

Witness in the University

In the EU the desire for youth to lead was still strong after the Second World War. The EU was no longer seen as a sectarian fundamentalist group, but as evangelical mainstream and it grew rapidly. The leadership of the organization was strengthened by the servicemen who returned to university and by the mentoring of the IVF staff. Confidence grew with the strengthening of intellectual credibility of evangelicals, bolstered by T. C. Hammond and the evangelical writing that was read by EU members.[27]

20. Hilliard, "Church, Family and Sexuality," 135–36.
21. "Evangelism Has New Vigour," *Sydney Morning Herald*, October 9, 1950.
22. Hilliard, "God in the Suburbs," 418.
23. Chilton, "Evangelicals," 2.
24. "Church Attendance, Australia 1947–1983," in Goot, "Public Opinion, 438.
25. Mol, Faith of Australians, 56.
26. Vamplew, *Historical Statistics*, 428–35.
27. Stuart Piggin in *National Soul*, 303, states that "between 1943 and 1964 the IVF through the Tyndale Press published at least 47 academic monographs. Four of them were by young Australian authors destined to make a big impact in Australia: Alan Cole, The New Temple. A Study in the Origins of the Catechetical 'Form' of the Church in the New Testament (The Tyndale Press: London, 1950); Leon Morris, The Biblical Doctrine of Judgement (London: Tyndale Press, 1960); Leon Morris, The Wages of Sin. An Examination of the New Testament Teaching on Death (London: Tyndale Press,

Some members were concerned, however, that the growth in numbers and the presence of IVF staff could undermine engagement of everyday members and damage the close fellowship that was important to the ministry. The EU responded by restructuring around small groups (cell groups) with faculty-based leaders. Although fellowship continued to be important, the clarion call for EU members was *witness* which was best expressed by the university mission of 1951. Although the focus of this study has been on the EU, the SCM remained active after the war and represented a different stream of university ministry. The SCM opposed the intellectual narrowness of the EU and continued to favor fellowship over witness. In the 1950s, while the EU grew exponentially, SCM numbers remained constant, and in the late 1960s, declined quickly.[28]

The EU was an expression of the success of the newer youth ministry model at this time; it grew in vitality and confidence and was successful in recruiting new members. The number of students at the University of Sydney grew dramatically,[29] but the EU more than kept pace. Membership rose from around one hundred at the end of the war to four hundred and fifty in 1955.[30] There was effective recruitment amongst Christian students graduating from high school ministries, the ISCF, and Crusader Union. High school students were directed to attend the EU and lists of names of imminent graduates were sent to the EU to follow up.[31] The EU also recruited at orientation week, connecting with students who were not yet Christians, but interested in the Christian message. EU members invited friends to house parties and challenged them there to become Christians. The most dramatic push for

---

1955); Donald William Bradley Robinson, *Josiah's Reform and the Book of the Law* (London: Tyndale Press, 1951)."

28. Howe, *Century of Influence*, 336. Hilliard explains that in the 1960s, "In Australia, as in Britain, the Student Christian Movement, which had been the standard-bearer of liberal Christianity in universities, faded in the late 1960s to virtual extinction. Alienated from the religion of their parents, almost an entire generation of teenagers and young adults seems to have dropped out of the Protestant churches. The socialisation process by which religious affiliation was transmitted from parents to the next generation broke down." Hilliard, "Religious Crisis," 221.

29. The increase of students overall was the result of government scholarships to returned service men to place them in the workforce. In 1940 the university had 3,269 day students and by 1950 this had grown to 8,309, stabilized back to around 6,000 by 1955. Connell et al. *Australia's First*, 454.

30. In the EU at the end of the war there were about 100 members, in 1950 there were 250 members, in 1952, 326 members, and by 1955, 450. "SUEU Membership Book," and Anderson, "A Brief History," Box 316, SUEU, Sydney University Archives.

31. "SUEU Membership Book," and Anderson, "A Brief History," Box 316, SUEU, Sydney University Archives.

recruitment were the university missions. These were seen by the EU as a way to publicly proclaim Jesus as Savior and Lord.

The EU continued to be a ministry *of* youth rather than *for* youth. It was still led by a student president and committee with the advice and encouragement of IVF staff. Some of the key leaders were perhaps stretching the definition of *youth* as they were returned servicemen finishing their degrees. For example, Donald Robinson returned from the war to be Vice President in 1946 at the age of twenty-three, and then President in 1947.[32] The returned servicemen brought skills of management and administration they had learnt in the war to the EU and many members attributed growth in the EU to the able leadership of these returned servicemen.

The IVF staff worked hard to advise, teach, and mentor rather than take responsibility away from the students. In 1944, Basil Williams[33] who had been a student leader and then IVF travelling secretary in New Zealand was made the travelling secretary in the Australian IVF and he regularly preached to the students on the doctrinal basis to give them a strong theological foundation. Paul White remained the General Secretary of the IVF and was another encouraging presence and mentor to young leaders. He regularly spoke to the EU on topics such as "Witnessing," "The Quiet Time," or "The Stewardship of Money."[34] He introduced the idea of "Blokes Worth-Watching" or BWW for short. The BWW was a younger man who had potential as a minister or missionary. White would write the names of BWWs in his prayer diary and would spend time investing in them as leaders.[35] White continued Guinness's strategic thinking about who might be a future leader in church and society. Charles Troutman[36] joined White and became the General Secretary of the IVF in 1953 and he had a similar strategic mindset to White.

---

32. He was an able leader of the EU and future Archbishop of Sydney. John Prince writes that under his presidency there was a healthy membership of 130 and conversions occurring at EU house parties. Prince, *Out of the Tower*, 25.

33. Williams had been a student leader and then IVF travelling secretary in the New Zealand student movement. Prince, *Out of the Tower*, 21.

34. Prince, *Out of the Tower*, 30.

35. Paul White interview.

36. Troutman was one of the founders of the IVF in Canada and the US. He was trained at Wheaton College, and was one of the "new evangelicals" who sought to communicate the traditional gospel message within a modern context. He came to Australia in 1953 to build the work of the IVF in all the universities of Australia in a time of increasing complexity as it grew after the war. He was asked to help with the work by Paul White and worked for the IVF in Australia as General Secretary from 1953 to 1961. Hutchinson, "Troutman, Charles Henry Jr. (1914–1991)," Australian Dictionary of Evangelical Biography.

The confidence of EU leaders was buoyed by the robust T. C. Hammond who reassured them that conservative evangelical faith had intellectual credibility. Hammond's book *Abolishing God: A Reply to Professor John Anderson* was published in 1943 and one hundred copies were bought and distributed within the EU.[37] This was an apologetic response to the attacks of Prof. Anderson, the atheist philosopher and faculty member at Sydney University. Hammond also took part in a very public debate with Anderson in 1946 on the topic, "Are Christians Credulous?" EU leaders recall the story of EU President Donald Robinson excitedly accompanying Hammond to the debate. He asked Hammond about his preparation. "I imagine you have been giving a lot of thought to this particular subject prior to the debate." Hammond's cheery answer was "no, he was just going to wait and hear what Anderson had to say, and respond." The students believed Hammond had the "full bag," including the ability to quote Plato by heart.[38] He was their "kingpin when it comes to debate"[39] with his gold medal in philosophy from Trinity College, Dublin. Although the student paper *Honi Soit* claimed Anderson as the victor, the EU members believed their contender was the true winner and this gave them more intellectual confidence.[40] Hammond emphasized the role of the mind in Christian belief and was impatient with shallow emotionalism. In 1940 he wrote:

> The fundamentals of the Christian faith have not been taught with sufficient care for years. As a result, the youth of our day are often ill-instructed. We have too many purveyors of a cheap gospel which makes its appeal solely to the emotions and does not supply a solid background of Bible fact on which the awakened soul may confidently rest.[41]

He instructed young people in the Reformed faith with rigorous biblical reasoning.

The growth in numbers in the EU was a challenge to the continued engagement in peer ministry and fellowship of every member. Those who

---

37. "Sydney University Evangelical Union Minutes, March 11, 1943," Samuel Marsden Archives.

38. Bill Andersen interview.

39. Paul White interview.

40. As well as the writings of Hammond, many other IVF books came to Australia and were enthusiastically read by students. For example, Troutman and White obtained three thousand copies of The New Bible Handbook (published by IVF in 1948) for five thousand pounds, kept them in a garage, and sold them to university students and at churches when they visited. Troutman, "Notes to Mark Hutchinson," June 30, 1990.

41. "A Century of Service," Dublin, YMCA, 1940. Cited in Nelson, *T. C. Hammond*, 42.

were involved in the committees were a dominant minority, and their influence could disempower other members. At times the minutes express concern at the low engagement of members. In 1954, for example, the EU committee stated that their aim was that each EU member should have "a deeper consecration to Christ, and through attending consecration, each member was to engage in personal evangelism with a view to winning one soul for Christ."[42] In 1947, the committee tried to solve the problem by creating faculty groups with faculty leaders in charge. In 1952, they formed faculty prayer groups called "cell groups." The cell group was an attempt to retain the small group DNA. It was the foundational core of the EU, "The small group that meets for prayer, witness and study is the basic cell which constitutes the foundation of the EU."[43] It was a place for accountability, to develop intimate relationships, and to grow and witness together. The cell group was an effective way to maintain peer engagement and warm fellowship.[44]

Although fellowship was important in the EU, witness was the fundamental task of each member, and their mentors Paul White and Howard Guinness were exemplars. White was a gifted evangelist who worked hard at effective communication. He taught the students to "Entertain, Educate and Evangelise," to really get into the head of your listener.[45] White also developed a method for students to talk about the Christian faith at the university through "Two Ways to Live," a clear and comprehensive summary of traditional evangelical doctrine with a call at the end to respond. It argued that there were two ways to live, either having Jesus as your Lord and Saviour or being your own boss.[46] A decision had to be made and the consequences were either eternal life or God's judgment. Howard Guinness was also a persuasive evangelist who mentored the students in their witness. In 1949, Guinness reentered the EU scene when he returned to Sydney to become the rector of the nearby parish of St. Barnabas, Broadway. He was an excellent communicator and at the time was experimenting with a

---

42. "Sydney University Evangelical Union Committee Retreat Minutes, January 6-10, 1954," Samuel Marsden Archives.

43. "Sydney University Evangelical Union Committee Retreat Minutes, January 6-10, 1954."

44. "History of Sydney University Evangelical Union," in "EU Committee Handbook 1955," General and IVF, Box 3, Samuel Marsden Archives.

45. His commitment to communicating Christian truths in cultural context then current is evidenced in the very popular children's "Jungle Doctor" book series. Paul White interview.

46. Paul White interview.

"devil's advocate" method of evangelism.⁴⁷ He heard that the campus mission of 1948 was regarded as a failure with only two students becoming Christians and believed the reason was that all the responsibility was left to the missioner rather than EU members.⁴⁸ Guinness sought to reinvigorate the engagement of EU members by running training sessions at the rectory in "personal work" (that is, evangelism) and encouraged students to be part of mission teams to regional areas.⁴⁹ He tried to teach students to communicate creatively with the context in mind.

Witness by students at the university was stimulated by missions, and the EU mission of 1951 was particularly important. Dudley Foord, who was president in 1950, took a year off from his studies in order to organize the mammoth mission, ably helped by Warren Adkins, then president. The EU began to organize eighteen months beforehand and involved local churches by sending them prayer letters and requests for financial support. The letters sent out in March 1951 by Adkins show the strategic nature of student ministry.

> Who knows what might happen in this sin-stricken world if these professional men and women of tomorrow are brought into saving knowledge of Christ. As teachers, doctors, lawyers, scientists, politicians and leaders in business and industrial spheres, they will have a marked influence on national policy and the moulding of future generations.⁵⁰

Howard Guinness was the key speaker of the mission giving lunchtime talks with the theme "God has spoken." There were a further one hundred and thirty subsidiary meetings, in every faculty, for every academic year, where thirty different "Assistant Missioners" spoke, including Stuart Barton Babbage, T. C. Hammond, Marcus Loane (later Archbishop of Sydney), Paul White, Graham Delbridge, and six women.⁵¹ These meetings included social time, so the EU members invited friends, catered, ran book stalls, and chatted to visitors, thereby facilitating "every member participation."⁵² The EU served four thousand cups of tea, twelve thousand

---

47. Guinness, *Journey among Students*, 152–53.

48. "Hyman Appleman Mission to the University, 1948," in "SUEU Various Missions," Box 5, Samuel Marsden Archives.

49. "EU Committee Handbook 1955," in "History of SUEU," General and IVF Box 3, Samuel Marsden Archives.

50. "1951 Mission," in Various Missions EU Box 5, Samuel Marsden Archives.

51. "1951 Mission," in Subsidiary Meetings Folder, Various Missions EU Box 5, Samuel Marsden Archives.

52. Rickard, "SUEU Mission in the University Report, June 20–28, 1951," in Various

sandwiches, five thousand scones, nine thousand pieces of cake and three thousand sausage rolls.[53] The mission was supported by the EU members and other Christians and there were reports of four hundred people attending daily prayer meetings. About five thousand students attended the mission, in a campus of around 9,500 students. It led to at least one hundred professions of Christian faith and the EU doubled in size. The level of organization was extraordinary, no doubt benefitting from the fact that as a returned serviceman, Foord had been trained in organization and in the management of people.[54]

The mission invigorated student engagement in ministry and evangelism. Dudley Foord recalled the attitude of the students who believed that they were co-workers with God:

> We are the co-workers, our task is to befriend people, and bring them along and then talk with them and explain... we expected that God would stop people in their tracks, that he would make people think and address the matter of the person of Christ and what would they do about it, and there would be those who God would put his hand upon them and turn them around and give them a new birth, and he did.[55]

The Annual Report recorded that students also contributed to the costs of the mission which came to 1,300 pounds.[56] Mission revitalized the EU members with a confidence in God's work in the world. Foord remembered the students saying to one another, "we just can't be the same again."[57] The mission also led to the formation of a new group, the Sydney University Volunteers Movement (SUVM), modelled on the old SVM of the Moody days. It began as a group of seventy students who committed themselves to full-time Christian ministry. They signed a manifesto of nine points,[58]

Missions EU Box 5, Samuel Marsden Archives.

53. This was according to Graham Delbridge. "Supporters Letter No. 56," January 1952, EU Box 5, Samuel Marsden Archives.

54. Smith, "Reviving Sydney University," 14. The numbers were very high at that time because of the exservicemen and women on scholarships.

55. Dudley Foord, cited in Smith, "Reviving Sydney University," 14.

56. "Sydney University Evangelical Union Annual Report," September 12, 1951, Samuel Marsden Archives.

57. Dudley Foord, cited Smith, "Reviving Sydney University," 14.

58. "Sydney University Evangelical Union Minutes, September 7, 1952," Samuel Marsden Archives.

which included: "I give myself to God freely and without reserve to serve Him on the foreign mission field."[59]

The EU also invigorated witness by sending teams of students to missions into churches throughout NSW. Guinness organized a mission in 1952 to Penrith called "Life at its Best," coordinating with the local churches in an extensive campaign. There were forty EU members involved who organized and spoke at evening meetings, after-school meetings, ladies' teas, open-air meetings, and there was also a big football game between the EU and Penrith. At the first meeting, four thousand people attended and there were reports of about one hundred conversions. This mission also directly led to the formation of the United Churches Committee in Penrith, an organization intent on continuing the evangelistic efforts.[60] For this and other missions, teams of students were trained for these missions at the university on Friday afternoons. A teams secretary was appointed who organized students to read the Bible, pray, sing, and speak. Members were told that they did not have to be "a polished speaker," and that there were many different ways to serve and be trained: "Experience plus training yields quicker and better results."[61]

The EU excelled in giving students a clear vision of glorifying God as a witness. An example of this enthusiastic witness was Michael Barratt in 1958. Barratt was a second-year medical student who lived at one of the university colleges. Charles Troutman reported that after an EU mission, Barratt felt that the Lord spoke to him "very specifically and gave him a sense of responsibility and leadership and personal work training among the men of the EU."[62] He spent his Saturday afternoons taking other EU members to the city, "milk-bar crawling" to talk to motorcycle gang members about Jesus. He was particularly attracted to evangelism with the "most unlikely," and Charles Troutman found his success "amazing." Michael's example to the other EU members was "quite startling," and he encouraged them in their personal witness in the university.[63]

59. "Sydney University Evangelical Union Committee Retreat Minutes, January 28–February 2, 1953," Samuel Marsden Archives. Many of these seventy did, in fact, spend their lives in full-time Christian ministry. Dudley Foord, cited in Smith, "Reviving Sydney University," 15.

60. "Sydney University Evangelical Union Annual Report, July 3, 1952," Samuel Marsden Archives.

61. Shellard, "Letter to EU members, March 27, 1947," in Various Missions, EU Box 5, Samuel Marsden Archives.

62. "Charles Troutman Letter to Ian Burnard, August 11, 1958," IVF in "Ian Burnard," Box 9, Samuel Marsden Archives.

63. "Charles Troutman Letter to Ian Burnard, August 11, 1958," IVF in "Ian Burnard" Box 9, Samuel Marsden Archives.

The EU was an example of the paradigm of youth ministry at its most effective. Its activities led to many conversions and the recruitment of Christian leaders who were actively engaged in Christian leadership once they left the university. The theology of the EU, however, was contested by the SCM. The SCM in many ways used the same model of ministry as the EU, namely leadership of the young, peer ministry, and fellowship and witness. But the SCM regarded the EU as fundamentalist and narrow in its view of salvation and witness. David Garnsey critiqued the EU in 1947 for its view of substitutionary atonement and the infallibility of the Bible. He believed that the EU sometimes did great damage in its witness of the Christian life, "By concentrating on sudden emotional conversion and on a narrow individualistic view of sin."[64] After the war, the goal of the SCM was to be involved in the reconstruction of Christian civilization and its theology led its members to emphasize fellowship over witness. There were times when the SCM was involved in university missions, but witness was understood as more ethical, focused on living out a Christian life and values rather than on an individual's salvation.[65] By the end of the 1950s, the SCM began to decline as it struggled to communicate a clear message that would attract the postwar generation.[66]

The EU growth and the SCM demise are evidence of the dominance of the conservative evangelical approach in youth ministry in NSW. The growth in members and vitality of the EU after the war was the fruit of combining effective methods of ministry with conservative theology. There was a strong young leadership, engaged members that sought to do peer ministry, and a commitment to effective communication of the gospel message to others.

Growth and Witness in the Schools Ministry

The model of youth ministry that was so effective in university ministry continued to bear fruit in the schools ministry as well. During the war, Scripture Union membership and activity had slowed down, as did other activities of the church, as many leaders were serving overseas in the armed forces. After the war, however, the basic structures for growth were still in place: ISCF groups, beach missions, camps, and leadership training. The

64. David Garnsey, "The Australian Student Christian Movement and the Intervarsity Fellowship," IVF and SCM Box 53, Samuel Marsden Archives.

65. For example, the "Christian Life Mission" of 1949, Howe, *Century of Influence*, 295.

66. Howe, *Century of Influence*, 336.

Crusader Union continued its ministry but was overshadowed by the ISCF work which grew rapidly as secondary education expanded. The model employed by both organizations was based on active student leadership of students, the significance of peer ministry and the importance of witness. They continued to be theologically conservative organizations.

In the Scripture Union, the latter half of the 1950s and the early 1960s were glory days. The impact of Scripture Union is hard to gauge in terms of actual growth in numbers. In 1950, bi-monthly Bible reading notes were produced for 15,600.[67] In 1958 this had grown to 30,750, and in 1959 to 52,000 (largely due to a big promotional push in NSW through rallies and meetings as well as the Billy Graham Crusade).[68] But this was not only an indication of ministry to youth, as Scripture Union provided adults with SU study notes too. In the school ISCF groups, there was also growth. In 1946, there were thirty-nine secondary school ISCF groups, twenty-six girls' groups and thirteen boys.[69] By 1953, there had been an incredible multiplication of groups, with 107 senior ISCF groups and twenty-two junior groups, and six thousand members receiving *ISCF News*.[70]

The Crusader Union, however, was smaller and struggling with fewer leaders and groups. They lacked the integration that Scripture Union had with beach missions and camps, and the number of independent schools was low. There was, however, good cooperation between the two organizations and even an effort to amalgamate the ministries. To work towards amalgamation a combined camps and schools committee of ISCF and CU was formed under the leadership of Bill Andersen in 1948.[71] Ian Holt, however, the General Secretary of the Crusader Union, opposed the amalgamation. He argued that this was not because of private school snobbishness but because the "work in the ISCF was so great that the small number of independent schools would become insignificant and the impact would

---

67. Prince, *Tuned In to Change*, 143.

68. Prince, *Tuned In to Change*, 143.

69. "CSSM and Scripture Union Annual Report 1946," Scripture Union Archives. The predominance of the girls' work can be explained by the disruption of the war, when many male leaders left, and some did not return to the ministry. There were also many young female teachers who came through the universities and Teachers' Colleges on Commonwealth scholarships after the war and helped to set up and support ISCF groups at their schools.

70. "CSSM and Scripture Union Annual Report 1953–1954," Scripture Union Archives.

71. "Minutes of the CSSM and Scripture Union Council," February 15, 1948, Scripture Union Archives.

diminish" and "we'd get lost in the wash."[72] By 1952, the merger was abandoned at the insistence of the Crusader Union.[73]

Due to the large numbers involved, Scripture Union could now focus on deliberate leadership training of its volunteers. The hoped-for outcome was that a school child might be reached at a beach mission or invited to an ISCF house-party and become a Christian. The student would then be nurtured to take up leadership of the group within their senior years. Then, once at university, the IVF encouraged its members to continue leadership ministry at their old school and to be leaders at ISCF camps and beach missions. After university, those students that went on to become teachers were able to continue their support of ISCF groups. This was the vision of Paul White and Charles Troutman who talked about the "unbroken circle" of IVF and SU.[74] The strength of the Scripture Union movement was in the ISCF groups and their interconnectedness with the IVF and the Teachers Christian Fellowship (TCF).

There was a great deal of training to raise up good leaders in the ISCF. Although there were two travelling secretaries who encouraged school students in their leadership at school, the actual leadership of the ISCF groups remained the responsibility of senior students.[75] Bill Andersen and his wife led training camps held each year with a mix of "theological, administrative and outreach" instruction. At these camps, there were expositional talks on the Bible, practical sessions such as "how to give a talk" and "how to reach your mates at school." The training covered every aspect of camp and ISCF leadership.[76]

The Scripture Union continued to see its key priority as the evangelism of the young. Bill Andersen stated that the goals of the Scripture Union were implicit, but the first priority was "to witness to young people wherever they might be, particularly in schools."[77] It was still accepted that adolescence was a time of heightened spiritual openness. At the Australian CSSM and SU staff conference in 1945, Miss R. Chapman said, "Adolescence is God's greatest opportunity in the human soul . . . and the ISCF is one of the means God is using in Australia today to grasp that opportunity."[78] Students were

72. Ian Holt interview.

73. "Minutes of the CSSM and Scripture Union Council," May 19, 1952, Scripture Union Archives.

74. Troutman, "Notes to Mark Hutchinson," June 30, 1990, Audio Archives, Donald Robinson Library.

75. The travelling secretaries were Margaret Hydamen and Brian Hill.

76. Bill Andersen interview.

77. Bill Andersen interview.

78. "Australian Staff Conference notes March 19–26, 1945," Scripture Union

encouraged to exercise a witness by inviting friends to the ISCF meetings and to camps. Beverly Kemp, for example, was invited to the St. George Girls ISCF by a friend in the 1950s. The ISCF met for Bible study, sometimes proudly in the middle of the playground as a witness. Beverly became a keen member and witness herself and she wore the SU badge proudly as an outward sign of her allegiance.[79]

Camps were also central to the goal of witnessing. The Grange, a stately old home in Mount Victoria, had been purchased as a property to conduct girls' and boys' camps in 1941.[80] In the Annual Report of 1953 to 1954 it was heralded that over the Christmas break, six hundred and thirty-two girls had attended Scripture Union camps as well as three hundred and sixty boys.[81] The report stated that:

> The aim of these camps has always been and continues to be not only the provision of a happy and healthy holiday but also the presentation of the Gospel message so that boys and girls will be won to the saviour. Frequently commandants, in their reports, have told of the young folk coming to trust the saviour and of entering into new life in him.[82]

The Crusader Union also invested resources in campsites. In 1946, a property at Lake Macquarie was donated to the Crusader Union.[83] In 1949, a property at Galston was bought by Paul White for Crusader camps and developed by senior Crusaders led by Stuart Braga.[84] In 1955, nine different camps were organized with an attendance of three hundred and fifty students. The Annual Report recorded that, "As usual, these activities resulted in numbers of boys and girls coming to know the Lord Jesus Christ, and it is gratifying to see that so many have since given evidence of the reality of their faith."[85]

Council Minutes Vol. V, 1941–1947, Scripture Union NSW Archives.

79. Beverly Kemp interview.

80. Prince, *Tuned In to Change*, 121.

81. "Annual Report of the CSSM and SU 1953–1954," Scripture Union Council Minutes Vol. VI, 1947–1956, Scripture Union NSW Archives.

82. "Annual Report of the CSSM and SU 1953–1954," Scripture Union Council Minutes Vol. VI, 1947–1956, Scripture Union NSW Archives.

83. "Crusader Union NSW 21st Annual Report, 1946–1947," Crusader Union NSW Archives.

84. "Crusader Union NSW 21st Annual Report, 1949–1950," Crusader Union NSW Archives.

85. "Crusader Union NSW 25th Annual Report, 1955," Crusader Union NSW Archives.

It is hard to judge the effectiveness of the witness of the Scripture Union and the Crusader Union, but there are many reports of conversions, particularly through ISCF camps and beach missions. It is noteworthy that Charles Troutman, while General Secretary of both IVF and SU, was struck by the comparative strength of Scripture Union in bringing about conversions through its witness and was tempted to give up the university ministry and concentrate on high school students.

> ... I am almost tempted to throw in the IVF sponge and concentrate exclusively on the high school and beach mission work. I can see more clearly now than I did five years ago that our recruiting strength lies to a large measure in the character and the numerical size of the ISCF and beach mission work. The same is true of the TCF as it seems that nothing can be done except rescue operations unless there is that constant flow from the high schools into the teaching profession.[86]

It was in the schools and beach missions that the majority of young people were converted and recruited into ministry, rather than the university or through professional ministries such as the Teachers Christian Fellowship.

The Crusader Union and the Scripture Union both remained committed to a conservative priority on witness and evangelism. In 1958, three hundred supporters of the Crusader Union gathered to celebrate the opening of campsite cabins at Galston and Howard Guinness gave the address. Guinness spoke of how Crusaders began twenty-nine years ago "because Christian leaders realised from their own experience how essential it was to share their faith." He explained that at school, young Christians needed to make their faith personal and have a practical outlet to grow. It was the Crusader Union (and ISCF in government schools) that provided opportunities in "effective evangelism and training in leadership."[87]

Leadership Training and Mission in the Local Churches

The youth ministry in the local churches was more varied and complex than that of the schools and universities. It is difficult to judge the overall vitality as there were many denominations and organizations involved. There does

---

86. "Charles Troutman, Letter to Ian Burnard, October 20, 1958," IVF "Ian Burnard" Box 9, Samuel Marsden Archives.

87. "Crusader Union NSW 29th Annual Report, 1958," Crusader Union NSW Archives.

seem to have been growth in the CEFDOS groups and the PFA that can be attributed to the model of youth ministry. In the Methodist and Congregational Churches, however, the earlier "youth society" model was languishing and the new fellowship model did not flourish. Those groups that were conservative evangelical or were able to combine social engagement with a spiritual warmth were able to reach the outsider and grow. Those with more of a traditional liberal commitment, like the Congregational Youth Fellowship, declined like the SCM. In the PFA there was a battle for leadership as younger leaders sought to wrest the overall direction of the ministry from the old guard. They aimed to reinvigorate the fellowship model by focusing on Bible study and witness, yet still engage with social issues. In the Church of England, the fellowships continued to focus on witness, and this outreach was stimulated by the "Youth to Youth Missions" and the camping ministries.

After the war, all Protestant denominations began to focus on youth ministry in various ways. They were influenced by the context of reconstruction and wanted to invest in the young following the devastation of the war. Now was the time to pray for a revival, to witness to young people and to establish a more Christian civilization. New resources were raised in order to build upon the work already established, particularly to build youth departments to assist and resource the local parish. Denominations also resourced youth ministry through building facilities, offices, campsites, and by providing film services.

Church of England

The vitality of youth ministry within the Church of England was partly due to the charisma of the chaplain for youth, Graham Delbridge. His approach was to gather young people around him and encourage and facilitate their leadership rather than doing it on his own. He chose four young women and three men to meet weekly with him and his wife.[88] Meeting on "butter boxes" in the basement of the Chapter House to plan the ministry, this group would later develop into the Youth Advisory Council.[89] The chaplain and his team became the "Youth Department" in 1949 with five goals:

1. Assist youth work in parishes
2. Provide facilities for the guidance and help of youth

---

88. They were Juliet Backhouse (later a missionary to Tanganyika), Charles Chambers, Brenda Miller, Don Noble, Dorothy Robinson, Gwen Robinson, and Alan Yuill. Harris, et al., *Delbridge Years*, 47.

89. Harris et al., *Delbridge Years*, 46.

3. Train youth in leadership
4. Encourage cooperation and activities amongst youth
5. All things incidental to the above.[90]

The goal was for the administrative center of the diocese to facilitate the ministry of young people in their local parishes, rather than take responsibility for the ministry. The Youth Department was partially funded by young people themselves. The Home Mission Society supplied the salary of the chaplain, and the remainder was supplied by fundraising.

The numbers of CEFDOS groups increased as did the number of overall members. In 1946 there were fifty active branches and 1,700 active members, with 1,100 of those aged between fourteen and eighteen years.[91] There were also events organized on a diocesan level including a launch picnic, rallies on Saturday nights, topic nights, an annual sports day, and a tennis tournament.[92] The fellowship groups continued to spread, and in some cases grew quite large. By 1951, there was a fellowship group in almost every parish.[93] Rex Harris, who became an inner-city youth worker for the Youth Department, recalled growing up in Auburn in the early 1950s. He claimed that at the local Anglican Church there were four fellowship groups including junior, intermediate, and senior, and waiting lists to become a member. There were also one thousand kids in Sunday school. The churches were the center of activity in the district, with midweek meetings, socials, sports on Saturday, and fellowship teas as well as church on Sunday. Rex recalled, "if you didn't go to a youth group when I grew up in Auburn, there was something wrong with you ... nothing else was being offered."[94]

Delbridge believed his key responsibility to be the training of young people in Christian leadership. In 1947, some of the surplus funds of the CENEF (Church of England National Emergency Fund) were used to buy a large office building on Castlereagh Street in central Sydney, which was called the CENEF building. It was used for training leaders and to provide a place where young people could gather. On the first floor, there was an auditorium where lectures, concerts, screening of Christian films, and training could take place. On the second floor, there were beds provided as

---

90. "Youth Department," *Year Book of the Diocese of Sydney* (1950), 105.

91. "Annual Report, 1945/46," Sydney Diocese Board of Education Minutes, Youthworks Archives.

92. "Board of Education Report," *Year Book of the Diocese of Sydney* (1946), 107.

93. Mowll, "Presidential Address," *Year Book of the Diocese of Sydney* (1951), 48.

94. Rex Harris interview. The Anglican parishes that had booming youth ministries at the time included Auburn, Peakhurst, Manly, Kingsgrove, Mosman, and Narrabeen.

hostel-type accommodation for country boys and ex-servicemen. On the third floor, there was office space for different youth organizations: CEBS, GFS, the Board of Education, CEFDOS, IVF, TCF, and the Crusader Union, as well as a Christian library. This shared space led to a fertile cross-pollination in the separate youth organizations who were often working with common student leaders. On the fourth floor, there was a restaurant that was a gathering point, particularly for young workers in the city on their lunch break. In the basement, there was a photographic laboratory which became a film strip library to resource youth groups.[95] The CENEF building became an open house facilitating a network that inspired a sense of belonging and being part of something bigger. It connected not only the Anglicans but those from other denominations too, including the Baptist, Presbyterian, and Methodist youth leaders. This created an energy which was then taken back into the local parishes.

Delbridge recommitted himself to the priority of training Christian leaders after he returned from the World Conference of Christian Youth in Oslo in 1947. This conference was organized by the YMCA, YWCA, World Council of Churches, and WSCF. Delbridge's inspiration from the conference was to play his part in building a youth movement that opposed the materialism of the age by winning the young generation for Christ. To do this, young people needed to be enlisted as Christian leaders. Delbridge explained that young people needed to be more than "hangers-on," that they had to become *leaders*. Each person could become a leader if they played their part and led others to Christ. What was needed was leadership training.

> . . . Leaders sometimes are born, but even when they are born they have to train, and those of us who are not born leaders can train to become Christian Youth Leaders.[96]

---

95. This attempt to engage in the new media illustrates the commitment of these people to communicate the gospel in a way that would engage a young audience. Paul White and Graham Delbridge used to take filmstrips out to local churches and fellowships when they spoke or conducted missions, for example, the film *Barabbas*. They also obtained "Fact and Faith" films from the Moody Institute of Science as a resource for fellowship groups. There was a group of men with creative abilities that embraced the new media. White wrote the Jungle Doctor books and converted them into comic books, filmstrips, radio scripts, and later television. Clifford Warne was a puppeteer and ventriloquist who created pantomimes, concerts, and radio plays. Graham Wade was an artist who also assisted in this creative work. Harris et al., *Delbridge Years*, 51–52. There were many evangelicals in Australia who used the radio particularly to communicate the Christian message. The new evangelicals in the US similarly used the new media extensively. See Carpenter, *Revive Us Again*.

96. Delbridge, "Are You a Hanger-On?" in "Preview and Review, Church of England Fellowship Magazine, South Coast," March–July 1949, Youthworks Archives.

A leadership course was developed to run for seventeen weeks on the basic doctrines of Christian faith.[97] In 1953, there were forty young men and women doing the course facetoface and another forty by correspondence.[98] A full-time two-year youth leaders' class was also developed in conjunction with Moore Theological College with two female students, Betty Wood, and a female student from India. Delbridge took them through subjects in Psychology, Sociology, and Education, and they joined Moore Theological College for classes in Old Testament, New Testament, Church History, and Pastoralia.[99]

As well as leadership by young people, the model of youth ministry continued to emphasize the centrality of witness. Whereas Sunday fellowship meetings were often inhouse affairs that focused on the spiritual growth of the members, house parties focused on outreach and witness. The Youth Department continued to buy properties and develop them. Once the properties had been renovated, they were used for Youth Department house parties on public holiday weekends, over the summer, and at Easter. Properties near Katoomba were also used for house parties at the time of the Katoomba convention.[100] The Youth Department house parties were always evangelistic, and Delbridge mentored future evangelists such as John Chapman[101] who helped him. Chapman was the leader of the fellowship at St. Paul's Oatley Anglican Church. He took his fellowship down to the campsite properties whenever he could: "It never crossed my mind that I could take kids down and they would not come back saved. And it never crossed my mind because it never happened."[102] Chapman had confidence in the preaching of Delbridge at the house parties, considering him a "wonderful evangelist who also inspired me to think that we could evangelise Australia if we really tried! Like Wesley of old, the world was Graham's parish."[103]

Along with the camping ministries, witness and evangelism were fortified by the many missions run by the Church of England during the 1950s. One of note was the weeklong Bryan Green mission in St. Andrew's Cathedral in July 1951.[104] The event was extensively advertised and many

97. Harris et al., *Delbridge Years*, 55.
98. "CENEF Centre 1953," Youthworks Archives.
99. Harris et al., *Delbridge Years*, 53.
100. Harris et al., *Delbridge Years*, 19.
101. John Chapman (1930–2012) was an Anglican minister and evangelist. He ran the Sydney Anglican Department of Evangelism for twenty-five years. Orpwood, *Chappo*.
102. John Chapman interview.
103. Orpwood, *Chappo*, 17.
104. Green was a famous Anglican evangelist. Lawton, "Winter of Our Days,"

young people attended and were brought by friends. Each morning Green would speak at high school meetings, then meetings were held in the Sydney Town Hall during the day, and at the Cathedral at night. Howard Guinness recalled how crammed the building became. "Every foot of space was occupied and those under thirty were on cushions, rugs or hassocks in the Chancel."[105] At the end of the week, he claimed that the Town Hall was full to overflowing, with over six thousand attending.[106] One of the outcomes of this mission was enormous Scripture classes at Fort Street Boys' High where Stuart Barton Babbage gave talks and showed films from the Moody Bible Institute.[107] As a result, Graham Delbridge was assigned one hundred and fifty young people of Anglican background to follow up.[108]

The "Youth to Youth" missions were an initiative championed by Archbishop Mowll in 1951 and held at the same time as family missions in local parishes. Mowll had a passion for outreach that encouraged an assertive evangelism in the new suburbs. The historian Bill Lawton claims that for Mowll, "evangelism was the key to progress, with the under twenty fives as the main target group."[109] Mowll wrote a letter to every young person confirmed in the previous year, to invite them to give money and to pray for the 1951 mission.[110] The diocesan missioner, George Rees,[111] worked alongside the Youth Department. Rees had gathered together a group of about three hundred young people as "the Ambassadors" who gave him prayer and financial support.[112] In the new housing areas such as Balgowlah, Punchbowl, Herne Bay, and Padstow, teams of young people joined the rector and missioner to visit every Church of England family in the area, inviting them to church and giving them literature supplied by

---

12–30.

105. Guinness, *Journey among Students*, 152.

106. Guinness, *Journey among Students*, 152.

107. Babbage, *Memoirs*, 81.

108. Delbridge, "Supporters Letter No. 56, January 1952," EU Box 5, Samuel Marsden Archives.

109. Lawton, "Winter of Our Days," 14.

110. Mowll, "Presidential Address," *Year Book of the Diocese of Sydney, 1951, NSW, Australia*, 54.

111. Rees worked for the Board of Diocesan Missions (BDM) for nine years between 1946 and 1954. In the BDM news bulletin, his ministry was summed up: "4,401 addresses have been given to aggregate attendances of 270,273 people. Decisions registered for conversion and dedication totalled approximately 5,215; of that number 3,660 were children." Cited in Orpwood, *Chappo*, 63.

112. Orpwood, *Chappo*, 62.

the Youth Department.[113] Based on these missions, new properties were subsequently purchased, and "mobile churches" met the temporary needs of the church.[114] The priority of evangelizing young people was central to Mowll's strategy and he dreamed of appointing a youth worker for every parish and evangelizing every young person in Sydney.[115]

The missions continued throughout the 1950s and illustrate the way that young people were mobilized in witness and were expected to step up and take initiative, "youth to youth." For example, a mission was held in the suburb of Guildford in 1954. Arthur Deane, who had just taken over from Delbridge as head of the Youth Department, gave the main evangelistic talks. Teams of young people from the fellowships of Chatswood, Hurstville, Campsie, and Northbridge organized concerts, social nights, quizzes, and film nights. On Saturday night, they watched the film "What's your excuse?" starring Billy Graham, the Youth for Christ star from the US.[116] These missions involved young fellowship members in both outreach and Christian leadership.

The Church of England Youth Department encouraged a conservative evangelicalism that was vibrant and sought to equip Christian teens to live a passionate Christian life and to witness to their friends. The heart of the ministry was in the fellowships, the CEFDOS. Before 1950, there had been a split between the conservative and liberal evangelical groups, some CEFDOS (blue) and others CEF (red), as described in chapter five. By 1950, the CEF was no longer active in Sydney and the conservative strain of Anglican evangelicalism was predominant.[117]

Presbyterian Church

Whereas the Church of England fellowships were theologically conservative, in the Presbyterian Church there was an influential group in the PFA that sought to engage with social issues and the task of reconstructing Christian society after the war as well as witness. The leaders of the PFA were often "middle of the road" theologically. They sought social engagement and were influenced by neoorthodox theology, but they were also committed to reading the Bible and evangelism. The PFA continued to grow in numbers and spiritual vitality after the war. In 1950, numbers returned

113. Lawton, "Winter of Our Days," 14.
114. Lawton, "Winter of Our Days," 14.
115. Lawton, "Winter of Our Days," 14.
116. "Youth Campaign," *The Broadcaster*, October 20, 1954, 1.
117. Arthur Deane interview.

to the pre-war level of about five thousand. By 1959, these had grown to six thousand members and the all-time peak was in 1964 with seven thousand members.[118] In individual parishes, there were some very large fellowship associations of one hundred and fifty to three hundred members. The District Committees were also very active, organizing swimming carnivals, choral festivals, and athletic carnivals.[119]

One of the key reasons for the vitality of the PFA at this time was its new leadership at the executive level. In chapter five the takeover by the Young Turks was described. The PFA leadership had been growing older, but this takeover reinstigated the leadership of younger people. Many of these younger leaders were influenced by neoorthodox theology. Bruce Mansfield, for example, attended the Oslo Youth Conference that was concerned with both the study of the Bible and the problems of youth around the world. It encouraged an ecumenical spirit and concern to rebuild the world based on Christian principles. The key speakers such as Reinhold Niebuhr and Martin Niemoller were neoorthodox. Mansfield attended this conference and then took a year off his studies in order to travel around NSW speaking at many rallies of Methodist and Presbyterian Youth. Catching the train from one spot to another to speak at churches and fellowships in a "whistle-stop tour,"[120] he sought to open the eyes of young Christians to the worldwide youth movement and to inspire young people to renewed service. He came back with a sense that the Presbyterian Fellowship was failing in its God-ordained goal. After discussion with key leaders, the fellowship published a motion of penance for their failure in witness and service at the PFA annual conference.

> The Presbyterian Fellowship Union of New South Wales, in conference assembled, confesses its failure to be a true witness to its Lord and admits its share of responsibility for the suffering and helplessness of youth everywhere. It seeks God's guidance in its task of witness and service and asserts its solidarity with Christian Youth of every nation and confession.[121]

A commission, including the Youth Director, the Reverend H. F. Peak, Bruce Mansfield, and some of the Young Turks, was then set up to investigate the problems in the PFA.[122] It concluded that there were seven symptoms

118. Prentis, "Fellowship," 18.
119. Prentis, "Fellowship," 18.
120. Bruce Mansfield interview.
121. "The Report of the Commission to the Annual Conference of the Presbyterian Fellowship Union," 5.
122. Prentis, "Fellowship," 17.

of ineffectiveness. These were: poverty in worship and prayerlessness, degeneration in Bible study, ignorance of the faith, lack of vocation and social witness, lack of responsibility, lack of decisions, and lack of evangelism.[123] The fellowship groups were critiqued as social groups where "the entertainment element is made supreme and the spiritual is often subordinated."[124] In response, fellowships sought to reactivate service efforts such as food drives, support for missions, and social welfare.[125] The PFA was concerned for the social order and the development of the ecumenical movement, "building a new kind of society."[126]

Methodist Church

The Methodist Church was also involved in mission during these years. The youth fellowship or club idea was used, for example, by Alan Walker in Waverley. Here he built a community center which included a gymnasium, library, and other rooms for youth. The club had three hundred members in 1947 and seventy on the waiting list. It offered forty-five minutes of free fellowshipping, two hours of structured games/activities, and twenty minutes of Christian devotion. In Walker's youth club, many of these young people came from unchurched backgrounds, so Christians were in the minority.[127] This youth group excelled in its evangelism to those outside of the church.

In 1949 the Methodist Church began its Commonwealth Campaign for Christ which was to last three years. Methodists were buoyed by the 1947 census results that ranked them as the third largest denomination, now ahead of the Presbyterian Church. However, all was not well in NSW. Overall church membership since 1933 had increased by 13 percent, but Sunday attendance had decreased by 26 percent and Sunday school numbers since 1933 were down by 25 percent.[128] In the Methodist youth organizations in Australia, there was also a decline in numbers (this was the sum of youth in Christian Endeavor, Girl's Comrades, MOK, Crusaders and fellowship groups). In 1921 there had been forty-five thousand young people involved, in 1933 this had increased to ninety-two thousand, but in

---

123. "The Report of the Commission to the Annual Conference of the Presbyterian Fellowship Union."

124. "The Report of the Commission to the Annual Conference of the Presbyterian Fellowship Union."

125. Prentis, "Fellowship," 18.

126. Bruce Mansfield interview.

127. Wright, *Conscience of the Nation*, 63.

128. Hyde, *When Youth Crusades*, 6.

1945, only fifty-six thousand were involved.[129] These observations motivated leaders to encourage young people in the campaign to bring in their friends: "You can witness, you can win others"[130] and to establish youth community centers.[131] They were encouraged to write to local newspapers, contact local radio stations, organize open-air meetings, and to be involved in visitational ministry from house to house.[132] The first year of the campaign was to be a time of revitalizing and preparing local churches. The intention of the second year of the campaign was to challenge lay people to visitation ministry to bring non-attending Methodists back into the church and reactivate "every member" evangelism. Finally, in the third year, there was to be a "mission to the nation" with intensive outreach conducted over the country.[133] Groups of lay people were trained to do "visitation evangelism," visiting locals in their area and inviting them to come to church and church events to hear evangelistic preachers.

In April 1953, the Methodist "Mission to the Nation" was launched as a six-month evangelistic campaign led by the Reverend Alan Walker, who had since become the head of the Youth Department and continued to have an affinity with and ability to talk to youth. It was a new kind of campaign for two reasons. First, it was financially resourced so it could make use of radio and advertising. Second, it was concerned with social justice and with Christianizing institutions.[134] Walker's campaign included programs for youth.[135] He often gave evening sessions on "Love, Courtship and Marriage" for young people to talk about sexual purity and following Jesus.[136] In July 1954, Walker visited the secondary schools in all of the capital cities.[137] The purpose of the mission was twofold according to Walker. It was to "try and bring men and women, one by one, to follow Jesus and to accept through repentance and faith the Christian way of life." But the other part of its purpose was to be a "Mission to the *Nation*, not just to individuals. And therefore it consistently raised the issues that

129. Trenaman, "Whither Are We Bound?," *The Methodist*, June 9, 1945, 1.
130. Hyde, *When Youth Crusades*, 28.
131. Trenaman, "Whither Are We Bound?," *The Methodist*, June 9, 1945, 1.
132. Hyde, *When Youth Crusades*, 29.
133. Frappell, "Post-War Revivalism," 249; Wright, *Conscience of the Nation*, 93.
134. Frappell, "Post-War Revivalism," 93.
135. Walker believed that the Youth Convention was "the greatest single event in the witness of the Mission to the Nation." Walker, "Significance of the Youth Convention," *The Methodist*, October 30, 1954.
136. Wright, *Conscience of the Nation*, 101.
137. "The Churches Mission to Secondary Schools Opens Next Week," *Sydney Morning Herald*, July 24, 1954, 7.

confronted Australia."[138] It was vocal on issues such as race, peace and war, work conditions, and sex and marriage.

Walker was seeking to engage with Australian culture. He continued to emphasize the work of the Spirit, the importance of conversion. However, he encouraged a "new evangelism."

> The time is overdue for Christians to find a new, saner, larger evangelism. The new evangelism must express the fruits of biblical scholarship and appeal to the mind as well as the emotions of modern people. It must draw together the personal and social elements of the gospel, seeking at the same time the conversions of men and women and the building of a society fit for people to live in.[139]

This evangelism would not exclude the social aspects of the Christian gospel as he believed the older evangelical gospel did with its emphasis on individual salvation. There was still a definite message of salvation through Christ, but conversion was no longer to be motivated through a fear of hell and judgment. Instead, young people would consider the purpose and meaning of their life and the answer the Christian gospel held for the problems they were facing.

Although the campaign brought big numbers of enthusiastic young people together, it did not succeed in reinvigorating the Methodist Church and its youth organizations. Early goals had been to see an increase of twenty thousand Methodists in Australia or an increase of 15 percent.[140] As Samantha Frappell has argued, it did not lead to a revival evidenced by measures such as "dramatic increase in membership, finances and ministerial candidates."[141] At times Walker's message of Christian values was at odds with the conservative government, and opposition within the Methodist leadership grew because of a fear of political backlash. Church leaders were also concerned about the costs of radio and production which led them to close the mission in March 1957.[142]

The Methodist Youth Fellowship, Congregational Youth Fellowship and Baptist Youth Fellowship never captured the hearts of young people in the same way that the Church of England Fellowship and the Presbyterian Fellowship Union did. The fellowship groups were shaped by the congregations in which they grew. Sometimes they were able to retain a spiritual

138. Frappell, "Post-War Revivalism," 254.
139. Cited in Parker, "Fundamentalism," 291.
140. "Crusade for Christ," *The Methodist*, November 26, 1949, 3.
141. Frappell, "Post-War Revivalism," 225.
142. Frappell, "Post-War Revivalism," 225.

vigor and commitment to social justice as Walker did. Other groups were more social. The fellowships of the Congregational Church in Australia more than any other church, were heavily influenced by liberal evangelical thinking. The emblem on their badge was the Mayflower, "symbolising the spirit of freedom and adventure, and loyalty to God and the truth, as it is progressively revealed."[143] This expressed an independence of thought and progressive revelation that was fundamental to liberal thought. They were involved heavily in the Christian Social Order Movement and its concern for work conditions and reconstruction.[144]

In all fellowship groups at the end of the 1950s, there were many who attended for social reasons or who had not yet decided to embrace the Christian faith for themselves. In 1958 a report in *The Witness* stated that evangelistic missions were needed for the fellowship groups themselves! The editor argued that, there were two groups within the fellowships. The first was "attracted by the healthy social life" and therefore would often grow out of the group. The second "is essentially 'hereditary' Christians," that is, those that have grown up in the church with Christian families. The editor claimed that in both cases "a decision has yet to be made,"[145] and so, to encourage young people to make decisions, an evangelistic group should go to each fellowship, give talks, play gospel music, and perform dramas.

Rallies

The late 1940s and 1950s saw the rise of big campaigns and missions to evangelize youth, and the rallies were established as another boost to the denominational youth ministry. The rallies (sometimes called squashes) were large meetings on a Friday or Saturday night in the city to which young people could invite their non-believing friends. At the event, there would be games, choir singing, dramas, movies, as well as an evangelistic talk. There were many stories of conversion, for example, Maureen Coleman, who was taken to a rally at the age of eighteen. She had attended an Anglican Sunday school as a child but "had no assurance of salvation." At the rally, she watched a Billy Graham film and when it had finished, her friend asked her, "Are you saved?" Not long after, she made a commitment and felt a sense of assurance about her salvation. She was determined to serve, perhaps as a missionary nurse.[146]

---

143. *The Congregationalist*, July 1951.
144. For example: "Youth Looks at Marriage," *The Congregationalist*, February 1951.
145. *The Witness*, March 18, 1958.
146. Maureen Coleman interview.

The most successful rallies were the "This is Life" rallies founded by Alex Gilchrist,[147] a representative of the parachurch evangelism organization, Campaigners for Christ. His rallies used a simple format, Christian music, and a short evangelistic message and a film, making particular use of Billy Graham films, and they were regularly broadcast on 2CH radio.[148] Rowdy fellowship groups would come together on the train and would invite their friends to attend too.[149] Behind the rallies was the presumption that young people wanted fun and entertainment along with a Christian message, the same *modus operandi* of the Youth for Christ movement.

Conclusion

The methodology of modern youth ministry was established before the war, and after the war, the youth organizations who applied it were flourishing. The EU, ISCF, Crusader Union, PFA, and CEFDOS all grew in numbers, while staff and other adults continued to nurture student leadership and initiative. The greatest advances were in the conservative evangelical stream while the more liberal stream in the CYF, MYF, and SCM declined. The leaders of denominations recognized the need to pour resources into youth and embraced the methodology with an emphasis on witness to peers seen in the "youth to youth" campaigns and the Alan Walker campaign. Denominational resources also created youth departments, directors, central offices like the CENEF building, and campsites. There were new advances in leadership training with courses and training camps. Ambitious new initiatives in mission combined with formidable organization in mission resulted in "big" events like the 1951 mission, and the rallies which stimulated every member engagement and witness. All of these initiatives and activity would lead to the biggest event of all—the Billy Graham Crusade of 1959.

---

147. Alex Gilchrist was perhaps the best known Australian youth evangelist who became the head of Campaigners for Christ. He also organized youth camps associated with the Katoomba Convention and became the chairman for the Sydney Billy Graham Crusade. "Gilchrist, Arthur Alexander (1907–1987)," *Australian Dictionary of Evangelical Biography*.

148. Alex Gilchrist interview.

149. Piggin and Linder, *National Soul*, 275.

8

Epilogue: The Billy Graham Crusade 1959

THE BILLY GRAHAM CRUSADE in Sydney was the high point of a decade of growth in mission amongst young people in the Protestant churches in NSW. After more than two decades of nurturing the institutions that sought to reach youth, the crusade was a time of harvest. The majority of those who made decisions to become Christians at the crusade were young people, and most of these converts had participated in youth ministry at some point. The crusade did not take place in a vacuum but was dependent upon the NSW context of flourishing youth ministry. Indeed, it was only possible because of the prior ministry at the university, schools, and church fellowships. The model of youth ministry that was developed in the 1930s and 1940s had been flourishing and led to a culture that encouraged the leadership of young people, with active witness and ministry to peers. The crusade itself closely reflected the values of the youth ministry model: a focus on witness, the leadership of young people, and the importance of peer ministry. What it added was the challenge for young people to make a decision. The ongoing impact of the crusade was significant growth in these ministries as young people who decided to become Christians in the crusade were channeled into the EU, Scripture Union, and the Crusader Union, as well as into their local fellowship groups.

The crusade was led by the internationally renowned evangelist Billy Graham and his organizing team, the Billy Graham Evangelistic Association. Billy Graham was a conservative American Baptist pastor and speaker who became a global celebrity. As a young man, he was an evangelist in the Youth for Christ movement. He became well known and supported as an evangelistic speaker in the US and overseas, speaking over the course of his career at

400 crusades in 185 countries.[1] The Billy Graham Crusade in Sydney lasted four weeks in April and May, and meetings were held at the Sydney Showground and the Sydney Cricket Ground, the biggest auditoriums in Sydney. Each night of the crusade there was a service which included a time of singing led by large choirs that sang old-time gospel songs, an evangelistic message by Billy Graham, followed by an appeal. In the appeal, people were asked to make a "decision for Christ," demonstrated by coming to the front to talk to a counsellor, and to fill out a decision card as a concrete expression of commitment to Jesus as Lord and Savior. The numbers at the Sydney crusade were astonishing; in total ninety-eight thousand people attended. The number of people who registered a "decision for Christ" was 56,780, the biggest response of any of Graham's Crusade's up to this date.[2]

Billy Graham himself was a seasoned speaker with much experience in giving evangelistic talks to youth. In many of his talks he directly addressed young people in the crowd. In a press conference in Melbourne in 1959, he argued that:

> I think young people today are searching for something. Something to believe in. The President of Harvard University recently said about American teenagers that they were searching for a creed to believe in and a song to sing. And I believe that's true all over the world. And I think thousands of teenagers are turning to Christ in many parts of the world. Just as thousands of young people are turning to Communism. They're searching for something that they can believe in and give their lives to.[3]

The crusade often focused its attention on youth. Stuart Barton Babbage and Ian Siggins who wrote a firsthand account of the crusades claimed that the youth nights were the most memorable and fruitful part of the crusade.[4] Graham empathized with young people and their "problems" and tried to communicate that he understood youth culture: "Teenagers have a language and a style and a philosophy of their own. In the United States, to the teenager, grown-ups are 'squares' because they can't 'dig the jive.'"[5] In his appeal, Graham reassured youth that they were created by God and understood by him. He called young people to give their life to Christ, to

---

1. He was a key leader amongst the new evangelicals and he led a "revival of revivalism" in the 1950s. Carpenter, *Revive Us Again*, 211–32. See also Graham, *Just As I Am*; Pollock, *Billy Graham Story*; Smart, "Evangelist as Star," 165–75.
2. Alleyne and Fallding, "Decisions," 32–41.
3. Quoted in "Billy Graham Down Under," *Compass*, February 15, 1990, ABC iview.
4. Siggins and Barton Babbage, *Light Beneath the Cross*, 81.
5. Siggins and Barton Babbage, *Light Beneath the Cross*, 83.

live a more challenging, but also a more joyful life. He also exhorted young people to dedicate their life to gospel ministry. In crusade meetings, he included a separate appeal to youth to witness and dedicate their lives to the Lord before the main appeal.[6]

The response by young people to Billy Graham's preaching was unprecedented. In a statistical analysis of the Sydney Crusade, Alleyne and Fallding have shown that the 60 percent of those who filled out the decision card were under the age of twenty-one.[7] Almost half of those who made decisions were from the Church of England, and the other denominations were also represented roughly in proportion to their strength of numbers in the population.[8] Almost two-thirds of those who responded were already churchgoers, and of the young people we can assume that many were already members of youth organizations. It seems that the crusade was a place where those nurtured in the Christian faith came to make a decision for themselves. Whilst the weekly activities of the organizations taught young people the basics of the faith and how to live as a Christian, the crusade was a time of decision-making. It served a similar function to the house parties, evangelistic fellowship teas, and the Katoomba Convention. They were events where a response was called for and conversions were expected. Many young people had participated in youth ministry organizations to some extent. At the crusade, however, they were called to make a formal commitment rather than just being "hereditary" or social Christians. The fellowships, school groups, and university ministries were fields that had been sown; the harvest was in the crusade.

One of the young people who made this commitment was Peter Jensen, who would later become the Anglican Archbishop of Sydney. In 1959 he was fifteen years old, had been attending an Anglican church, and was a member of the youth fellowship. At a crusade meeting, he heard Graham speak from the story of Noah's Ark about the judgment of sin and the need for personal salvation through Jesus. By the end of the talk, Jensen realized that he "was not actually in a personal relationship with God" and "needed to do something about it."[9] He went to the front and "prayed the prayer." This response shaped how he thought about his future plans and a call to

---

6. Siggins and Barton Babbage, *Light Beneath the Cross*, 96.

7. Alleyne and Fallding, "Decisions," 3–37. The age most highly represented was 12 to 15 years at 28 percent, followed by 16 to 21 years at 19 percent.

8. Apart from the Baptists who were overrepresented relative to church membership (46.7 percent Church of England, 17.4 percent Methodist, 11.6 percent Presbyterian, 11.6 percent Baptist, and 3.7 percent Congregational). Alleyne and Fallding, "Decisions," 37.

9. Robson, "Peter Jensen."

ministry was planted in his heart. After the crusade, Jensen saw many opportunities for ministry. He claims that:

> We had to run the Sunday School, we had to run the youth group, and then we got involved in Scripture Union camps. So life for us was mostly revolved around ministry.[10]

He later embraced Anglican ministry as his full-time vocation.

The impact of the crusade was evident in the schools with large numbers of school students making decisions and joining Crusader or ISCF groups. Associate evangelists went to the high schools and spoke at assemblies and lunchtime groups and many school children came to the large crusade meeting with their Crusader or ISCF group or were invited by a school friend. The model of youth ministry in which they had been trained prioritized witness and peer ministry. According to the analysis of Fallding and Alleyne, 25 percent of those who signed the decision card were secondary students.[11] When a school student responded by signing the decision card, a counsellor would contact them. They were encouraged to become regular members of a church and be active in their youth fellowship. They were also given a gospel of John and a booklet called "How to succeed in the Christian life." Many of these converts then joined their school Christian group, and there were dramatic increases in numbers.[12] By the end of May, attendances at the Crusader groups were "increased considerably," and at several schools, there were now more than one hundred in the group with an average of sixty.[13] Members of Scripture Union in NSW grew from 30,750

---

10. Robson, "Peter Jensen." Other examples of teenagers who made decisions at the 1959 Crusade and were to have influential roles in the church are: Phillip Jensen, Peter's brother who was to run an Anglican church that he grew from about thirty to over one thousand and became the Dean of Sydney. Cameron, *Phenomenal Sydney*, 191–99; Canon Bruce Ballantine-Jones who grew an Anglican church from seventy-five to five hundred. Ballantine-Jones, *Inside Sydney*, ix–xix; also, John Hirt, a Baptist minister who established an influential evangelistic ministry for young people in the 1970s by seeking to connect with the counterculture. He was a founder of the "Australian Jesus Movement" and the "House of the New World." Chilton, "Evangelicals," 146–47.

11. Alleyne and Fallding, "Decisions," 33. Although there were large numbers of school students making decisions, there was a minority who dropped out after the initial decision, more than other age groups. Charles Troutman explained that some of the children went up the front to make a "decision" as a group, so "many of the decisions were simply mass movements." "Charles Troutman Letter Charles Riggs," June 16, 1959, IVF, Box 8, Samuel Marsden Archives.

12. Barton Babbage, *Light Beneath the Cross*, 95; Parker, *Vision of Eagles*, 53.

13. "Crusader Union NSW 30th Annual Report," 1959, Crusader Union NSW Archives.

in March 1958, to 52,000 in November 1959.[14] At some schools, those who had made a decision met in small groups in the school yard and read their copies of John's gospel with their friends.

The Crusader Union and Scripture Union ministries grew because of the crusade, but it can be argued that the success of the crusade was also a result of the model of ministry already being used in the schools. What the crusade added was a clear opportunity for students to witness to their friends by bringing them to the crusade where they would be asked to make a decision for Christ. The crusade also motivated student leaders who volunteered to become counsellors who could answer questions and direct school students who had signed the decision card. The Crusader Union Annual Report of 1959 stated that this opportunity had been the "experience of a lifetime ... we have a strong team of men and women who know their God and who by His grace, intend to do exploits for Him."[15] They were already enthusiastic leaders, but this training refreshed them and gave them new impetus.

Like the schools ministries, the local church youth ministry was also invigorated by the crusade. The crusade was seen by those involved in youth ministry as affirming the evangelistic work which they were already doing amongst youth. Don Robertson who worked for the Anglican diocese and the Youth Department in the early 1960s and who was on the Youth Council for thirty-three years, believed that the crusade was "critical to the expansion of Anglican youth ministry in Sydney."[16] Numbers of young people attending Sydney churches increased dramatically, and more fellowships, Bible studies, and confirmation classes began.

What the crusade specifically contributed was the challenge of making a "decision for Christ." Young people went along with their youth fellowship to the crusade, and many like Jensen realized that they needed to make a personal decision to follow Jesus. For example, Margaret Papst attended the crusade with her fellowship with a conviction that she would not go forward. But when she heard the message, she realized that she needed Jesus's forgiveness and went to the front to "witness to her decision." She felt that it was God himself who brought her forward to make a decision

14. Prince, *Tuned In to Change*, 166. Scripture Union membership entailed making a commitment to reading the Bible daily and members were sent copies of Scripture Union notes to guide them in this. Part of the Billy Graham follow-up encouraged people to become members. These membership numbers include adults, children, and teenagers. It is not only the Billy Graham Crusade that explains the exponential growth in numbers, but also the membership push in 1958 of a "Scripture Union Week" campaign with rallies and meetings in churches, Sunday Schools, and fellowships.

15. "Crusader Union NSW 30th Annual Report," 1959, Crusader Union NSW Archives.

16. Don Robertson interview.

for Christ.[17] In Sans Souci, the Anglican rector received 270 cards, 164 of these from people under the age of thirty. Most were already in casual or regular attendance at Sunday school or fellowship, but the crusade was a time of decision. The crusade "fostered a spiritual alertness in his congregation and among his young people."[18] At Lindfield, the Presbyterian minister reported that 150 cards were sent to him by people who had made decisions, most of them young people.

> Something has happened in our church that hasn't been in existence before. At our service yesterday morning if a number had not been away for school holidays we would have had to put in extra chairs. Our Church is different. I think perhaps I'm different.[19]

What was different was the enthusiasm of the new converts and the commitment to witness. The churches were being shaped by the same commitment to peer ministry and witness that was characteristic of the youth ministries.[20]

The university ministry was also deeply affected by the crusade. The EU embraced the crusade, while SCM remained aloof, unsure of the fundamentalist message that Graham would preach. The different responses reflect the different theological perspectives of the two groups. Charles Troutman was appointed the chair of the Crusade Student Committee, formed six months before the crusade to prepare for it.[21] He described "fun and games with our friends from the SCM," as he invited them to help in the crusade preparation. Later, some SCM members became more enthusiastic and Troutman

---

17. Anon, "Billy Graham Crusades."

18. Loane, "The Diocese of Sydney and the Graham Crusade," Stuart Piggin files.

19. Another example is that of Gordon Powell at St. Stephen's Presbyterian Church, Macquarie St. He was sent 615 decision cards, the majority being young people. He began new youth ministries. Graham Delbridge, who was now the rector of St. Matthews, Manly, reported 480 cards and he started confirmation classes to ensure these young people understood their decision and to help them belong to the church. "Statements from the Sydney Area Ministers," May 18 (one week after the close of the Sydney Crusade), Stuart Piggin files.

20. It must be conceded that the impact was much greater in the Anglican and Baptist Churches because of their higher participation.

21. Part of Graham's way of operating was to encourage denominations and different organizations to work together. The student committee at Sydney University was to be as wide as possible and include the SCM, Anglican Club, Methodists, and Presbyterian clubs. It was only the EU and the Baptists who turned up to the meetings. Though all were invited, the General Secretary of the IVF, Charles Troutman, stated that they were unsupportive of the crusade and did not turn up to the meetings. Charles Troutman, "Memories recorded for Mark Hutchinson," June 30, 1990.

was delighted to hear that several of them were converted during the counselling classes.[22] EU members unreservedly embraced the crusade, with one hundred of them becoming counsellors at the crusade, ready to talk to any student who made a response of faith, and to help the new Christians settle into churches and fellowship groups.[23]

The ongoing impact of the crusade on the EU was growth in numbers and more graduates planning to undertake vocational ministry. Students were invited to the main meetings of the crusade, but there was also a special meeting at the university, where Graham spoke to a huge crowd of four thousand students and staff standing on the lawn outside the Great Hall.[24] In response, there were 350 "first decisions" amongst Sydney University students and thirty enquirers joined the EU. The EU organized follow-up house parties and additional faculty Bible studies for new Christians to join.[25] Troutman claimed there was a 60 percent permanent response from those who filled out response cards. The aim of the crusade was not only to evangelize young people but to raise up a new group of potential Christian leaders. One of the crusade team leaders, Dean Piatt, claimed that:

> Our purpose in pressing a man-to-man type of ministry was to try and impart to these new Christians a New Testament principle which they, in turn, can pass on to others. I believe with all my heart that the Lord is going to take many of the young people who were converted in the Australian-New Zealand tour and send them out as missionaries, especially to the countries of Asia.[26]

Many students felt this call and after the crusade, there was a surge in applications to theological colleges and to missionary societies.[27]

The Billy Graham Crusade exemplified a trend that was a characteristic of the youth ministries; the engagement of each person in witness and peer ministry. One of the remarkable aspects of the crusade was the engagement of everyday people in prayer and follow-up. There were around five thousand cottage prayer meetings in Sydney leading up to the crusade.

22. "Charles Troutman Letter to Ian Burnard, October 15, 1959," EU Archives, Samuel Marsden Archives.

23. "Minutes of the IVF," June 27, 1959, EU Archives, General and IVF, Box 3, Samuel Marsden Archives.

24. Some students sought to disrupt the proceedings with a smoke bomb and heckling by a student dressed as a devil with a red cloak, horns, and a tail. Barton Babbage, *Light Beneath the Cross*, 133.

25. "Minutes of the IVF," June 27, 1959, EU Archives, Box 3 General and IVF, Samuel Marsden Archives.

26. Barton Babbage, *Light Beneath the Cross*, 97.

27. Barton Babbage, *Light Beneath the Cross*, 96.

There were also nine thousand counsellors enrolled in the counsellor training course before the crusade, and six thousand who became counsellors to personally follow-up those who made the decision.[28] Marcus Loane said, "We were all taught in a new way the strength and value of individual Christians in all walks of life."[29] The strengths of youth ministry were now influencing the rest of the church through the crusade, reinforcing that every member had the responsibility to witness and to be active in their faith. Loane believed one of the greatest achievements of the crusade was that members of churches "were made to realise afresh that evangelism, winning men and women for Christ, is the great primary task which our risen and ascended Lord has committed to us."[30]

Why was there such a positive response by young people to the Sydney crusade in 1959? Apart from less tangible spiritual reasons for conversions, Hilliard has argued that the reason that Australians were so receptive to the Billy Graham conservative Christian message was because of a desire for social stability, an anxiety about the lowering of moral standards and juvenile delinquency, and the fear of communism and the Cold War.[31] Young people were particularly fearful of a potential nuclear war and were craving moral certainty and life direction. The social context inclined people to listen to the message. The other key reason for the success was the ongoing ministry of the church, and in particular, the youth ministries that had developed since the 1930s and their preparatory work. Alleyne and Fallding show that almost two-thirds of those who signed the decision card were churchgoers before the crusade. Therefore, part of the success of the crusade was that there was a fertile ground cultivated by the instruction that young people had received in their churches, fellowships, and schools. The depth of the youth ministry before the crusade helped to cultivate knowledge of Christian belief and practice. What was needed, however, was "the challenge of commitment to what they had been taught."[32] The crusade was the stimulus to make a "decision for Christ" in the same way that house parties and rallies had attempted to invite a decision.

The call to make a decision, Christians came to believe, was what Australians needed to hear. Australians generally thought that being a Christian

---

28. Loane, "The Diocese of Sydney and the Graham Crusade," 11, Stuart Piggin files.

29. Loane, "The Diocese of Sydney and the Graham Crusade," 11, Stuart Piggin files.

30. Loane, "The Diocese of Sydney and the Graham Crusade," 11, Stuart Piggin files, 14.

31. Hilliard, "God in the Suburbs," 419.

32. Alleyne and Fallding, "Decisions," 38.

was being a good bloke, or "doer of the word."³³ Hansen argues that the public saw Christianity as a "subscription to a set of beliefs or conformity to a prescribed pattern of conduct," a practical religion.³⁴ Graham helped many to see that they needed to make a decision to repent of past sin and put their faith in Jesus Christ, a decision which shaped their life direction. He showed them that salvation was not about belonging to a church or being a good bloke but having a personal relationship with Christ. There was urgency in Graham's preaching: each crusade service was an *hour of decision*.

The Billy Graham Crusade was the culmination of trends within youth ministry and it capitalized on the strength of the youth ministry already evident in NSW. After the war, the youth organizations established in the 1930s were growing and healthy, particularly those shaped by conservative evangelical belief. The model of ministry was bearing fruit, with good numbers and new young people brought to faith and included into their groups. The years 1945 to 1959 were characterized by a focus on witness and revival. Young people were encouraged to bring their friends to events like rallies in the city as well as house parties and camps in order to hear the Christian message. Those involved in youth ministry longed for revival, individuals being saved, and a society transformed by Christian values. In the Billy Graham Crusade of 1959, their hopes were partially realized.

It was the Billy Graham Crusade of 1959 that has been celebrated as the high tide of conservative evangelicalism. Australian historian, Stuart Piggin has persuasively argued that it can be categorized as one of the few Australia-wide revivals, in the mold of the Wesley and Whitefield revivals.³⁵ Moreover, the crusade can readily be understood as a youth event, as the majority of conversions were amongst youth. It followed thirty years of effective youth ministry and was a harvest time for the work that had been done. The crusade is the culmination of the four trends of the modern paradigm of youth ministry.

---

33. Hansen, "Churches and Society," 5, 6.
34. Hansen, "Churches and Society," 5, 6.
35. Piggin, *Spirit, Word and World*, 153–71.

9

Conclusion

THIS STUDY ARGUES THAT societies working with the young before the 1930s operated with goals and methods that were influenced by a psychological theory of human development as well as by liberal evangelical theology. The writings of Horace Bushnell, G. Stanley Hall, and the Religious Education Association were particularly important. The societies sought to nurture the character of young people and were often motivated by a fear of the dangers of juvenile delinquency. The theory of the Foursquare shaped the priorities as well as the activities of the societies.

During the 1930s and 1940s, leaders of youth ministries in Sydney began to challenge the Foursquare and new methods were practiced in new institutions. In the university ministries, the schools ministry, and the local church fellowships, young people were encouraged to lead and take initiative in ministry to their peers. As well as leadership of the young, these ministries emphasized fellowship, peer ministry, witness, and a collaboration between the sexes. The reasons for this change in model were social forces: the impact of world war and depression, the expansion of secondary education, and the resurgence of conservative evangelicalism. The key instigators of change and growth were individuals such as Howard Guinness, Howard Mowll, John Jamieson, Paul White, and Graham Delbridge.

This model of youth ministry developed within the university ministry and spread to other youth ministries. Howard Guinness raised up a generation of leaders from Sydney University who were committed to extraordinary self-sacrificial service of others. They developed a subcultural identity that was strong and resilient as they defined themselves as evangelical, created a defining story of origins, and emphasized fellowship ties and responsibilities. Guinness also established this model in the schools through the Crusader Union, and university students established the ISCF. The schools ministry also helped to create for members a strong subcultural identity through the name of the organization, membership, and badge. The schools were a feeder for the university ministry, and the university students often continued to lead within the schools ministry in an "unbreakable circle" that thrived. In the local church fellowships, a similar model was put into place. The difference in this ministry was a clear distinction between those who were more towards the liberal end of the spectrum of evangelicalism and those who were on the conservative side. Those who were more liberal advocated a new social order and the ongoing importance of nurturing the character of young Christians. Those who were more conservative advocated the priority of evangelism and witness.

During World War II in Australia, heterodox theology and the loss of leaders who enlisted to serve challenged the viability of this model. The theology of the sinless perfection movement in the university and schools ministry exposed the potential weaknesses of the model. The empowerment of young leaders had been wonderfully productive for youth ministry, but this movement displayed the potential for destructive behavior by charismatic leaders who were unconstrained by adult mentors or denominational discipline. Amongst the sinless perfectionists, the fellowship which had formed a strong subcultural identity was distorted, becoming exclusive and manipulative. Conversely, women and younger male members were encouraged to take up leadership roles that would otherwise have been taken by young men who were now at war. Due to the loss of leaders in wartime, activities were curbed, and numbers fell. Despite these setbacks, resources were put into youth ministry by churches, and campsites were bought and developed. Many recognized the need to invest in young people after the war, who were the hope of the nation. There was also a call to consider the place of young people in creating a new social order after the war, based upon Christian principles.

The Billy Graham Crusade represented the high point of modern Protestant youth ministry in Sydney. There were many new converts, a new energy, and new leaders in the youth organizations. Young people were reading the Bible, witnessing to friends, committed to peer ministry, and actively living out their faith. Many of those young people eventually took up significant roles of leadership in their denominations as lay leaders, full-time ministers, and bishops. Many believed the crusade to be the "Morning Star" suggesting further revival and the hoped-for Christianization of Australia.

The model of youth ministry developed in the 1930s and 1940s was effective in a society which was yet to face challenges such as postwar consumerism, multiculturalism, and the sexual revolution of the late 1960s.[1] Between 1965 and 1975 there was a collapse in the numbers in Sunday schools,[2] which were the feeders of many of the youth organizations. The collapse was at least in part due to alternative entertainments: the widespread ownership of TVs, cars facilitating Sunday drives, and sport on Sunday.[3] Other factors which help explain the decline are the advent of birth control and therefore the decrease in the birth rate, the rebellion against institutions by those influenced by an "expressive revolution,"[4] and the desertion of women from the church.[5] By the early 1970s, as a consequence of the departure from Sunday

---

1. Macleod attributes the religious crisis of the 1960s to a growing tension between the sexual ethics of the church and society, greater affluence and individualism which undermined communal institutions, the civil rights movement, and the Vietnam War. McLeod, *Religious Crisis*. Callum Brown argues that in the early 1960s it was women, who had been the foundation of the church, who broke with the church. There was a change in conventional popular culture and conventional discourse that was no longer shaped by Christian values, propped up by the "angel in the house." These changes took place as women joined the workforce; there were new sexual relations (particularly because of the availability of the contraceptive pill in 1961) and new recreational opportunities. Brown, "Religious Crisis," 468–79; Brown, *Death of Christian Britain*. Australian histories of the 1960s include Cockington, *Mondo Weirdo*; Gerster and Bassett, *Seizures of Youth*; Robinson and Ustinoff, *1960s in Australia*; Horne, *Time of Hope*; and Townsend, *Baby Boomers*. David Hilliard addressed the religious crisis in Australia. Hilliard, "Religious Crisis." He highlights TV and cars providing alternate entertainment, the expansion of higher education, radical theology, and Vatican II (particularly opposition against its stand on contraception), as reasons for the crisis. See also the contribution of Hugh Chilton. Chilton, "Evangelicals."

2. The Australian sociologist Mol states that the number of children attending Sunday school in the major Protestant denominations halved in the 1960s and 1970s based on a report by the Commission on Christian Education of the Australian Council of Churches. Mol, *Faith of Australians*, 128. For Sunday school enrolments for each state, see Phillips, "Religion," 432–35.

3. Piggin and Linder, *National Soul*, 326; Hilliard, "Religious Crisis," 211. The same factors were influential in the rest of the Western world. See McLeod, *Religious Crisis*.

4. Hilliard argues that the key to secularization in Australia was an intellectual revolution: "At the centre was a rebellion by the young against the values, conventions and authorities of the older generation and the emergence of a new cultural style—the 'expressive revolution'—based on individual self-exploration and self-transformation, informality, spontaneity and immediate experience." Hilliard, "Religious Crisis," 210.

5. Callum Brown in his book on secularization in Britain has argued that the reason for secularization was the desertion of women from the church. It was women who sent their children to Sunday school and volunteered their services to the church. When more women entered the workforce, and when sex and gender values changed in the 1960s, it was women who left the church in response. Brown, *Death of Christian Britain*. It could be argued that the same phenomena happened in Australian in the 1960s.

schools, numbers in the youth organizations such as the EU, fellowships, the PFA, CU, and ISCF also declined. Hilliard has argued, however, that the decline was not spread evenly across all denominations and organizations. The decline was felt disproportionately in the more liberal churches (Methodist, Congregational, and Presbyterian) as well as the SCM. The more conservative churches such as the Baptist and Anglican in Sydney were more "conversionist," "less likely to affirm the secular world", and therefore "more successful at holding on to what they had."[6]

In the twenty-first century the youth organizations, particularly the more conservative evangelical among them, have not died out but continue in their mission to evangelize young people and deepen the faith of young people who are already members of the church. Numbers of young people within local churches are much lower than the heyday of the 1950s. Sociologists have noted a decrease in both church attendance and the religious affiliation of "Generation Y"[7] while at the same time numbers involved in university ministries, the Crusader Union, and ISCF continue to increase,[8] although this must be tempered by a recognition of the increasing proportion of students involved in higher education and independent schools.[9]

The findings of McAllister support this theory, as he demonstrates that the greatest decline in numbers in the 1960s was amongst young women in their late 20s, the age when many would have children. The outcome of this decline would be a decline in Sunday school membership as mothers are the primary agents in the socialization of children. McAllister, "Religious Change," 249–63.

6. Hilliard, "Religious Crisis," 227.

7. Generation Y is generally agreed by demographers and sociologists as the generation after X, born between 1981 and 1995. Gen Y is characterized as a generation shaped by rapid advances in information technology as well as an increasingly pluralistic society. Singleton et al., "Practice of Youth Ministry," 37, 52.

8. The Crusader Union has kept pace with the expansion of independent schools in NSW. In the last ten years it has increased the number of school groups from 129 to 186 and increased the number of young people on camps by 57 percent from 2502 to 3931. "Crusader Union of Australia 2007/08 Annual Report, August 23, 2016," and "Crusader Union of Australia 2016 Annual Report," documents received from the Crusader Union Office. In the EU, numbers in small groups have grown from 658 in 2009 to 927 in 2016. "CEO's Report to EU Graduates Fund Meeting," June 14, 2016. Numbers at the Annual Conference have grown from 444 in 2008 to 683 in 2016. "CEO's Report to EU Graduates Fund Board Meeting," August 23, 2016.

9. For example, in the last ten years, student numbers at Sydney University have risen from 46,000 in 2006, to 61,000 in 2016. Australian Government, "Selected Higher Education Statistics"; "Selected Higher Education Statistics." In 2017, 37 percent of young people between the ages of 25 and 34 have a bachelor degree or higher. This is a huge increase to that of under 10 percent in the 1930s. Universities Australia, "Data snapshot 2017."

A current sociological study from Melbourne has gathered the views of youth ministers on what methods they use in their ministry and how "successful" the methods are. It shows that there are still two basic strategic goals in the ministry: to evangelize young people and to assist in the faith development of those young people within the church.[10] The methods used are largely those developed in the 1930s and 1940s, though now the youth program is run by a paid youth minister rather than a volunteer. The fellowship meeting, now called youth group, typically meets on Friday night and often focuses on evangelism and outreach. The small group meeting for faith formation generally happens at a Bible study on Sunday morning.[11] Some youth ministers have advocated a rethinking of methods within the new cultural context where it doesn't seem to be working, especially the Friday night meeting. The failure of this method, however, appears to be the lack of a critical mass of young people rather than a problem with the method itself.[12]

The key markers of youth ministries that are successful according to this study include youth ownership and empowerment, a "bottom-up" leadership model, support from key people, and engagement with schools and local communities.[13] These markers closely correspond to some of the key characteristics of the model developed in the 1930s and 1940s.

First, young people need to be empowered and to feel a sense of ownership of the youth ministry program. Singleton et al. suggest offering opportunities to plan the program and take up leadership roles. They quote a youth minister who notes:

> I'd say most of my youth groups and groups that I've had have grown. They grow because young people feel empowered and like that they own it . . . like that they belong and that they can shape what they do. So, therefore, they decide how a program will look . . . And the reality of them participating and shaping it. So that's an initial point that they need to have for them to go on to actually leading the younger ones, or leading some musical, doing some stuff in the school . . . when people are left to do

---

10. Mason, et al, *Spirit of Generation Y*, 37.

11. Singleton et al., "Practice of Youth Ministry," 42.

12. Singleton et al., "Practice of Youth Ministry," 43. The study describes a solution to this problem initiated by a larger Protestant church. They gathered together a small group of young people as a team to partner with other local churches to reinvigorate youth ministry there through the agency of other young people.

13. Singleton et al., "Practice of Youth Ministry," 47–50.

nothing, and to just be catered to, I find that's where the young kids just disappear.[14]

We have noted in this study the importance of the agency of youth and the significance of peer groups and peer ministry. An implication for youth ministry is to continue to nurture this agency by nurturing small groups where individuals can find their place. Youth groups tend no longer to be called "fellowships." Has something been lost in this change? The older name reminded youth of the significance of relationships, particularly the value of relationships within the peer group. These were relationships of mutual enjoyment and spiritual growth. The name "fellowship" also had a theological foundation. It conveyed to young Christians that they were indeed comrades, united spiritually by the spirit of God, both men and women. They were interdependent and responsible for the flourishing of others in the group, not just themselves, and that the fellowship was a spiritual enterprise, not merely a youth "group" or "club."

A further marker of effective youth ministry according to the study is nurture of the leadership of young people. Singleton et. al. note that a "bottom-up" style with young people leading suits today's culture.[15] But this study shows that this methodology, in fact, originated in the 1930s and 1940s when a distinctive youth culture began to emerge. In the university ministry, the schools ministry, and fellowships, young people displayed conspicuous leadership and engagement. They ran the groups and committees, gave talks, organized events and house parties. They sought to witness to their friends and to promote a society based on Christian principles. They demonstrated the activism that has always been a trait of evangelicalism. An implication for today is a warning not to underestimate the capabilities of young people and particularly their ability to lead. In the 1980s, youth ministry in Australia began to be professionalized, which has led to better thinking and practice about youth ministry. There is a danger, however, that a professional youth minister can result in young people becoming passive rather than active participants and "owners." This can undermine the agency and activism of those participating in the ministry. Young people have shown themselves to be more capable than their elders sometimes assume.

Another marker of effective youth ministry, according to the 2010 study was support from key people such as ministers, diocesan leaders, and parish councils.[16] This study has noted the significance of key individuals in resourcing, supporting, and mentoring those who do ministry with youth.

14. Singleton et al., "Practice of Youth Ministry," 47–48.
15. Singleton et al., "Practice of Youth Ministry," 50.
16. Singleton et al., "Practice of Youth Ministry," 48.

In the Anglican Diocese of Sydney, Archbishop Mowll and other diocesan leaders invested financial resources into youth departments, camping sites, and training. Leaders such as Howard Guinness, Paul White, John Jamieson, and Graham Delbridge were vital in thinking strategically, establishing new methods, and mentoring young leaders.

The final marker to be noted is the importance of links with local schools and communities. It is at schools through religious education, or lunchtime groups, or in social relationships, that bridges are made with the local church. These bridges enable young people who are not churched but interested in the Christian faith to have questions answered and become part of a Christian community. This study has noted that it was the schools ministry that was the feeder to the university ministry and to local churches. Learning about the Christian faith at school or having a Christian friend at school who invited a young person to church was often the first step towards faith.

A marker that the researchers in the study do not mention, and which current youth ministers probably take for granted, is that of coeducation. This research notes the way that youth ministries in the 1930s and 1940s brought the sexes together and created a "safe place" where relationships with the young people of the opposite gender could be nurtured as comrades and chums. The fellowship or university cell group also functioned as a place to find a potential marriage partner, as men and women came to know each other through discussions and social events, and by leading and serving together. Youth ministries continue to have the potential to play a role in developing healthy male/female relationships in a safe place where there are boundaries and a commitment to the spiritual growth of the other. The golden age of youth ministry in the 1950s may be over, but there are lessons to be learnt from our past.

Bibliography

Interviews

Personal Collection

Bill Andersen interviewed by Richard Ford on June 30, 2000.
Bill Andersen interviewed by Ruth Lukabyo on June 27, 2012.
Bill Andersen interviewed by Ruth Lukabyo on July 24, 2014.
Bryde Beman interviewed by Ruth Lukabyo on September 12, 2013.
Allan Bryson interviewed by Richard Ford on June 28, 2000.
Peter Boase interviewed by Ruth Lukabyo on October 14, 2015.
Maureen Coleman interviewed by Ruth Lukabyo on June 12, 2012.
Arthur Deane interviewed by Ruth Lukabyo on May 23, 2012.
Harry Goodhew interviewed by Ruth Lukabyo on June 18, 2012.
Rex Harris interviewed by Ruth Lukabyo on June 6, 2012.
Beverly Kemp interviewed by Ruth Lukabyo on May 21, 2012.
Bruce Mansfield interviewed by Ruth Lukabyo on April 27, 2016.
Jean Porter interviewed by Richard Ford on June 23, 2000.
Don Robertson interviewed by Ruth Lukabyo on June 5, 2012.
Marcus Loane interviewed by Richard Ford on June 29, 2000.
Donald Robinson interviewed by Richard Ford on June 28, 2000.

Oral History Collection, Donald Robinson Library, Newtown, NSW

Allan and Elsie Bryson interviewed by Margaret Lamb on October 29, 1986.
Win Dunkley interviewed by Margaret Lamb on December 13, 1981.
Win Dunkley interviewed by Stuart Piggin and Margaret Lamb on April 5, 1990.
Win Dunkley interviewed by Margaret Lamb on August 12, 1990.

Alex Gilchrist interviewed by Margaret Lamb on July 31, 1987.
Alison and Ken Griffiths interviewed by Margaret Lamb on May 20, 1988.
Marjorie Hercus interviewed by Mark Hutchinson on November 10, 1993.
Ian Holt interviewed by Margaret Lamb on March 9, 1987.
Alwyn Prescott interviewed by Stuart Piggin on December 23, 1987.
Paul White interviewed by Margaret Lamb on April 3, 1986.

Archives

Youthworks Archives, Ingleburn, NSW. Including the Sydney Diocese Board of Education Minutes, papers related to CEFDOS.
Ferguson Memorial Library and Archives of the Presbyterian Church NSW, Surry Hills, NSW. Including minutes of the PFA and pamphlets.
Sydney University Evangelical Union Archives, Boxes 309, 314, 316, 317; Sydney University Archives, Level 9, Fisher Library, University of Sydney, Camperdown, NSW.
Samuel Marsden Archives, Donald Robinson Library, Moore Theological College, Newtown. For SUEU archives and IVF archives.
Donald Robinson Archives, Donald Robinson Library, Moore Theological College, Newtown.
Crusader Union NSW Archives, Eastwood, NSW.
Scripture Union Archives, Rydalmere, NSW.
Billy Graham Center Archives, Wheaton Illinois. Notes were taken by Dr Stuart Piggin.

Newspapers and Journals

Australian Church Record
The Argus
The Broadcaster
Clarence and Richmond Examiner
The Congregationalist
The Courier Mail
The Edifier
The Friend
The Methodist
Newcastle Morning Herald and Miner's Advocate
Northern Star
Riverine Herald
The Sydney Gazette and NSW Advertiser
Sydney Diocesan Magazine
Sydney Morning Herald.
The Witness, Journal of the Presbyterian Fellowship Union of NSW

Websites

Australian Dictionary of Evangelical Biography. http://webjournals.ac.edu.au/ojs/index.php/ADEB.

"Billy Graham Down Under." *Compass*, February 15, 1990. ABC iview. http://www.abc.net.au/compass/s2484481.htm.

Braga, Stuart. "Guinness, Howard Wynham (1903-1979)." *Australian Dictionary of Evangelical Biography*. http://webjournals.ac.edu.au/ojs/index.php/ADEB/article/view/1197/1194.

———. "Holt, Ian Wellesley (1913-1989)." *Australian Dictionary of Evangelical Biography*. http://webjournals.ac.edu.au/ojs/index.php/ADEB/article/view/1147/1144.

Burnard, Ian. "Hercus, John Mackay (1912-1986)." *Australian Dictionary of Evangelical Biography*. http://webjournals.ac.edu.au/ojs/index.php/ADEB/article/view/1132/1129.

"C250 Celebrates Columbians Ahead of Their Time." *Columbia 250*. http://c250.columbia.edu/c250_celebrates/remarkable_columbians/v_k_wellington_koo.html.

"Data Snapshot 2017." Universities Australia. file:///C:/Users/ruthl/Downloads/Data%20snapshotv6%20webres.pdf.

Dickey, Brian. "Delbridge, Graham Richard (1917-1980)." *Australian Dictionary of Evangelical Biography*. http://webjournals.ac.edu.au/ojs/index.php/ADEB/article/view/1256/1253.

Dougan, Angus Alan. "Angus, Samuel (1881-1943)." *Australian Dictionary of Biography*. http://adb.anu.edu.au/biography/angus-samuel-5032.

"Enrolments in Government Schools (1848-2015). NSW Department of Education." https://education.nsw.gov.au/about-us/our-people-our-structure/history-of-government-schools/media/documents/enrolment_rates_AA.pdf.

"From Generation to Generation." Australian Bureau of Statistics, 2006. http://www.ausstats.abs.gov.au/Ausstats/subscriber.nsf/0/FCB1A3CF0893DAE4CA25754C0013D844/%24File/20700_generation.pdf.

Garnsey, David A. "Garnsey, Arthur Henry (1872-1944)." *Australian Dictionary of Biography*. http://adb.anu.edu.au/biography/garnsey-arthur-henry-6280.

"Government Schools from 1848." NSW Government. http://www.governmentschools.det.nsw.edu.au/story/early.shtm.

Gunson, N. "Hassall, Thomas (1794-1868)." *Australian Dictionary of Biography*. http://adb.anu.edu.au/biography/hassall-thomas-2167.

Higgins, Matthew. "Australians at War." Australian Bureau of Statistics. http://www.abs.gov.au/ausstats/abs@.nsf/Previousproducts/1301.0Feature%20Article61988?opendocument&tabname=Summary&prodno=1301.0&issue=1988&num=&view=.

King, Madeline. "Alumni Remembered." *Sydney University Website*. https://secureau.imodules.com/s/965/index.aspx?sid=965&gid=1&pgid=1426.

"KYC." http://www.kyck.kcc.org.au/.

Little, Sara. "Youth Ministry: Historical Reflections Near the End of the Twentieth Century." The Princeton lectures on youth, church and culture. http://www.ptsem.edu/lectures/?action=tei&id=youth-1997-02.

Loane, Marcus. "Mowll, Howard West Kilvinton (1890–1958)." *Australian Dictionary of Evangelical Biography*. http://webjournals.ac.edu.au/ojs/index.php/ADEB/article/view/1027/1024.

———. "White, Paul Hamilton Hume (1910–1992)." *Australian Dictionary of Evangelical Biography*. http://webjournals.ac.edu.au/ojs/index.php/ADEB/article/view/737/734.

National Church Life Survey. *Occasional Paper 3, 2001 Church Attendance Estimates* (2004). http://www.ncls.org.au/default.aspx?sitemapid=2260.

Nelson, Warren. "Howard, Thomas Chatterton (1877–1961)." *Australian Dictionary of Evangelical Biography*. http://webjournals.ac.edu.au/ojs/index.php/ADEB/article/view/1113/1110.

"Number of Government Schools 1848–2010." NSW Education and Communities. http://www.governmentschools.det.nsw.edu.au/files/number%20of%20govt%20schools%202011.pdf.

O'Neil, William M. "Anderson, John (1893–1962)." *Australian Dictionary of Biography*. http://adb.anu.edu.au/biography/anderson-john-5017.

"Post-Primary Enrolments." NSW Education and Communities. http://www.governmentschools.det.nsw.edu.au/files/post_1908_1948.pdf.

"Register of New Zealand Presbyterian Ministers, Deaconesses and Missionaries." *Presbyterian Research Centre*. http://www.archives.presbyterian.org.nz/page143.htm.

"Robert Raikes, Founder of Sunday Schools (1736–1811)." *Museums Victoria Collections*. https://collections.museumvictoria.com.au/articles/2403.

Robson, Geoff. "Peter Jensen on Books, Billy Graham and Finding Spiritual Refreshment." The Bible Society. http://www.biblesociety.org.au/news/peter-jensen-books-billy-graham-finding-spiritual-refreshment#sthash.

"Selected Higher Education Statistics 2016, Student Data." Australian Government Department of Training. https://www.education.gov.au/selected-higher-education-statistics-2016-student-data.

"Students, Selected Higher Education Statistics, 2006, 2007, Full Year." Australian Government Department of Training. https://docs.education.gov.au/node/34207.

Troutman, Charles. "Notes to Mark Hutchinson." Audio Archives, Donald Robinson Library (June 30, 1990). https://myrrh.library.moore.edu.au/handle/10248/8635.

"UCA Historical Society Newsletter March 2016." http://historicalsociety.unitingchurch.org.au/wp-content/uploads/2014/03/Newsletter-Mar.2016.pdf.

Wilkinson, John. "Education in Country and City New South Wales." NSW Parliamentary Library Research Service, 2008. https://www.parliament.nsw.gov.au/researchpapers/Documents/education-in-country-and-city-new-south-wales/Education2FINALINDEX.pdf.

Primary

Allen, Roland. *Missionary Methods: St. Paul's or Ours?* London: Lutterworth, 1912.

Angus, Samuel. *Truth and Tradition: A Plea for Practical and Vital Religion and for a Reinterpretation of Ancient Theologies*. Sydney: Angus & Robertson, 1934.

Anonymous. *The Challenge of Youth, the Report of the Youth Work Commission of the Young People's Department, NSW, 1933–1936*. Sydney: Methodist Young People's Department, 1936.

———. *Lo! Here Is Fellowship, the Methodist Crusaders 1929–1979, 50 Years of Crusader Camping*. Sydney: Colprint, 1981.

———. *Methodist Order of Knights, Commanders Handbook*. Sydney: Methodist Dept. of Christian Education, 1957.

———. *Old Paths in Perilous Times: An Account of the Cambridge Inter-Collegiate Christian Union*. Cambridge, 1933. http://www.tertullian.org/rpearse/scanned/old_paths_in_perilous_times.htm.

———. *The Report of the Commission to the Annual Conference of the Presbyterian Fellowship Union*. Presbyterian Fellowship Union: Crows Nest, 1949.

———. "St Andrew's Fellowship Eastwood: Fifty Years." Pamphlet, 1959.

———. "Verbatim Report, Youth in Action, Report of National Youth Parliament." Macquarie University Library, 1941.

———. *Youth's Job in the Parish. Some Practical Suggestions for Youth Groups*. London: Anglican Young People's Association, 1941.

Blackwood, Donald Burns, and Frederick Arthur Walton, eds. *Our Greatest Asset: A Handbook for Australian Sunday Schools*. Sydney: Angus & Robertson, 1932.

Bryson, Allan. "Letter from Allan Bryson to Margaret Lamb 12.12.89." Private Papers of Prof. Stuart Piggin.

Bushnell, Horace. *Christian Nurture*. New Haven: Yale University Press, 1947.

Clark, Francis E. *The Children and the Church and the Young Peoples Society of Christian Endeavour as a Means of Bringing Them Together*. Boston: Boston Congregational and Sunday School, 1882.

———. *The Christian Endeavor Manual: A Text-Book on the History, Theory, Principles, and Practice of the Society, with Complete Bibliography and Several Appendixes*. Boston: United Society of Christian Endeavor, 1903.

Clover, J. Owen. *The Senior Department Handbook*. London: National Sunday School Union, 1930.

———. *The Youth Fellowship Handbook*. London: National Sunday School Union, 1948.

Coe, George Albert. *What Ails Our Youth?*: New York: C. Scribner's Sons, 1927.

Coggan, F. D. *Christ and the Colleges: A History of the Inter-Varsity Fellowship of Evangelical Unions*. London: Inter-Varsity Fellowship of Evangelical Unions, 1934.

"Crusader Union of Australia 2007/08 Annual Report, 23 August 2016." Personal email.

"Crusader Union of Australia 2016 Annual Report." Documents received from the Crusader Union Office, personal email.

"Crusader Union Boys Division Camp Brochure 1937." The Crusader Forces Fellowship of Australia Circular, Circular 20, November 1945, Donald Robinson Library.

"CEO's Report to EU Graduates Fund Meeting." June 14, 2016, personal email.

"CEO's Report to EU Graduates Fund Board Meeting." August 23, 2016, personal email.

Delbridge, Audrey. *My Life with Graham Delbridge*. Self published, 1981.

Forbush, William B. *The Boy Problem*. Boston: Pilgrim, 1907.

Gallacher, Charles. *Forward—Youth, A Developmental Programme for Youth Work*. Sydney: Methodist Young People's Dept., 1944.

Guinness, Howard. *Journey among Students*. Sydney: Anglican Information Office, 1978.

———. *Sacrifice*. Downers Grove: InterVarsity Press, 1975.
———. *Swords Drawn*. Sydney: Crusader Unions of the Commonwealth of Australia, 1934.
Hall, Grant Stanley. *Adolescence—Its Psychology and Its Relations to Physiology, Anthropology, Sociology, Sex, Crime, and Religion (1931)*. New York: Hesperides Press, 2008.
Hammond, C. K. "The History of the Church of England Fellowship." Sydney. Edited by Board of Education, date unknown.
Hancock, H. Lipson. *Modern Methods in Sunday-School Work*. Adelaide: Methodist Book Depot, 1916.
Harford, Charles F. *The Keswick Convention, Its Message, Its Method and Its Men*. London: Marshall Brothers, 1907.
Harner, Nevin C. "A Decade of Youth Work in the Church." *Religious Education* 38, no. 1 (1943) 25–30.
———. *Youth Work in the Church*. New York: Abingdon-Cokesbury Press, 1942.
Harris, W. J. *Problems of Youth: Text Book for Teacher Training Classes, Study Groups and General Use*. Melbourne: Joint Board of the Graded Lessons of New Zealand for the National Council of Religious Education, 1933.
Hayes, E. H. *The Child in the Midst: A Guide to New Sunday School Methods*. New York: Religious Education, 1936.
Hyde, Dudley. *When Youth Crusades*. Sydney: Youth Publications, Methodist Church of Australasia, 1949.
Jamieson, James C. *The Modern Fellowship Association: A Manual of Methods for Bible Classes, Guilds and Fellowships*. Sydney: Presbyterian Fellowship Union, 1913.
———. *The Unique Fellowship: Daily Readings and Studies*. Melbourne: Presbyterian Board of Christian Education, 1936.
Johnston, George. *My Brother Jack*. Sydney: HarperCollins, 2013.
Lewis, Wyndham. *Doom of Youth*. London: Chatto & Windus, 1932.
Lindsey, Ben B., and Wainwright Evans. *The Revolt of Modern Youth*. London: J. Lane, 1932.
Mannheim, Karl. *Essays on the Sociology of Knowledge*. New York: Oxford University Press, 1952.
Mansfield, Bruce. *Summer Is Almost Over: A Memoir*. Canberra: Barton, 2012.
Mott, John Raleigh. *The Evangelization of the World in This Generation*. New York: Student Volunteer Movement for Foreign Missions, 1900.
———. *The Student Missionary Uprising and Its Message to Australasia: Addresses Delivered at the Student Conferences on Home and Foreign Mission*. Melbourne: Australasian Student Christian Union, 1903.
Niles, Katherine Evelyn. "A Survey and Critique of Young People's Societies." *Religious Education* 24, no. 6 (1929) 526–35.
Parry, Alice Fox. *Girls on the Highway, Studies for Girls Fellowships and Clubs*. Melbourne: Board of Religious Education Presbyterian Church of Australia, 1938.
Parsons, Talcott. "Age and Sex in the Social Structure of the United States." *American Sociological Review* 7, no. 5 (1942) 604–16.
Porter, George. *The Methodist Order of the Knights and the Methodist Girls Comradeship: Formation of the Orders*. Morphett Vale, South Australia: G. W. Porter, 1997.
Presbyterian Fellowship Union NSW Reports. Christ College Library, NSW.
Rogers, T. G. *Liberal Evangelicalism*. London: Hodder & Stoughton, 1923.

Studd, C. T. *The Chocolate Soldier*. Project Gutenberg, 2007. http://www.gutenberg.org/files/22331/22331-h/22331-h.htm.

"The Early Years." March 19, 2012. Anecdotes given by those involved in the camping ministry in its early days at the 70th anniversary celebration at Port Hacking, Youthworks, Youthworks Office.

Vodden, H. T., and C. A. Martin. *Youth in World Service*. Edinburgh: Edinburgh House, 1926.

Walker, Alan. *Australia Finding God: The Message of the Mission to the Nation*. Sydney: Methodist Church of Australia, Central Conference Literature and Publications Committee, 1953.

White, Paul. *Alias Jungle Doctor: An Autobiography*. Surry Hills: Anzea, 1977.

Wilberforce, Robert I., and Samuel W. Wilberforce. *The Correspondence of William Wilberforce*. London: J. Murray, 1840.

Wilberforce, William. *A Practical View of the Prevailing Religious System of Professed Christians in the Higher and Middle Classes in This Country Contrasted with Real Christians*. Philadelphia: Key and Biddle, 1835.

Year Book of the Diocese of Sydney, NSW, Australia. Sydney: Wm. Andrews, 1923.
Year Book of the Diocese of Sydney, NSW, Australia. Sydney: Wm. Andrews, 1932.
Year Book of the Diocese of Sydney, NSW, Australia. Sydney: Wm. Andrews, 1935.
Year Book of the Diocese of Sydney, NSW, Australia. Sydney: Wm. Andrews, 1942.
Year Book of the Diocese of Sydney, NSW, Australia. Sydney: Wm. Andrews, 1946.
Year Book of the Diocese of Sydney, NSW, Australia. Sydney: Wm. Andrews, 1948.
Year Book of the Diocese of Sydney, NSW, Australia. Sydney: Wm. Andrews, 1950.
Year Book of the Diocese of Sydney, NSW, Australia. Sydney: Wm. Andrews, 1951.

Secondary

Alleyne, Faith, and Harold Fallding. "Decisions at the Graham Crusade in Sydney: A Statistical Analysis." *Journal of Christian Education* 3, no. 1 (July 1, 1960) 32–41.

Ariès, Philipe. *Centuries of Childhood: A Social History of Family Life*. New York: Vintage, 1965.

Arnett, Jeffrey Jensen. "G. Stanley Hall's Adolescence; Brilliance and Nonsense." *History of Psychology* 9, no. 3 (2006) 186–97.

Babbage, Stuart Barton. *Memoirs of a Loose Canon*. Sydney: Acorn Press, 2004.

Babbage, Stuart Barton, and Ian Siggins. *Light Beneath the Cross: The Story of Billy Graham's Crusade in Australia*. Melbourne: The World's Work, 1960.

Ballantine-Jones, Bruce. *Inside Sydney: An Insiders View of the Changes and Politics in the Anglican Diocese of Sydney, 1966–2013*. Sydney: BBJ, 2016.

Barcan, Alan. *Radical Students: The Old Left at Sydney University*. Melbourne: Melbourne University Press, 2002.

———. *A Short History of Education in New South Wales*. Sydney: Martindale Press, 1965.

Barclay, Oliver R., and Robert M. Horn. *From Cambridge to the World: 125 Years of Student Witness*. Leicester: InterVarsity, 2002.

Barnes, Peter. *Living in a Half-Way House: The Rise of Liberal Evangelicalism in the Presbyterian Church of New South Wales, 1815–1915*. Sydney: Revespress, 2007.

Bebbington, David W. *The Dominance of Evangelicalism: The Age of Spurgeon and Moody*. InterVarsity Press, 2005.

———. "Evangelical Conversion C. 1750-1850." *Scottish Bulletin of Evangelical Theology* 18 (2000) 102-27.

———. *Evangelicalism in Modern Britain: A History from the 1730s to the 1980s*. London: Routledge, 1989.

Bebbington, David W., and David Ceri Jones, eds. *Evangelicalism and Fundamentalism in the United Kingdom during the Twentieth Century*. Oxford: Oxford University Press, 2013.

Bellanta, Melissa. *Larrikins: A History*. QLD: University of Queensland Press, 2012.

Berger, Peter L. *The Sacred Canopy: Elements of a Sociological Theory of Religion*. New York: Doubleday, 1967.

Bergler, Thomas. *The Juvenilization of American Christianity*. Cambridge: W.B. Eerdmans, 2012.

———. *Winning America: Christian Youth Groups and the Middle-Class Culture of Crisis, 1930-1965*. PhD diss., University of Notre Dame, US, 2000.

Bessant, Judith. "A Patchwork: The Life-Worlds and 'Cultures' of Young Australians 1900-1950." In *Youth Subcultures Theory, History and the Australian Experience*, edited by Robert Douglas White, 80-86. Hobart: National Clearinghouse for Youth Studies, 1993.

Boobbyer, Philip. *The Spiritual Vision of Frank Buchman*. US: Penn State University Press, 2013.

Boylan, Anne. *Sunday School: The Formation of an American Institution, 1790-1880*. New Haven: Yale University Press, 1990.

Braga, Stuart. *A Century Preaching Christ*. Sydney: Katoomba Christian Convention, 2003.

Braithwaite, John and Michelle Barker. "Bodgies and Widgies, Folk Devils of the Fifties." In *Two Faces of Deviance: Crimes of the Powerless and the Powerful*, edited by Paul R. Wilson and John Braithwaite, 26-45. St. Lucia, QLD: University of Queensland Press, 1978.

Brake, Micheal. *The Sociology of Youth Culture and Youth Subcultures: Sex and Drugs and Rock 'N' Roll?* London: Routledge, 1980.

Brett, Judith. *Robert Menzies' Forgotten People*. Melbourne: Melbourne University Publishing, 2007.

Brown, Callum. G. *The Death of Christian Britain: Understanding Secularisation, 1800-2000*. New York: Routledge, 2001.

———. "What Was the Religious Crisis of the 1960s?" *Journal of Religious History* 34, no. 4 (2010) 468-79.

Brown, Callum. G., and Michael Snape. *Secularisation in the Christian World*. Farnham, UK: Ashgate, 2010.

Bruce, Steve. "The Student Christian Movement and the InterVarsity Fellowship: A Sociological Study of the Two Student Movements." PhD diss., University of Stirling, 1980.

Cameron, Donald. "Donald William Bradley Robinson: An Appreciation." In *In the Fullness of Time: Biblical Studies in Honour of Archbishop Donald Robinson*, edited by David Peterson and John Pryor, xi-xvi. Homebush, NSW: Lancer, 1992,

Cameron, Marcia. *Living Stones: St Swithun's Pymble 1901-2001*. Wahroonga, NSW: Helicon, 2001.

———. *Phenomenal Sydney: Anglicans in a Time of Change, 1945–2013*. Oregon: Wipf & Stock, 2016.
Campbell, Richard. "The Character of Australian Religion." *Meanjin Quarterly* 36, no. 2 (1977) 178–88.
Cannister, Mark. "Youth Ministry's Historical Context: The Education and Evangelism of Young People." In *Starting Right: Thinking Theologically About Youth Ministry*, edited by Chap Clark, Kenda Creasy Dean, and Dave Rahn, 78. Grand Rapids: Zondervan, 2001.
Carey, Hilary M. *Believing in Australia: A Cultural History of Religions*. Sydney: Allen & Unwin, 1996.
Carpenter, Joel. *Revive Us Again: The Reawakening of American Fundamentalism*. New York: Oxford University Press, 1997.
Carroll, Jackson W., and Wade Clark Roof, eds. *Beyond Establishment: Protestant Identity in a Post-Protestant Age*. Louisville: Westminster/John Knox Press, 1993.
Chapman, Alister. *Godly Ambition: John Stott and the Evangelical Movement*. Oxford: Oxford University Press, 2012.
Chilton, Hugh. "Evangelicals and the End of Christian Australia, Nation and Religion in the Public Square 1959–1979." PhD diss., Sydney University, 2014.
Cleverley, John Farquhar, and John Richards Lawry. *Australian Education in the Twentieth Century: Studies in the Development of State Education*. Camberwell, VIC: Longman Australia, 1972.
Cliff, Philip B. *The Rise and Development of the Sunday School Movement in England, 1780–1980*. Surrey: National Christian Education Council, 1986.
Cockington, James. *Mondo Weirdo: Australia in the Sixties*. Melbourne: Mandarin, 1992.
Cohen, Phil. *Rethinking the Youth Question: Education, Labour and Cultural Studies*. Basingstoke, UK: Macmillan, 1997.
Comacchio, Cynthia. *The Dominion of Youth: Adolescence and the Making of a Modern Canada, 1920–1950*. Waterloo: Wilfred Laurier University Press, 2006.
Connell, William Fraser, et al. *Australia's First: A History of the University of Sydney, Vol. 2*. Sydney: Hale & Iremonger, 1995.
Curthoys, Anne, and John Merritt. *Australia's First Cold War, 1945–1953: Society, Communism, and Culture*. Sydney: Allen & Unwin, 1984.
Cusack, Carole M. "Some Recent Trends in the Study of Religion and Youth." *Journal of Religious History* 35, no. 3 (2011) 409–18.
Daniels, F., and Mitchell, R., eds. "St Phillip's Anglican Church Eastwood—Centenary. History 1907–2007." Self-published pamphlet, 2007.
Dean, Kenda Ceasy, et al. *Practicing Passion: Youth and the Quest for a Passionate Church*. Grand Rapids: Eerdmans, 2004.
———. *Starting Right: Thinking Theologically About Youth Ministry*. Grand Rapids: Zondervan, 2001.
Deane, Arthur Davidson. "The Contribution of the New Evangelical Movements of the Late Nineteenth Century to Evangelical Enterprise in Australia, 1870–1920." MA diss., Sydney University, 1983.
Dickey, Brian. "Evangelical Anglicans Compared: Australia and Britain." In *Amazing Grace: Evangelicalism in Australia, Britain, Canada, and the United States*, edited by George A. Rawlyk and Mark A. Noll, 215–40. Montreal: McGill-Queen's University Press, 1994.

Dunk, James. "Creating an Atmosphere of Joy and Pleasure: The Curious Combination of Work and Play in Scripture Union Beach Mission." BA Hons diss., Sydney University, 2007.
Dyhouse, Carol. *Girls Growing Up in Late Victorian and Edwardian England*. Boston: Taylor & Francis, 2012.
Earnshaw, Beverly. *Fanned into Flame: The Spread of the Sunday School in Australia*. Sydney: Board of Education, Diocese of Sydney, 1980.
Eddison, John. *'Bash': A Study in Spiritual Power*. Basingstoke: Marshalls, 1983.
Edwards, Mark. "Can Christianity Save Civilisation?: Liberal Protestant Anti-Secularism in Interwar America." *Journal of Religious History* 39, no. 1 (2015) 51–67.
Egan, Paul. *St John's Darlinghurst*. Sydney: Self-published, 2000.
Emilsen, Susan. *A Whiff of Heresy: Samuel Angus and the Presbyterian Church in New South Wales*. Sydney: New South Wales University Press, 1991.
Erb, Frank Otis. *The Development of the Young People's Movement*. Chicago: University of Chicago Press, 1917.
Evans, John H. "The Creation of a Distinct Subcultural Identity and Denominational Growth." *Journal for the Scientific Study of Religion* 42, no. 3 (2003) 467–77.
Evans, Robert. "Collecting for Revival." In *Reviving Australia: Essays on the History and Experience of Revival and Revivalism in Australian Christianity*, edited by Michael Hutchinson and Stuart Piggin, 58–74. Sydney: Centre for the Study of Australian Christianity, 1994.
Evensen, B. J. *God's Man for the Gilded Age: D. L. Moody and the Rise of Modern Mass Evangelism*. Oxford: Oxford University Press, 2003.
Fabian, Sue, and Morag Jeanette Loh. *Children in Australia: An Outline History*. Melbourne: Oxford University Press, 1989.
Fass, Paula. *The Damned and the Beautiful: American Youth in the 1920's*. New York: Oxford University Press, 1977.
Fielder, Geraint. *Lord of the Years*. London: InterVarsity Press, 1988.
Fowler, David. *The First Teenagers: The Lifestyle of Young Wage-Earners in Interwar Britain*. London: Woburn, 1995.
Frappell, Samantha. "Post-War Revivalism in Australia: The Mission to the Nation, 1953–1957." In *Reviving Australia: Essays on the History and Experience of Revival and Revivalism in Australian Christianity*, edited by Michael Hutchinson and Stuart Piggin, 249–261. Sydney: Centre for the Study of Australian Christianity, 1994.
Franklin, James. *Corrupting the Youth: A History of Philosophy in Australia*. Sydney: Macleay, 2003.
Garland, Jon, et al. "Youth Culture, Popular Music and the End of 'Consensus' in Post-War Britain." *Contemporary British History* 26, no. 3 (2012) 265–71.
Garnsey, David Arthur. *Arthur Garnsey: A Man for Truth and Freedom*. Sydney: Kingsdale, 1985.
Gerster, Robin, and Jan Bassett. *Seizures of Youth: The Sixties in Australia*. Melbourne: Hyland House, 1991.
Gillis, John R. *Youth and History: Tradition and Change in European Age Relations, 1770–Present*. New York: Academic, 1981.
Godman, P. W. "Mission Accomplished? The Rise and Decline of the Christian Endeavour Movement, 1878–1988." MA diss., Queensland University, 1989.

Goodhew, David. "The Rise of the Cambridge Inter-Collegiate Christian Union 1910–1970." *Journal of Ecclesiastical History* 54, no. 1 (2003) 62–88.
Graham, Billy. *Just As I Am: The Autobiography of Billy Graham*. New York: HarperCollins, 2011.
Griffiths, Steve. *East End Youth Ministry 1880–1957*. UK: Lulu, 2007.
Grubb, Norman. *C. T. Studd*. London: Lutterworth Press, 1960.
Hall, Stuart, and Tony Jefferson. *Resistance through Rituals: Youth Subcultures in Post-War Britain*. New York: Taylor & Francis, 2006.
Hansen, David, "The Churches and Society in NSW 1919–1939." PhD diss., Macquarie University, 1978.
Harder, Ben. "The Student Volunteer Movement for Foreign Missions and Its Contribution to Overall Missionary Service." *Christian Higher Education* 10, no. 2 (2011) 140–54.
Harris, Jonathan. *Trinity Grammar School: A Centenary Portrait*. Sydney: Third Millennium, 2013.
Harris, Rex. *The Vision Splendid: Anglican Diocese of Sydney Children's and Youth Ministry 1943–2003*. Sydney: CEP, 2016.
Harris, Rex, et al. *The Delbridge Years: Youth Work in the Anglican Diocese of Sydney from 1942–54*. Sydney South: Anglican Press Australia, 2012.
Hawes, J. M. *Children Between the Wars: American Childhood, 1920–1940*. New York: Twayne, 1997.
Hebdige, Dick. *Subculture: The Meaning of Style*. London: Taylor & Francis, 2012.
Heilbronner, Oded. "From a Culture for Youth to a Culture of Youth: Recent Trends in the Historiography of Western Youth Cultures." *Contemporary European History* 17, no. 4 (2008) 575–91.
Hendrick, Harry. *Images of Youth, Age, Class and the Male Youth Problem, 1880–1920*. Oxford: Clarendon, 1990.
Henry, Nelson B., ed. *Adolescence: 43rd Year Book of the National Society for the Study of Education*. Chicago: University of Chicago Press, 1944.
Heredia, Rudolf C. "Education and Mission: School as Agent of Evangelisation." *Economic and Political Weekly* 30, no. 37 (September 16, 1995) 2332–40.
Hession, Roy. *My Calvary Road*. Fort Washington: CLC, 1978.
Hicks, Lesley. *A City on a Hill: A History of St Paul's Anglican Church, Chatswood, 1901–1991*. Sydney: St Paul's Chatswood Parish Council, 1991.
Hilliard, David. "Church, Family and Sexuality in Australia in the 1950s." *Australian Historical Studies* 27, no. 109 (1997) 133–46.
———. "God in the Suburbs: The Religious Culture of Australian Cities in the 1950s." *Australian Historical Studies* 24, no. 96 (1991) 399–419.
———. "The Religious Crisis of the 1960s: The Experience of the Australian Churches." *Journal of Religious History* 21 (1997) 209–27.
Hindmarsh, D. Bruce. *The Evangelical Conversion Narrative: Spiritual Autobiography in Early Modern England*. Oxford: Oxford University Press, 2005.
Hodkinson, Paul, and Wolgang Deicke. *Youth Cultures: Scenes, Subcultures and Tribes*. London: Routledge, 2007.
Hopkins, C. Howard. *History of the Y. M. C. A. In North America*. New York: Association, 1951.
———. *John R. Mott 1865–1955: A Biography*. Grand Rapids: Eerdmans, 1979.
Horne, Donald. *Time of Hope: Australia, 1966–72*. Sydney: Angus & Robertson, 1980.

Howe, Renate. *A Century of Influence: Australian Student Christian Movement 1896-1996*. Sydney: University of New South Wales Press, 2010.
Humphries, Stephen. *Hooligans and Rebels?: An Oral History of Working-Class Childhood and Youth 1889-1939*. Oxford: Blackwell, 1995.
Hunt, Arnold Dudley. *This Side of Heaven: A History of Methodism in South Australia*. Adelaide: Lutheran, 1985.
Hutchinson, Mark P. "An American Evangelical in Australia: C. H. Troutman and the Perception of Cultural Difference." In *CSAC Working Papers*. North Ryde, date unknown.
———. *Iron in Our Blood: A History of the Presbyterian Church in NSW, 1788-2001*. Sydney: Ferguson, 2001.
Hutchinson, Mark P., and Stuart Piggin. *Reviving Australia: Essays on the History and Experience of Revival and Revivalism in Australian Christianity*. Sydney: Centre for the Study of Australian Christianity, 1994.
Irving, T. H., et al. *Youth in Australia: Policy, Administration, and Politics: A History Since World War II*. Melbourne: MacMillan, 1995.
Jarlert, Anders. *The Oxford Group, Group Revivalism, and the Churches in Northern Europe, 1930-1945: With Special Reference to Scandinavia and Germany*. Lund, Sweden: Lund University Press, 1995.
Johnson, Douglas. *Contending for the Faith: A History of the Evangelical Movement in the Universities and Colleges*. Downers Grove: InterVarsity, 1979.
Johnson, Lesley. *The Modern Girl: Girlhood and Growing Up*. Buckingham: Open University Press, 1993.
Judd, Stephen. "Defenders of Their Faith: Power and Party in the Anglican Diocese of Sydney 1909-1938." PhD diss., University of Sydney, 1984.
Judd, Stephen, and Kenneth Cable. *Sydney Anglicans: A History of the Diocese*. Sydney: Anglican Information Office, 1987.
Kalapati, Joshua. "The Early Educational Mission of the Scottish Missionaries in Madras Presidency: Its Social Implications." *Scottish Bulletin of Evangelical Theology* 16 (1998) 140-55.
Kathan, Boardman W. "Horace Bushnell and the Religious Education Movement." *Religious Education* 108, no. 1 (2013) 41-57.
Keen, David S. "Feeding the Lambs: The Influence of Sunday Schools on the Socialization of Children in Otago and Southland, 1848-1901." PhD diss., University of Otago, 1999.
Kelley, Brian. "Nurseries for Christians? A History of the Sunday School in Australia 1788-1988, with Special Reference to South Australian Methodism." PhD diss., Flinders University, 1988.
Kelley, Dean. M. *Why Conservative Churches Are Growing: A Study in Sociology of Religion*. Georgia: Mercer University Press, 1977.
Kepel, Gilles. *The Revenge of God: The Resurgence of Islam, Christianity and Judaism in the Modern World*. Cambridge: Polity, 1994.
Kett, Joseph. *Rites of Passage: Adolescence in America, 1790 to the Present*. New York: Basic, 1977.
Kociumbas, J. *Australian Childhood: A History*. Sydney: Allen & Unwin, 1997.
Koester, Nancy. "The Future in Our Past: Post-Millennialism in American Protestantism." *Word and World* 15 (1995) 137-44.

Krahn, John H. "Nurture Vs. Revival: Horace Bushnell on Religious Education." *Religious Education* 70, no. 4 (1975) 375–82.
Kuan, Wei-Han. *Foundations of Anglican Evangelicalism in Victoria: Four Elements for Continuity, 1847–1937*. Oregon: Wipf & Stock, 2019.
Lacquer, Thomas W. *Religion and Respectability: Sunday Schools and Working Class Culture, 1780–1850*. New Haven: Yale University Press, 1976.
Lake, Marilyn. "Historical Reconsiderations IV: The Politics of Respectability: Identifying the Masculinist Context." *Historical Studies* 22, no. 86 (1986) 116–31.
Lake, Meredith. "Faith in Crisis: Christian University Students in Peace and War." *Australian Journal of Politics and History* 56, no. 3 (2010) 441–54.
———. *Proclaiming Jesus Christ as Lord: A History of the Sydney University Evangelical Union*. Sydney: Evangelical Union Graduates Fund, 2005.
Lange, Stuart. *A Rising Tide: Evangelical Christianity in New Zealand 1930–65*. Dunedin: Otago University Press, 2013.
Laqueur, Walter. *Young Germany: A History of the German Youth Movement*. New Brunswick: Transaction, 1962.
Lawton, William J. *The Better Time to Be: Utopian Attitudes to Society among Sydney Anglicans, 1885 to 1914*. Sydney: New South Wales University Press, 1990.
———. "The Better Time to Be: The Kingdom of God and Social Reform." PhD diss., University of New South Wales, 1985.
———. "The Winter of Our Days: The Anglican Diocese of Sydney, 1950–1960." *Lucas: An Evangelical History Review* 9 (March–April 1990) 12–30.
Lee, Michael. "Higher Criticism and Higher Education at the University of Chicago: William Rainey Harper's Vision of Religion in the Research University." *History of Education Quarterly* 48, no. 4 (2008) 508–33.
Linder, Robert Dean. *The Long Tragedy: Australian Evangelical Christians and the Great War, 1914–1918*. Adelaide: Open Book, 2000.
Loane, Marcus L. *Archbishop Mowll: The Biography of Howard West Kilvinton Mowll, Archbishop of Sydney and Primate of Australia*. London: Hodder and Stoughton, 1960.
———. *Mark These Men*. Sydney: Acorn, 1985.
Lukabyo, Ruth. "Protestant Youth Ministry at the University of Sydney in the 1930s." *Journal of Youth and Theology* 15, no. 1 (2016) 3–22.
Macleod, David. "Act Your Age: Boyhood, Adolescence, and the Rise of the Boy Scouts of America." *Journal of Social History* 16, no. 2 (1982) 3–20.
———. *Building Character in the American Boy: The Boy Scouts, YMCA, and Their Forerunners, 1870–1920*. Madison: University of Wisconsin Press, 2004.
———. "A Live Vaccine, the YMCA and Male Adolescence in the United States and Canada 1870–1920." *Histoire Sociale/Social History* 11, no. 21 (1978) 5–25.
MacLeod, Donald. *C. Stacey Woods and the Evangelical Rediscovery of the University*. Downers Grove: InterVarsity, 2007.
Manley, Ken R. *From Woolloomooloo to "Eternity": A History of Australian Baptists: Volume 1: Growing an Australian Church (1831–1914), Volume 2: A National Church in a Global Community*. Oregon: Wipf & Stock, 2006.
Mansfield, Joan. "The Christian Social Order Movement 1943–51." *The Journal of Religious History* 15, no. 1 (June 1988) 109–27.
———. "The Social Gospel and the Church of England in New South Wales in the 1930s." *Journal of Religious History* 13, no. 4 (December 1985) 432–33.

Marsden, George M. *Fundamentalism and American Culture*. New York: Oxford University Press, 2006.
Mason, A. J. "A History of the Board of Education 1919–1949." MEd. Diss., Sydney University, 1973.
Mason, Micael, et al. *The Spirit of Generation Y: Young People's Spirituality in a Changing Australia*. Mulgrave, Victoria: John Garratt, 2007.
Massey, John Toley. *The Y.M.C.A. In Australia*. Melbourne: F. W. Cheshire, 1950.
Matthews, Jill Julius. *Dance Hall and Picture Palace: Sydney's Romance with Modernity*. Sydney: Currency, 2005.
McAllister, Ian. "Religious Change and Secularization: The Transmission of Religious Values in Australia." *Sociological Analysis* 49, no. 3 (1988) 249–63.
McDannell, Colleen. *Material Christianity: Religion and Popular Culture in America*. New Haven: Yale University Press, 1998.
McIntosh, John. *Anglican Evangelicalism in Sydney 1897 to 1953: Nathaniel Jones, D. J. Davies, and T. C. Hammond*. Eugene, Oregon: Wipf & Stock, 2018.
McLeod, Hugh. *The Religious Crisis of the 1960s*. Oxford: Oxford University Press, 2007.
Millikan, David. *Imperfect Company: Power and Control in an Australian Christian Cult*. Sydney: William Heinemann, 1991.
Milson, Fred. *Youth in a Changing Society*. London: Routledge & K. Paul, 1972.
Mintz, Steven. *Huck's Raft: A History of American Childhood*. Cambridge: Belknap, 2004.
Mitterauer, Micheal. *A History of Youth*. Oxford: Blackwell, 1993.
Mol, Hans. *The Faith of Australians*. Studies in Society. North Sydney, NSW: Allen & Unwin, 1985.
Murphy, John. *Imagining the Fifties: Private Sentiment and Political Culture in Menzies' Australia*. Sydney: University of New South Wales Press, 2000.
———. "Shaping the Cold War Family: Politics, Domesticity and Policy Interventions in the 1950s." *Australian Historical Studies* 26, no. 105 (1995) 54–67.
Nelson, Warren. *T. C. Hammond: Irish Christian: His Life and Legacy in Ireland and Australia*. Edinburgh: Banner of Truth Trust, 1994.
Nobbs, Raymond. *You Are God's Building: A History of St. Paul's Church Wahroonga, 1862–1987: First Anglican Church on Sydney's Upper North Shore*. Wahroonga, NSW: St. Paul's Church, 1987.
Nock, A. D. *Conversion: The Old and the New in Religion from Alexander the Great to Augustine of Hippo*. Baltimore: Johns Hopkins University Press, 1998.
Noll, Mark A., et al. *Evangelicalism: Comparative Studies of Popular Protestantism in North America, the British Isles, and Beyond, 1700–1900*. New York: Oxford University Press, 1994.
O'Brien, Anne. "'A Church Full of Men': Masculinism and the Church in Australian History." *Australian Historical Studies* 25, no. 100 (1993) 437–57.
Oddie, Geoff. *Religious Conversion Movements in South Asia: Continuities and Change, 1800–1990*. New York: Taylor & Francis, 2013.
Orchard, Stephen, and John H. Y. Briggs. *The Sunday School Movement: Studies in the Growth and Decline of Sunday Schools*. Bletchley, England: Paternoster, 2007.
Orpwood, Michael. *Chappo: For the Sake of the Gospel: John Chapman and the Department of Evangelism*. Russell Lea, NSW: Eagleswift, 1995.
Pahl, Jon. *Youth Ministry in Modern America: 1930 to the Present*. Peabody, MA: Hendrickson, 2000.

Parker, David. "Fundamentalism and Conservative Protestantism in Australia, 1920–1980." PhD diss., University of Queensland, 1982.
Parker, Joy. *A Vision of Eagles*. Sydney: Pilgrim, 1980.
Percy, Martyn, and Ian Markham. *Why Liberal Churches Are Growing*. Oxford: T. & T. Clark, 2006.
Piggin, Stuart. "The American and British Contributions to Evangelicalism in Australia." In *Evangelicalism: Comparative Studies of Popular Protestantism in North America, the British Isles, and Beyond, 1700–1900*, edited by Mark A. Noll et al., 290–309. New York: Oxford University Press, 1994.
———. "The Properties of Concrete: Sydney Anglicanism and Its Recent Critics." *Meanjin* 65, no. 4 (2006) 184–93.
———. *Spirit, Word and World: Evangelical Christianity in Australia*. Brunswick East, Victoria: Acorn, 2012.
———. "Towards a Bicentennial History of Australian Evangelicalism." *Journal of Religious History* 15, no. 1 (1988) 20–36.
Piggin, Stuart, and Robert Linder. *Attending to the National Soul: Evangelical Christians in Australian History 1914–2014*. Clayton, Victoria: Monash, 2020.
———. *The Fountain of Public Prosperity: Evangelical Christians in Australian History 1740–1914*. Clayton, Victoria: Monash, 2018.
———. "Norman Makin, Holy Warriors, Peaceful Prophets, and the Great War 1914–1918." Unpublished manuscript.
Platt, Anthony M. *The Child Savers: The Invention of Delinquency*. Chicago: University of Chicago Press, 1977.
Pollock, John Charles. *The Billy Graham Story*. Grand Rapids: Zondervan, 2003.
———. *The Good Seed: The Story of the Children's Special Service Mission and the Scripture Union*. London: Hodder & Stoughton, 1959.
Potter, Sarah. "The Making of Missionaries in the Nineteenth Century." In *A Sociological Yearbook of Religion in Britain 8*, edited by Michael Hill, 103–21. London: SCM Press, 1975.
Potts, David. *The Myth of the Great Depression*. Carlton North, Victoria: Scribe, 2009.
Prentis, Malcolm. "Fellowship: A History of the Presbyterian Fellowship Movement in New South Wales, 1874–1977." Pamphlet, Sydney: Presbyterian Fellowship of Australia, 1977.
Prince, John. *Out of the Tower*. Homebush West, Sydney: Anzea, 1987.
———. *Tuned In to Change*. Sydney: Scripture Union, 1979.
Rambo, Lewis R. *Understanding Religious Conversion*. New Haven: Yale University Press, 1993.
Randall, Iann M. *Evangelical Experiences: A Study in the Spirituality of English Evangelicalism 1918–1939*. London: Paternoster, 1999.
Rawlyk, George A., and Mark A. Noll. *Amazing Grace: Evangelicalism in Australia, Britain, Canada, and the United States*. Montreal: McGill-Queen's University Press, 1994.
Reed, Colin. *Walking in the Light: Reflections on the East African Revival and Its Link to Australia*. Sydney: Acorn, 2007.
Reed, James E. and Ronnie Prevost. *A History of Christian Education*. Nashville: Broadman & Holman, 1998.
Robinson, Shirleen, and Julie Ustinoff. *The 1960s in Australia: People, Power and Politics*. Newcastle upon Tyne, UK: Cambridge Scholars, 2012.

Root, Andrew. *Revisiting Relational Youth Ministry: From a Strategy of Influence to a Theology of Incarnation*. Downers Grove: InterVarsity, 2007.
Rouse, Ruth. *The World's Student Christian Federation: A History of the First Thirty Years*. London: SCM, 1948.
Savage, Jon. *Teenage: The Creation of Youth Culture*. London: Chatto and Windus, 2007.
Schmidt, Darren W. "Crossing the Great Divide, the Student Christian Movement and the Inter-Varsity Christian Fellowship as Varieties of Canadian Protestantism, 1928–1939." MA diss., Queens University, 1998.
Schwarz, Hans. *Theology in a Global Context: The Last Two Hundred Years*. Grand Rapids: Eerdmans, 2005.
Senter, Mark. *When God Shows Up: A History of Protestant Youth Ministry in America*. Grand Rapids: Baker Academic, 2010.
Senyard, J., and S. Lees. *The 1950s: How Australia Became a Modern Society, and Everyone Got a House and Car*. Melbourne: Hyland House, 1987.
Setran, David P. "Morality for the Democracy of God, George Albert Coe and the Liberal Protestant Critique of American Character Education, 1917–1940." *Religion and American Culture: A Journal of Interpretation* 15, no. 1 (2005) 107–44.
Shedd, Clarence Prouty. *History of the World's Alliance of Young Men's Christian Associations*. London: SPCK, 1955.
Shelley-Sireci, L. M. *Developmental Psychology*. New York: Facts on File, 2012.
Singleton, Andrew, et al. "The Practice of Youth Ministry in a Changing Context: Results from an Australian Scoping Study." *The Journal of Youth Ministry* 9, no. 1 (2010) 35–54.
Sleight, Simon. "'For the Sake of Effect': Youth on Display and the Politics of Performance." *History Australia* 6, no. 3 (2010) 1–22.
Smart, Judith. "The Evangelist as Star: The Billy Graham Crusade in Australia, 1959." *The Journal of Popular Culture* 33, no. 1 (1999) 165–75.
Smith, Christian. *American Evangelicalism: Embattled and Thriving*. Chicago: University of Chicago Press, 1998.
Smith, Murray. "Reviving Sydney University: The Missions of the Sydney University Evangelical Union in Revival Perspective 1930–1952." BA Hons diss., Sydney University, 1999.
Sprange, Harry, and George Reed. *Children in Revival: 300 Years of God's Work in Scotland*. Rosshire, Scotland: Christian Focus, 2003.
Springhall, John. *Coming of Age: Adolescence in Britain, 1860–1960*. London: Gill and Macmillan, 1986.
———. *Youth, Empire, and Society: British Youth Movements, 1883–1940*. London: Croom Helm, 1977.
Springhall, John, Brian Fraser, and Michael Hoare. *Sure and Steadfast: A History of the Boys Brigade 1883 to 1983*. London: Collins, 1983.
Stackhouse, John G. *Canadian Evangelicalism in the Twentieth Century: An Introduction to Its Character*. Toronto: Regent College, 1998.
Stanley, Brian. *The Global Diffusion of Evangelicalism: The Age of Billy Graham and John Stott*. Downers Grove: InterVarsity, 2013.
Stratton, Jon. "Bodgies and Widgies—Youth Cultures in the 1950s." *Journal of Australian Studies* 8, no. 15 (1984) 10–24.
Sylvester, Nigel. *God's Word in a Young World: The Story of Scripture Union*. London: Scripture Union, 1984.

Tamney, Joseph B. *The Resilience of Christianity in the Modern World*. New York: State University of New York Press, 1992.
Terracini, Paul. *John Stoward Moyes and the Social Gospel: A Study in Christian Social Engagement*. Katoomba, NSW: Xlibris, 2015.
Thornton, Carol Dianne. "The Crusader Union of NSW: A Political and Administrative History 1930–1978." MA diss., Sydney University, 1978.
Todd, Selina. *Young Women, Work, and Family in England 1918–1950*. Oxford: Oxford University Press, 2005.
———. "Flappers and Factory Lads: Youth and Youth Culture in Interwar Britain." *History Compass* 4, no. 4 (2006) 715–30.
Townsend, Helen. *Baby Boomers Childhood Book: Growing Up in Australia in the 1940s, 50s and 60s*. East Roseville, NSW: Simon & Schuster, 1988.
Treloar, Geoff R. *The Disruption of Evangelicalism: The Age of Torrey, Mott, McPherson and Hammond*. Downers Grove: InterVarsity, 2017.
———. "Some Reflections on Writing the History of Early Twentieth Century Evangelicalism." Evangelical History Association Conference, July 2013.
Trimmer, Pam. "Children, the Band of Hope and the Temperance Movement." *Church Heritage* 16, no. 3 (2010) 146–55.
Tyron, Caroline. "The Adolescent Peer Culture." In *Adolescence, 43rd Year Book of the National Society for the Study of Education*, edited by Nelson B. Henry, 217–39. Chicago: University of Chicago Press, 1944.
Vamplew, Wray, ed. *Australians: Historical Statistics* Broadway, NSW: Fairfax, Syme & Weldon Associates, 1987.
Ward, Pete. *Growing Up Evangelical: Youthwork and the Making of a Subculture*. London: SPCK, 1996.
———. *Participation and Meditation: A Practical Theology for the Liquid Church*. London: SCM, 2008.
Ward, Russel B. *A Nation for a Continent: The History of Australia, 1901–1975*. Sydney: Heinemann Educational Australia, 1977.
Warren, Riley. "Instructing Them in 'the Things of God': The Response of the Bishop and the Synod of the Church of England in the Diocese of Sydney to the Public Instruction Act 1880 (NSW) Regarding Religious Education for Its Children and Young People, 1880–1889." MEd Diss., Sydney University, 2014.
Watson, Nick, et al. "The Development of Muscular Christianity in Victorian Britain and Beyond." *Journal of Religion and Society* 7 (2005) 1–21.
Watts, Michael. *The Dissenters: Volume II: The Expansion of Evangelical Nonconformity*. New York: Clarendon, 1995.
West, Janet. *Innings of Grace: A Life of Bishop W. G. Hilliard*. Sydney: Standard, 1987.
White, C. A. *The Challenge of the Years: A History of the Presbyterian Church of Australia in the State of New South Wales*. Sydney: Angus and Robertson, 1951.
Willis, Paul E. *Profane Culture*. Princeton: Princeton University Press, 2014.
Wohl, Robert. *The Generation of 1914*. Cambridge: Harvard University Press, 2009.
Wolffe, John. *The Expansion of Evangelicalism: The Age of Wilberforce, More, Chalmers and Finney*. Downers Grove: InterVarsity, 2007.
Wright, Don. *Conscience of the Nation*. Adelaide: Open Books, 1997.

www.ingramcontent.com/pod-product-compliance
Lightning Source LLC
Chambersburg PA
CBHW050848230426
43667CB00012B/2200

"Ruth Lukabyo's historical investigation into youth ministry in Sydney is fabulous. This study certainly fills a gap in our knowledge. In doing so it highlights a considerable area of neglect, and so initiates a new vista of research. The story is compellingly told and the analysis acute. Contemporary practitioners will benefit from not only learning about the past but also reflecting on the suggestive implications for their current practice."

—**Bill Salier**, Principal, Youthworks College, Sydney, Australia

"A sympathetic but not uncritical local study of youth ministry in a key center of the global evangelical movement, this engaging book has no parallel in the historiography of evangelicalism. It will be essential reading for people everywhere who are interested in evangelism and the practice of youth ministry, in both the past and the present."

—**Geoff Treloar**, Reader in the History of Christianity, Australian College of Theology, and author of *The Disruption of Evangelicalism*

"Against a backdrop of increased secularity since the 1960s, youth ministry has been an under-explored source of Australian evangelicalism's continued vitality. This important study explains how a distinctive and confident culture of leadership by young Christians developed from the 1930s in Sydney's university, schools, and church fellowships, laying a foundation for the remarkable 1959 Billy Graham crusade."

—**Hugh Chilton**, Vice-President, Evangelical History Association, and author of *Evangelicals and the End of Christendom: Religion, Australia and the Crises of the 1960s*

"This fine study makes sense of the present by examining the past. In particular it calls on the churches to sustain and improve their ministry to young people. I was both encouraged and challenged by reading it and warmly commend it."

—**Peter Jensen**, former Archbishop of Sydney, Anglican Church of Australia